Lincoln Christian College

P9-DFN-231

LINCOLN CHRISTIAN COLLEGE

THE LEGAL MIND IN AMERICA

From Independence to the Civil War

THE
LEGAL MIND
IN AMERICA

From Independence
to the Civil War

Edited by Perry Miller

Cornell Paperbacks

CORNELL UNIVERSITY PRESS

ITHACA, NEW YORK

Copyright © 1962 by Perry Miller

Published by arrangement with Doubleday & Company, Inc.

All rights reserved. Except for brief quotations in a review, this book, or parts thereof, must not be reproduced in any form without permission in writing from the publisher. For information address Cornell University Press, 124 Roberts Place, Ithaca, New York 14850.

First published, Anchor Books, 1962
First printing, Cornell Paperbacks, 1969

Standard Book Number 8014-9097-9
Library of Congress Catalog Card Number 62-15323

PRINTED IN THE UNITED STATES OF AMERICA
BY VAIL-BALLOU PRESS, INC.

Allenson

2.45

9 March 73

47034

For Felix Frankfurter

CONTENTS

FOREWORD

The major problem I confronted while compiling this anthology was the limitation of space. Legal spokesmen in the early decades of the nineteenth century were prolix. They were so not only because of their florid literary standards but because they had a lengthy case to argue upon every presentation. I do them injustice by extracting only what seem to me crucial passages. Were this edition to present the complete texts of all these documents, the work would run to volumes, and no reader of today would have the leisure to peruse them.

These manifestoes record a fundamental chapter in the history of the American intellect: the emergence, the formulation, and the inner divisions of an American legal mentality. Of course, this faculty was whetted upon the stone of courtroom disputation. A professional student would perhaps be better advised to trace the story in reports and in the opinions of the judges. For such a student, this sort of material is readily available in the "case books" used in almost all contemporary law schools—or at least as much of it as is still considered valuable. One may question, however, whether the forensic records of trials really reveal as much of the temper that lay behind the arguments as do the more rhetorical adventures in this volume. My aim has been to offer expressions that may appeal primarily to the hypothetical "general reader," and only secondarily to the specialist; and I have conceived that a collection of these texts may serve as a summary account of a brilliant episode in American intellectual history, an account which happens in this instance to center upon the legal profession but which is more concerned with the quality of its mind than with its technical competence.

With one exception, then—Webster's peroration over Dartmouth College—these pieces are what might be termed public or general discussions. They are efforts not to determine concrete issues but to discover a philosophy. In that sense I contend that they tell us more about the pattern of thinking and of feeling in the period than about the specific arguments and citations employed in the courtrooms.

The prose style of lawyers in this age was molded by their habits of speech, even when they were writing in the solitude of their libraries. Their punctuation was apt to be oral in nature, rather than strictly grammatical. The semicolon, for instance, indicated the rhythms of their breathing but not of the clauses. As far as possible I have left their "pointing" as they indicated it. Silently I have made a few editorial changes for the sake of clarity: I have regularized their occasional use of capitals for the Common Law when meaning the body of English precedent, and have left their references to indigenous growths uncapitalized. In general they themselves followed this method, though not always consistently.

Annotations can be an annoyance rather than a help. I have refrained from tagging obvious names—such as Chief Justice John Marshall—and endeavored to identify persons or references which I assume may not be familiar to a number of ordinary readers. These footnotes may in their variety serve to indicate as well the amazing range of achievement of the jurists of this provincial society, an achievement the more considerable given the complexities of English Common Law and the labyrinthine systems of continental civilians with which they had constantly to contend.

THE LEGAL MIND IN AMERICA

From Independence to the Civil War

THE LIBERAL MIND IN AMERICA

INTRODUCTION

In the portion of his *Autobiography* written in 1804, John Adams looked back to the year 1758, when he was admitted to the bar, remembering that the study of law was then "a dreary Ramble, in comparison of what it is at this day." Blackstone had not yet published the *Commentaries*, reports on English decisions were not available, copies of the classical treatises could hardly be found; and so, "I suffered very much for Want of Books." With characteristic energy, he set himself to remedy that situation and eventually, as he modestly but factually recorded, "I procured the best Library of Law in the State."

But even more deplorable, even more of a handicap, was the condition of ordinary legal practice in the colony of Massachusetts. He found that it "was grasped into the hands of Deputy Sheriffs, Pettyfoggers and even Constables, who filled all the Writts upon Bonds, promissory notes and Accounts, received the Fees established for Lawyers and stirred up many unnecessary Suits." Despite some exceptions, this passage describes the general condition of the profession of law throughout the colonies in this year. However, in the decade before the American Revolution diverse efforts were made to promote the dignity of the calling. In Virginia, for instance, the tuition administered by George Wythe at William and Mary aimed at a professionalism theretofore unknown in the genial county courts of the Old Dominion. In Pennsylvania and New York analogous efforts to create an ethos for the profession were undertaken, these being important chapters, though they need not be here recounted, in the nascent life of what would ultimately become the legal intellect of a new nation. The most concerted attempt was made in Massachusetts, led not surprisingly by the young John Adams immediately after his admission to the bar.

Every word and phrase Adams uses in his description of his predicament furnishes themes for this anthology, down as far even as the middle of the nineteenth century. There were, he says, a number of cultivated gentlemen in Boston who "resented" the way in which justice was administered—as there were in all the colonies. In Boston, at Adams's suggestion, members of the bar assembled and voted a number of regulations, not only for limiting admission to those properly qualified, "but to introduce more regularity, Urbanity, Candour and Politeness as well as honor, Equity and Humanity, among the regular Professors." Meetings of this group, held periodically, were ruled according to Adams by a spirit "of Solid Sense, Generosity, Honor and Integrity: and the Consequences were most happy, for the Courts and the Bar instead of Scenes of Wrangling, Chicanery, Quibbling and ill manners, were soon converted to order, Decency, Truth and Candor."[1]

By implication, Adams reveals what had been fatally lacking in all colonial jurisprudence, even in so relatively advanced a culture as that of Massachusetts. The amazing fact is that within just the few short years before the issue with Britain became inflamed the several bars of the colonies did indeed so improve their conditions as to supply lawyers in majority numbers to the Continental Congresses, to the signers of the Declaration of Independence, and to the drafters of the Constitution. Some of these were learned enough to pass for more than merely provincial students of rudimentary handbooks—Jefferson perhaps, John Adams assuredly, George Mason in a sense, and Alexander Hamilton by dint of three months' application of his genius to reading law in the 1780s.

But after the achievement of independence in 1783 and even more after the more tenuous achievement of union through the adoption of the Constitution in 1789, the profession was in a still more sorry state than Adams remembered it to have been in 1758. In the first place, the void which Adams had presciently felt that far back, the lack of books, was now intensely felt by every lawyer and backwoods judge: they simply did not know what the law was, whether it was the municipal law of the now sovereign states or the Common Law which supposedly was to serve them as precedent. Secondly, they had no reliable records of decisions by colonial courts. Thirdly, they had no notion whatsoever of what the federal law would be or in what relation it might stand to state law. Fourthly, and most ominously, the profession had to contend, in the post-Revolutionary years, with a deep hostility among the people to the whole conception of the Common Law, which patriots now identified with British tyranny and with Tory endeavors to hoodwink them out of their hard-won gains. The lawyers could hardly conduct a suit without appealing to the Common Law—or to what little they could learn of it —but in the very act laid themselves open to the charge of subversion; thus, they were invariably certain to inflame the emotions of democratic juries, and see their cases decided by chauvinistic passions, which ignorant judges could not control. Finally, these practitioners found themselves, as a consequence of all the other circumstances, up against the still-prevalent conviction among the dominant Protestant groups, and so of the majority of the population, that lawyers were by the very nature of their profession hypocrites, ready to defend a bad cause as well as a good one for a fee, inherently corrupt and therefore unworthy of the title of American. As was often remarked by observers of the young Republic, Americans were the most litigious people in the world, as well as the most contemptuous, or at least distrustful, of the lawyers they employed.

In this confused and confusing complex of emotions, traditions, and aspirations, the legal fraternity of the United

States commenced its national career. The documents here aligned relate the story of its tormenting problems and dilemmas, and also of its eventual and remarkable success.

NOTES

[1] *The Adams Papers. Diary and Autobiography of John Adams* (Cambridge, 1961), III, 274.

NATHANIEL CHIPMAN (1752–1843)

SKETCHES OF THE PRINCIPLES OF GOVERNMENT (Rutland, 1793)

[Chipman's little volume of 1793 provides an excellent starting point for the heroic story of the growth of the legal intellect in the first decades of the Republic, particularly because he was the leader of the bar in what was still a "frontier" community, Vermont. Chipman succinctly states the central problem for the new country and announces the themes with which the present collection is concerned.

Chipman was born in Salisbury, Connecticut, and graduated from Yale in 1777. He spent eighteen months in the Continental Army and endured the rigors of Valley Forge. He studied law in Litchfield, Connecticut, was admitted to the bar in 1779, and moved to Vermont, where he soon became a public figure. Appointed an assistant justice of the Supreme Court of the state in 1787, he was the first professional lawyer to serve on that bench. He was Vermont's Chief Justice for several terms, and served for six years in the United States Senate. He was a stout Federalist, devoted to the memory of Alexander Hamilton.

Blackstone—who had already become the Bible of the profession in America—had not been obliged to write a treatise on the nature of law in general, but merely to find out what the laws of England were. In America we were compelled to start anew. With virtually a *tabula rasa* to write upon, we had to commence with natural principles and, further, prove their appropriateness, as possible bases of a legal code, to the natural condition of our particular society.

The decision to return to natural principles was derived from two prior alternatives: whether, lacking any body of precedents, we should: 1) appropriate all English law up to the Revolution, or whether we should 2) work from universals to a more judicious adoption of such English rules as were suitable to our profoundly different situation. The first, given the temper of the population, was out of the question. If the second were chosen, then further and more radical declarations of independence from English law, and especially from the Common Law, would be needed. And where would this rejection of the Common Law lead? To a new and theoretical system, not backed up by centuries of experience? Or simply to lawlessness? In the older provinces the issue was not quite so dramatic as among, let us say, California vigilantes, because the older provinces had some records of the colonial courts. But even these were hard to come by, and there were as yet no printed reports. Still, the difference was merely one of degree: the intellectual problem for all the states, old or new, was just what Chipman outlines.

Hence the importance of Chipman's argument that even though the state of nature is wholly a myth, the concept has to be presumed in this country, that we are compelled to commence our thinking with the supposedly solitary individual who gradually enters into the complexities of social relations with other individuals. The unfolding of the rules for his behavior must, therefore, be a result of circumstances; yet the general course of the communal development must be posited upon the universal rules which prevailed in the hypothetical state of nature. Of these the most enduring is the sanctity of private property. This sanctity is not exclusive to any particular class. Nor does it resemble the vast amount of aristocratically biased English law, which is pronounced by Americans as inherently immoral. This sanctity of private property—the most enduring of natural laws—is the cornerstone of the democratic solution.

Given this basis, laws for an American society—and no man in America can live outside society—must so allow men to act according to their nature, unchecked by merely "political" or "artificial" restrictions, that they can continue to be in effect "natural." Here the American paradox emerges: the more we perfect our legal system, the more natural we shall become, in contrast to the European and English trend toward continuously increasing artificiality.

Another way of stating the problem—though Chipman would be dismayed to see it thus derived from his *Sketches* —is whether the law must be no more than an intellectual, complex mechanism for the intricate management of a civilized (and so by definition a corrupt) arena of human contention, or whether it is a clever means by which a civilization resists its own sophistication in order to preserve, in the midst of artificiality, the eternal virtues of pristine "Nature."

Hence, Chipman concludes, to work out the pattern for America, to construct a body of law for a democratic society without any mixture of "heterogeneous" principles, requires "genius." It demands as well (and Chipman was among the first to make this assertion) a gradual liberation of the American legal mind from the domination of Blackstone. But of course, until it could discover or manufacture contents of its own, it would, however reluctantly, have to derive its sustenance from Blackstone's *Commentaries*.]

SKETCHES OF THE PRINCIPLES OF GOVERNMENT, 1793

The learned Judge *Blackstone* in his Commentaries[1]*
says, "It hath been holden, and very justly, by the principal of our ethical writers, that human laws are binding on men's consciences." But afterwards he says, "True as this principle is, it must be understood with some restrictions. It holds, I apprehend, as to rights; and that when the law has

---

* Footnotes are given at the end of each selection.

determined the field to belong to Titius, it is matter of conscience no longer to withhold or invade. So also, in regard to natural duties, and such offences, as are *malae in se*.[2] Here we are bound in conscience, because we are bound by superior laws, before those human laws were in being, to perform the one, and to abstain from the other. But in regard to those laws, which enjoin only positive duties, and forbid only such things, which are not *mala in se*, but *mala prohibita*[3] merely, annexing a penalty to the non-compliance, here I apprehend conscience is no farther concerned, than by directing a submission to the penalty, in case of our breach of those laws. For otherwise the multitude of penal laws in a state, would not only be looked upon as impolitic, but would also be a very wicked thing, if every breach of such laws were made a snare for men's consciences. But in these cases, the alternative is offered to every man, either to do this, or submit to the penalty, and his conscience is safe, which ever side of the alternative he sees fit to take."

Judge Blackstone seems to have been drawn into this conclusion from the state of criminal law in Great-Britain. It was not his design to improve the laws of England; but to facilitate the study; not to write a criticism, or examine their merits, but to give the elements of a system, which was already formed. Had his subject led him to a close attention to the nature of laws, as founded in the principles of society, in a free government, and the only end, which can be admitted in penal laws, he would probably have found reason for a different opinion; especially, as far as respects the performance of those positive duties, which the general good of a well constituted society, in civil government, requires.

We have before seen, that man was formed for a state of civil government, and furnished with a disposition and principles which both allure and impel him to that state. Government may be originally formed upon different models; and each, in a course of improvement, may receive many and great alterations. There are, however, principles common to all, arising from their general nature.

From a variety of circumstances, situation of country, and different degrees of improvement, in arts, sciences, and manners, they may have particular principles arising from the particular nature of each.

When any individual acts in conformity to the laws of his nature, as constituted by the author of his being, taking in all connexions and dependencies, for every thing is relative, nothing stands alone, the actions of that individual are right and fit; so far as he deviates from those laws, they are wrong, or vicious. From the nature of man, it is impossible, that a society should, like an individual direct its actions by any common united volition. It must be done by rules or laws, by which the actions of every individual, as they concern the society at large, are to be directed. The same criterion holds here, as in the case of an individual. Those actions are right in any society, constituted upon natural principles, which are conformable to the principles and nature of that society. The actions of a society, which we call civil or political actions, are made up of the actions of individual members. It therefore clearly follows, that those are good laws, which require such actions of individuals as, taken together in all their connexions, are conformable to the principles and nature of the society; and those are bad laws, which deviate from this end.[4] Let it be observed here, that under action I comprehend both performance and forbearance.

Judge Blackstone, in another passage, defines municipal law to be, "a rule of civil conduct, commanding what is right, and prohibiting what is wrong." If laws command or prohibit that, which is absolutely indifferent to the state, they deviate from the true spirit and principles of legislation in a free government. They are arbitrary. They agree not with the definition, which is a good one, of "commanding what is right, and prohibiting what is wrong." If they go farther, and command the violation, or forbid the performance of any moral duty, they become tyrannically unjust. In the former instance, instead of feeling an obligation, we feel ourselves insulted; in the latter we are filled with the utmost abhorrence of the laws. When laws coin-

cide with the principles above laid down, when they fully
agree with the above, definition, they are strictly binding
on the consciences of men. They ought not to allow themselves an alternative.

The objection, that in this light the multiplicity of penal
laws would become a snare for men's consciences, does
not appear to me to be well founded. It lies with equal
weight against the moral obligation to the greater part of
social duties. Previous to a state of society, if man may
be supposed ever to have existed in such state, the duties
of the solitary individual must have been very few and
simple. In the first stages of society, in a simple state of
property, and a state of manners no less simple, duties must
be confined within very narrow limits. Still they would
greatly exceed those of the solitary individual. In the progress of society, the complex state of property, great improvements, numerous connexions, and extensive intercourse, introduce a great variety of social duties. These are left to
be discovered, as the result of situation, circumstances, and
relations; nor is the discovery and performance thought to
be a task too difficult. In matters which become the subject of civil laws, the case is easier. Many actions are considered as evil, only when they are forbidden. Hence the
duty of individuals arises on the requisition of the law, and
is explained in the law itself. We are not, however, to suppose, that civil laws constitute the ultimate fitness or morality of actions, in a strict sense; but as an individual may
allow others to reap advantage from the use of his property,
so government may allow the individual members to do
those things for their private advantage, which it is fitting
should be the right of the public. In the former case, if
the individual prohibit to others the farther use of his
property, it is their duty to forbear; to persist in the use,
will become a private injury. In the latter, if government
prohibit the doing of those things for private advantage,
which, though before allowable, by tacit consent, yet come
within the claim and right of the public, the actions, so
prohibited become wrong; morally so. It is to be observed
here, that we are upon general rules or laws, and that the

right of government is the right of the whole, not of any particular class, as distinct from the people.

To erect crimes upon actions wholly indifferent to society; to gratify the pride and caprice of one class of citizens, by allowing them what is forbidden to others; to inflict penalties to support a system of monopoly, or for fiscal purposes rather, than the purpose of preventing crimes, is to confound every idea of right and wrong in a criminal code. All this is to be found in a great variety of instances, in the laws of England. We need to instance only in the forest laws, the laws for the preservation of the game, and the penalties for not burying in woolen. In such cases, unable to find any moral restraint, men learn to make a distinction, between what is morally, and what is only politically wrong. Amid a great variety of laws, some arbitrary and some not, their minds are wearied with discriminations. They will readily adopt the distinction made above, and refer the violation of the primary duties in government, to the class of *mala in se;* the others to the class of *mala prohibita.* Probably, however, no two persons in any government would agree in classing.

Few actions, considered simply, are evil in themselves. They are relatively good or bad. They take their qualities from situation and circumstances. Reverence to the Supreme Being is, unchangeably, a duty. Such duties, however important, are few in number. Most actions of men are of the former kind. Murder, for instance is one of the most heinous crimes in society. Yet to kill a man is not always wrong. To kill one, who by violence and wrong, attempts my life, is, when the only probable means of saving it, in fact justifiable. We conceive an officer to do his duty, when he executes a criminal condemned to death, by the sentence of the laws. Should a private person, without authority, kill a criminal, though under a legal and just sentence of death, he would, by common consent, as well as by the laws of the land, be deemed guilty of murder. In every country, in the early stages of society, when any person is murdered, it is held to be the duty of the next of kin to avenge the blood of the slain, to put the man-slayer to death. This, in the ruder state of men in society, is right. It is, in such state, the only known, or practicable mode of punishment, or mean of restraint. In the progress of social improvement, this mode of punishment is accompanied with evils, which tend to sap the very foundation of society, and dissolve every bond of general union. The sole right therefore, of judging and punishing offenders, for the prevention of crimes, is at length entrusted with government. It then becomes a crime in the kindred, who had been called the avengers of blood, to attempt such punishment, by their own authority. These are instances, in which, not only the political, if I may use the expression, but the moral quality of the action is altered, and even reversed, by a change of social and political circumstances. If those only are to be esteemed natural duties, which arise antecedently to society, and independently of any relation to it, and their violation offences *mala in se;* they will be found, not only few in number, but the greater part will be found to be unnoticed by municipal laws, as being sufficiently guarded by the moral sense and the common principles of humanity. The principal of these are the duties of religion and self preservation; and though men are to be protected and secured in the observance of these duties, the observance cannot be enforced by human laws.

The laws of nature are not thus limited. When applied to man, the laws of nature are the laws of social nature. As, I have before shewn, man is formed for a state of society and civil government. He is furnished with appetites, passions, and faculties, which in no other state have either gratification or use. In society, in civil society only, can man act agreeably to the laws of his nature. It is the state pointed out in his formation; the state, to which most of his passions, appetites, faculties, and powers are directed. It is, in truth, his ultimate state of nature. The more perfect this state is, the more it harmonizes with the whole state of man; or rather, the more general operation it gives to the laws of his nature.

If society and civil government be founded in natural principles, the laws, which naturally and certainly result from such state, are laws of nature. There are certain principles, and relations, which are common to all societies, and governments, in the earliest and rudest state, and continue unchanged, through every successive degree of improvement. From these principles and relations result laws and duties, which, with one consent, are denominated, by way of eminence, laws of nature and natural duties. This eminence they have derived from their permanency and universality. In the progress of society, in the natural course of improvement, new and different connexions are formed; new principles and new relations arise. Hence result new laws, and a different class of duties. These laws and these duties will vary, or rather, they will exist in one society, and not in another, according to the various degrees of improvement in each. Still if they result from principles, relations, and connexions, which arise in a natural course of improvement, they are, with the former, equally laws of nature, and natural duties. They both, in fact result from a state of society, the natural state of man. Human laws, founded in these principles, as they arise in society, will have the force of moral obligation. Arbitrary laws; laws, which violate the principles of the society, for which they were made, will be obeyed with reluctance. Obedience, in such cases, will, sometimes, be considered as a matter of prudence, never as a matter of conscience.

Men would be in a deplorable condition, if the moral sense enforced obedience, alike, to every act of legislation. The worst laws, when once enacted, would be received with a degree of veneration. The facility of execution would supercede the necessity of repeated examination, and frequent recurrence to the principles of the government, and the rights, interest, and sentiments of the people, without which the best intentions of a legislature, can afford no security against the danger of tyrannical laws.

Where fear is the governing motive of every social action, all happiness in social intercourse, all social improvements, are not neglected only, but are opposed by the genius of the government. Blended with fear, however, *honor*, that principle of all the most capricious, sometimes irradiates, but more frequently obscures the social horizon. Neither of them have any principal regard to the happiness of the citizens, or to the interests of morality.

The principle of a democratic republic, a sentimental attachment to the community, its institutions and laws, needs not, neither can it endure, the intervention of the other two principles; principles which regard the whole society, as constituted to gratify the passions and appetites of one, or a few individuals. Such a mixture of heterogeneous principles in a government must, of necessity, have a very general effect upon its legislation, upon the interpretation, and execution of its laws. It will unavoidably dictate many acts and rules of civil conduct, which can, in no view, claim the sanction of the moral sense. Such is the government of Great Britain.

The spirit of laws is directed by the effective principle; the principle, by the constitution, or nature of the government. Perhaps, the laws of Great Britain are, in general, the best, which can consist with the heterogeneous principles of that government. If this be true, Judge Blackstone's distinction between those laws, which are morally, and those which are only politically binding, is, so far as it applies to those laws, just and necessary. Still it is a severe, though an undesigned stroke at the principles of that government.

Can there be a more sure, a more safe criterion for deciding the goodness of any government, than the tendency of its principles in legislation? That government, that constitution of society, the principles of which dictate those laws, and those only, which are adapted to the present state of men and manners, and tend to social improvement, which are influenced by a sense of moral obligation, and sanctioned by the laws of nature, not of savage solitary nature, but of social nature, in its improved and improvable state, is uncontrovertibly good. So far as it deviates, it is clearly faulty. Upon a candid examination, upon a fair comparison, it will be found, that a democratic republic is alone capable of this pre-eminence of principle. . . .

The governments of the several American states, as well as that of the Union, are of the democratic republican kind. We ought to know their principles, to study well their tendency, and to be able both in theory and practice to exclude all foreign principles.

Judge Blackstone was a British subject, highly in favor with the government. He was enamoured with its principles. He has blazoned them with all his rhetoric, and not the least those, which are the most faulty. Probably to these, notwithstanding his great abilities, he was chiefly indebted for his pre-eminence. Unhappily, his Commentaries are the only treatise of law, to which the law students, in these states, have access. In every section of the criminal code, and no less, in every question of a civil nature, where the prerogative of the Crown, or the privilege of the Peers intervene, the principles of the British government have given a cast to his reasonings. I wish not to detract from the merit of the author, as a British subject; a writer who has, in a masterly manner, delineated the laws and jurisprudence of a foreign nation, under a government very different from our own.

There are many things in his Commentaries, which accord with the principles of the American governments, and which are founded in the universal principles of jurisprudence. These, however, will be found to be derived from the democratic part of the British constitution. The student should carefully learn to distinguish those principles, which are peculiar to that government, or governments of a similar constitution; to distinguish the reasonings, which are accommodated to those principles, or solely dictated by them. He ought to know, that they are not universal; that in a democratic republic, they are wholly inadmissible. This is not enough. He should be led through a system of laws applicable to our governments, and a train of reasoning congenial to their principles. Such a system we yet want. Surely genius is not wanting in America. Can none be found equal to the arduous, the important task? Perhaps, we are not yet fully ripe for the undertaking. Years may be necessary for its completion. But he who shall only prepare the rudiments, will deserve highly of his country.

NOTES

[1] Sir William Blackstone (1723–80), Vinerian Professor of Law at Oxford, published his four volumes of *Commentaries* between 1765 and 1769. This immensely successful work became at once the standard text for legal education, and was even more piously venerated in America than in England.

[2] Wrong in themselves [Chipman's note].

[3] Evil as prohibited [Chipman's note].

[4] The foregoing observations may be extended as well to the fundamental laws or laws of the constitution, as to the municipal laws of the state. Both ought to be equally adapted to the state of society, and of social improvements [Chipman's note].

JESSE ROOT (1736–1822)

THE ORIGIN OF GOVERNMENT AND LAWS IN CONNECTICUT, 1798

[As early as 1798, just five years after the great question had been posed by Judge Chipman, an answer came from Jesse Root in a remarkable preface to the first volume of systematic *Reports* on Connecticut cases. Root was born in Coventry, Connecticut, graduated from Princeton, and at first intended to become a minister. He switched to the law, was admitted to the bar in 1763 and commenced a lucrative practice in Hartford. Like Judge Chipman, he served in the army; he was a member of Congress, an influential figure in Connecticut politics, and became Chief Justice of the Superior Court.

His pioneer effort to present a body of reports was an endeavor not only to fill the gap which John Adams and his confreres bemoaned, the lack of colonial records, but more decisively to commence working toward the independence of American from English law. Root is no impassioned chauvinist—as some of our later legalists will show themselves to be—but nonetheless he firmly inaugurates—in his stately manner—the theme which declares English law, especially the Common Law, to be utterly inapplicable to American society. He argues that the "common law" of Connecticut—and by implication that of all the other states—was derived from the Law of Nature, not from the vices of feudalism and commerce. Hence it is the perfection of reason and must be protected against the contaminating virus of the Common Law. Thereupon Root pursues the logic of this Americanism, of this appeal for self-reliance, to the conclusion which would repeatedly result from such a rejection of England: namely, that American law should escape the chaos of the accretion of contingent precedents by being reduced to a plain, simple, coherent statement of principles. Root is the first of our authors to proclaim the advantages of what some of our later agitators will magnify into a mighty slogan— "codification."]

THE ORIGIN OF GOVERNMENT AND LAWS IN CONNECTICUT, 1798

Our ancestors, who emigrated from England to America, were possessed of the knowledge of the laws and jurisprudence of that country; but were free from any obligations of subjection to them. The laws of England had no authority over them, to bind their persons. Nor were they in any measure applicable to their condition and circumstances here. Nor was it possible they should be: for the principle of their government, as it respected the prerogatives of the crown, the estates, rights and power of the lords, and the tenure of their lands, were derived from the feudal system. The privilege of sending members to parliament, from the towns, cities, and boroughs, to compose one branch of the legislature, called the House of Commons, and an exemption from taxation, only by their consent, was extorted from the kings by the barons, and is confirmed by the great charter of liberties as of his gift and grant. Their other laws were calculated for a great commercial nation. As to their criminal code, it was adapted to a people grown old in the habits of vice, where the grossest enormities and crimes were practised. In every respect therefore their laws were inapplicable to an infant country or state, where the government was in the peoples, and which had virtue for its principle, and the public good for its object and end, where the tenure of their lands was free and absolute, the objects of trade few, and the commission of crimes rare.

Our ancestors, therefore, as a free, sovereign, and independent people, very early established a constitution of government by their own authority; which was adapted to their situation and circumstances, and enacted laws for the due and regular administration of justice, for the propagation of knowledge and virtue, for the preservation of the public peace, and for the security and defense of the state against their savage enemies. New Haven did the same with little variation in point of form.

Their common law was derived from the law of nature and of revelation—those rules and maxims of immutable truth and justice, which arise from the eternal fitness of things, which need only to be understood, to be submitted to, as they are themselves the highest authority; together with certain customs and usages, which had been universally assented to and adopted in practice, as reasonable and beneficial. . . .

This constitution of our government, framed by the wisdom of our ancestors about 160 years ago, adapted to their condition and circumstances, was so constructed as to enable the legislature to accommodate laws to the exigencies of the state, through all the changes it hath undergone. And [it] is nearly coëval with our existence as a community, and analogous to the spirit of which all our laws have been made, from time to time, as cases occurred and the good of the public requires. And can it be said, with the least color of truth, that the laws of the state are not adequate to all the purposes of government and of justice?

We need only compare the laws of England with the laws of Connecticut, to be at once convinced of the difference which pervades their whole system. This is manifest in the spirit and principles of the laws, the objects, and in the rules themselves: with respect to the tenure of lands, descents, and who are heirs, and the settlement of insolvent estates, and of other estates testate and intestate, the probate of wills, registering of deeds, the arrangement and jurisdiction of our courts, the forms of civil processes, and the mode of trial, the appointing and returning jurors; and with respect to the settlement and support of the poor, the appointment and regulation of sheriffs, gaols and gaolers, the orderly celebration of marriages and granting of divorces; the means of propagating knowledge, and with respect to the punishments annexed to crimes; and in innumerable other instances, too tedious to mention, which every lawyer is acquainted with. May the citizens of Connecticut glory in this system of government and jurisprudence; which, at first, was the produce of wisdom, is perfected and matured by long experience; which has carried us safe through many a storm, withstood every attack, for more than a century and a half, is grown venerable by age and the wisdom of its regulations, and the rich profusion of blessings which it confers, as the noblest birthright of themselves and their children; and the highest interest and honor of the state as an independent member of a great nation, the rising empire of America!

These rights and liberties are our own, not holden by the gift of a despot. Our government and our rulers are from amongst ourselves; chosen by the free, uninfluenced suffrages of enlightened freemen; not to oppress and devour, but to protect, feed, and bless the people, with the benign and energetic influence of their power (as ministers of God for good to them). This shows the ignorance of those who are clamorous for a new constitution, and the mistake of those who suppose that the rules of the Common Law of England are the common law of Connecticut, until altered by a statute.

On the Common Law of Connecticut

These questions are frequently asked, What is the common law of America? Have we any common law in Connecticut? I know not how I can better resolve these questions than by answering another, (viz.) What is common law? And first, common law is the perfection of reason, arising from the nature of God, of man, and of things, and from their relations, dependencies, and connections: It is universal and extends to all men, and to all combinations of men, in every possible situation, and embraces all cases and questions that can possibly arise. It is in itself perfect, clear and certain; it is immutable, and cannot be changed or altered, without altering the nature and relation of things; it is superior to all other laws and regulations, by it they are corrected and controlled. All positive laws are to be construed by it, and wherein they are opposed to it, they are void. It is immemorial, no memory runneth to the contrary of it; it is co-existent with the nature of man, and commensurate with his being. It is most energetic and coercive, for every one who violates its maxims and precepts are sure of feeling the weight of its sanctions.

Nor may we say, who will ascend into heaven to bring it down, or descend into the depths to bring it up, or traverse the Atlantic to import it? It is near us, it is within us, written upon the table of our hearts, in lively and indelible characters; by it we are constantly admonished and reproved, and by it we shall finally be judged. It is visible in the volume of nature, in all the works and ways of God. Its sound is gone forth into all the earth, and there is no people or nation so barbarous, where its language is not understood.

The dignity of its original, the sublimity of its principles, the purity, excellency and perpetuity of its precepts, are most clearly made known and delineated in the book of divine revelations; heaven and earth may pass away and all the systems and works of man sink into oblivion, but not a jot or tittle of this law shall ever fall.

By this we are taught the dignity, the character, the rights and duties of man, his rank and station here and his relation to futurity, that he hath a property in himself, his powers and faculties, in whatever is produced by the application of them, that he is a free agent subject to the control of none, in his opinions and actions but to his God and the laws, to which he is amenable. This teaches us, so to use our own as not to injure the rights of others. This

enables us, to explain the laws, construe contracts and
agreements, to distinguish injuries, to determine their degree and the reparation in damages which justice requires.
This designates crimes, discovers their aggravations and
ill-tendency, and measures out the punishments proper
and necessary for restraint and example. This defines the
obligations and duties between husbands and wives, parents and children, brothers and sisters, between the rulers
and the people, and the people or citizens towards each
other. This is the Magna Charta of all our natural and
religious rights and liberties—and the only solid basis of our
civil constitution and privileges—in short, it supports, pervades and enlightens all the ways of man, to the noblest
ends by the happiest means, when and wherever its precepts and instructions are observed and followed—the usages and customs of men and the decisions of the courts of
justice serve to declare and illustrate the principles of this
law. But the law exists the same—nor is this a matter of
speculative reasoning merely; but of knowledge and feeling. We know that we have a property in our persons, in
our powers and faculties, and in the fruits and effects of
our industry. We know that we have a right to think and
believe as we choose, to plan and pursue our own affairs
and concerns, whatever [we] judge to be for our advantage, our interest or happiness, provided we do not interfere with any principle of truth or of reason and justice.
We know the value of a good name, and the interest we
have in it. We know that every man's peace and happiness
is his own. Nay, more when our persons are assaulted, our
lives attacked, our liberties infringed, our reputation scan-
dalized, or our property ravaged from us or spoiled, we feel
the injury that is done to us, and by an irrepressible impulse of nature, resent the violation of our rights, and call
upon the powerful arm of justice to administer redress. We
also know that other men have the same rights, the same
sensibility of injuries. When their rights are violated, this
law is therefore evidenced both by the knowledge and the
feelings of men. These ought to be the governing principles
with all legislators in making of laws, with all judges in

construing and executing the laws, and with all citizens in observing and obeying them.

Secondly, another branch of common law is derived from certain usages and customs, universally assented to and adopted in practice by the citizens at large, or by particular classes of men, as the farmers, the merchants, etc. as applicable to their particular business, and to all others of the same description, which are reasonable and beneficial.

These customs or regulations, when thus assented to and adopted in practice, have an influence upon the course of trade and business, and are necessary to be understood and applied in the construction of transactions had and contracts entered into with reference to them. To this end the courts of justice take notice of them as rules of right, and as having the force of laws formed and adopted under the authority of the people.

That these customs and usages must have existed immemorially, and have been compulsory, in order to their being recognized to be law, seems to involve some degree of absurdity—that is, they must have the compulsory force of laws, before they can be recognized to be laws, when they can have no compulsory force till the powers of government have communicated it to them by declaring them to be laws. That [is], so long as any one living can remember when they began to exist they can be of no force or validity whatever, however universally they may be assented to and adopted in practice; but as soon as this is forgotten and no one remembers their beginning, then and not until then they become a law.

This may be necessary in arbitrary governments, but in a free government like ours, I suppose, the better reason to be this:

That as statutes are positive laws enacted by the authority of the legislature, which consists of the representatives of the people, being duly promulgated, are binding upon all, as all are considered as consenting to them by their representatives: So these unwritten customs and regulations, which are reasonable and beneficial, and which

have the sanction of universal consent and adoption in
practice amongst the citizens at large or particular classes
of them, have the force of laws under the authority of the
people. And the courts of justice will recognize and declare
them to be such, and to be obligatory upon the citizens
as necessary rules of construction and of justice. The rea-
sonableness and utility of their operation, and the universality of their adoption, are the better evidences of their
existence and of their having the general consent and approbation, than the circumstance of its being forgotten
when they began to exist.

Thirdly, another important source of common law is, the
adjudications of the courts of justice and the rules of practice adopted in them. These have been learned by practice
only, as we have no treatises upon the subject, and but
one small volume of reports containing a period of about
two years only, and a treatise lately wrote by Mr. Swift,
containing a commentary on the government and laws of
this state. We learn from history, the constitutions of government and the laws of foreign countries, the adjudications and rules of practice adopted in their courts of justice.
But this will not give us the knowledge of our own, and
although we may seem to have borrowed from them, yet
ours is essentially different from all, in that it is highly improved and ameliorated in its principles and regulations,
and simplified in its forms, is adapted to the state of our
country, and to the genius of the people, and calculated in
an eminent manner to improve the mind by the diffusion
of knowledge, and to give effectual security and protection
to the persons, rights, liberties and properties of the citizens, and is clothed with an energy, derived from a source,
and rendered efficacious by a power, unknown in foreign
governments, (*viz.*) the attachment of the citizens who rejoice in being ruled and governed by its laws, for the
blessings it confers. Let us, Americans then, duly appreciate our own government, laws and manners, and be what
we profess—an independent nation—and not plume ourselves upon being humble imitators of foreigners, at home
and in our own country. But let our manners in all re-

spects be characteristic of the spirit and principles of our independence.

I trust by this time the reader has anticipated in his own mind the answer to the questions, what is the common law of America? And have we any common law in the State of Connecticut? These principles, as applied to the situation and genius of the people, the spirit of our government and laws, the tenure of our lands, and the vast variety of objects, civil and military, ecclesiastical and commercial, in our own state have been exemplified in practice, defined, explained and established by the decisions of the courts in innumerable instances, although reports of but few of them have been published. To these I think we ought to resort, and not to foreign systems, to lay a foundation, to establish a character upon, and to rear a system of jurisprudence purely American, without any marks or servility to foreign powers or states; at the same time leave ourselves open to derive instruction and improvement from the observations, discoveries, and experience of the literate, in all countries and nations, respecting jurisprudence and other useful arts and sciences. And indeed, a great part of our legal ideas were originally derived from the laws of England and the civil law, which being duly arranged, have been incorporated into our own system, and adapted to our own situation and circumstances.

It is of great importance to a country or state that the laws which regulate the intercourse among the citizens, determine property, construe and enforce contracts, define crimes and their punishments, and provide remedies for the recovery of rights, and for the redress of wrongs, should be just in principle, clear, concise, and unequivocal in expression, uniform, permanent, and consistent in their meaning and application, and energetic and coercive in their operation, extending to and embracing every possible case. This would enable the courts of law to do justice in all cases, and would supersede the necessity of the courts of chancery—in this state borrowed from a foreign jurisdiction which grew out of the ignorance and barbarism of the law judges at a certain period in that country, from whence borrowed. And would it not be as safe for the people to invest the courts of law with the power of deciding all questions and of giving relief in all cases according to the rules established in chancery as it is to trust those same judges as chancellors to do it? Those rules might be considered as a part of the law, and the remedy be made much more concise and effectual.

Further, would not this remedy great inconveniences and save much expense to suitors, who are frequently turned round at law, to seek a remedy in chancery? And as often turned round in chancery, because they have an adequate remedy at law? These are serious evils and ought not to be permitted to exist in the jurisprudence of a country, famed for liberty and justice; and which can be remedied, only by the interposition of the legislature. . . .

RICHARD RUSH (1780–1859)

AMERICAN JURISPRUDENCE (*Philadelphia, 1815*)

[Despite the sullen hostility of the mass of the population towards lawyers as a class, and despite the popular hatred of the Common Law (which became virulent among the more radical Jeffersonian Democrats, with every encouragement from Jefferson himself), the prestige of the profession steadily increased. In eastern centers the training of candidates became more rigorous, the *esprit* of the bar associations was reinforced by their uniting in denunciation of "pettyfoggers" and by their common measures to maintain and improve standards. Even in the wild new settlements beyond the mountains, attorneys, although still profoundly distrusted, began to acquire reputations for learning that made them figures as awesome to the pioneers as were the revivalistic clergy. Highly effective in this conquest of the common mind was the constant barrage of propaganda which the lawyers levied in their own behalf. The rise of the profession to the lofty eminence it attained by 1830 or thereabouts—to the peak which Tocqueville could describe as that of "the highest political class and the most cultivated portion of society"—was propelled not only by the brilliance of the great jurists and by their increasing displays of dazzling erudition but also by their propensity for advertising their own shining merits.

Richard Rush's contribution to this campaign is espe-

cially interesting because he, a man of varied accomplishments and highly distinguished in his career, wrote his
apologia for the profession in 1815 as a Jeffersonian. Later
he was similarly to maintain his pride in the calling after
becoming a Jacksonian Democrat in Philadelphia, where
the bar was overwhelmingly Whig and furiously anti-
Jackson. He was the second son of the famous Dr. Benjamin Rush, foremost of American physicians in the Revolutionary period, and grew up in a world of culture, literature, and rational strength. He graduated from Princeton
(then, of course, the College of New Jersey) at the age of
fourteen, and was admitted to the Philadelphia bar in
1800. He held many posts of honor: Attorney General of
the United States, Secretary of State, Minister to Great
Britain, Secretary of the Treasury, Minister to France. He
was popular, learned, and graceful. He was immensely
successful in London, where he found himself thoroughly
at home in aristocratic society without for a moment blunt-
ing his democratic convictions.

Rush's pamphlet of 1815 strives to reconcile the restless spirit of the democracy with the rigor of the law, or
rather to show wherein the two really coincide. America
may not yet be able to produce painters or poets equal to
those of Europe, but at the bar we have approached those
"excitements of mind" almost on a par with the luminaries
of the old world. Rush takes especial pleasure in explaining
the reasons for this excellence, dwelling (as subsequently
all defenders of the profession would do) upon the wonderful and strenuous variety of the American practice,
wherein there is no specialization, where every practitioner is obliged to be a legal jack-of-all-trades. His account of the tremendous labor required of the neophyte
lawyer had the effect, as did all other paeans in this key,
of impressing upon the American people the propriety of
the lawyers' claims to pre-eminence. And his conclusion,
comparing Chief Justice John Marshall to Sir William
Scott,[1] was a highly clever device, particularly as being
propounded by a Jeffersonian: Sir William Scott, though a
legend of erudition, was anathema in America for his

having enforced by his admiralty decisions the British Orders in Council directed against American shipping, and so for having forced us into the War of 1812. In Philadelphia, where the war was as much detested as it was in Boston, Rush had resolutely defended the course of President Madison, and had advocated the declaration of war. Yet at this time it was still considered proper form for Jeffersonians to damn John Marshall. Rush's self-possession and independence of spirit are exhibited in even this abbreviated selection from his eloquent pamphlet.]

AMERICAN JURISPRUDENCE, 1815

In the department of jurisprudence the United States probably approach if not in all of these yet in other great excitements of mind, nearer to a par with the old nations than in any other that could be named. Here the law is every thing. It makes its appeal to the strongest motives of interest and of ambition. In most instances it leads to a comfortable subsistence, and in many to independence and wealth. To public honors, if so they are to be denominated, it unquestionably opens a wider door than any other pursuit. But we do not mean to dwell upon the connexion in this country between politics and the law, which would open a space that it is not our purpose on this occasion to occupy. The unbounded freedom of our institutions begets, throughout every portion of the country, a corresponding latitude of conduct and of discussion which exultingly and fiercely disdains to acknowledge any limit or any regulator but the law. Hence the habit of bringing every thing to its test. The bolts of criticism shot from the most exalted heights of intellect on the one hand, and the shafts of unlettered simplicity upon the other, a Burke or a Jack Cade, may fall in eloquent vengeance or in harmless mirth upon this profession; but in a country of equal rights it has ever been a formidable engine of influence in public affairs, and scarcely less of credit and authority in private life. We can only mean, when it is associated with those strict prin-

ciples of probity and honor which not only constitute its
first ornament, but without which it is impossible that it
can ever in any country signally and ultimately prosper.
So endowed, it is, after all, in the beautiful words of the
first Vinerean lecturer, a profession which employs in its
theory the noblest faculties of the soul and exerts in its
practice the cardinal virtues of the heart.

As we outstrip England in her freedom, there is a still
greater call amongst us for those who are found to be so
usefully its ministers. It is like the rule of the political
economist in all other cases, where the supply of the commodity adapts itself to the demand. It may be that the
English loom makes a demand for ten or for twenty work-
men where the American as yet does for one. Hence the
comparative extent, variety, and perfection of their manufactures. But it is probable that the habits, the manners,
and the contentions, of the universally thriving and self-
supported freemen on this side of the Atlantic, call for at
least a couple of lawyers, take the two countries throughout, where the English do for one. Considering Burke's
assertion in 1775 that nearly as many of Blackstone's *Commentaries* were sold in the American colonies alone at that
period as in all England, we think it may be agreed that
we set down the proportion at a safe rate. The noble
definition of law, that nothing is so high as to be above its
reach or so low as to be beyond its care, is probably true
to a greater practical extent in this country than in any
other. The cause obviously is, not our liberty alone, but an
alliance between an active and restless spirit of freedom
and the comfortable condition of all classes of the community, not excepting, relatively considered, even the poor.
This encourages and provokes the disposition to go to law
by supplying it almost universally with the means. We
have honest blacksmiths suing banks for false imprisonment, and street cleaners fine gentlemen for assaults and
batteries as the common occurrences of our courts. Dear,
too, as law is supposed to be in this country, it falls short
of the expenses which are generally the concomitants of
its benefits in England. The sums which under the various

denominations of fees and costs fall upon the suitor by the
time he gets into the house of lords, when he carries his
claims to that final stage of appellate authority, sometimes
become enormous. A member of the House of Commons
stated in his place in 1810, that a bill of costs had been
presented in his court of one of their colonial dominions
three fathoms in length, and Sir William Scott himself
gives us to understand, that there are "some suits famous
in English juridical history for having outlived generations
of suitors. . . ."

The law itself in this country, is, moreover, a science of
great extent. We have an entire substratum of common
law as the broad foundation upon which every thing else
is built. It fills its thousand volumes like that of England,
whose volumes in this respect are at the same time ours.
But the extent of this law, its beginning, its termination;
upon what subjects precisely it operates and where it falls
short, where the analogy of situation holds and where not,
with the shades under which it may do the one or the
other, . . . these start questions upon which the nicest
discriminations of ingenuity and learning have been for a
century at work. Often therefore the American lawyer has
gone through but half his task when he has informed himself of what the common law is. The remaining and perhaps most difficult branch of inquiry is, whether it does or
does not apply to his case. Notwithstanding the determination of the Supreme Court in the case of the *United States*
v. *Hudson and Goodwin,* it is still by no means certain
that that tribunal would not sustain another and more full
argument at this day on the question in its nature so extensive and fundamental as whether or not the federal
government draws to itself the Common Law of England
in criminal matters. When we speak of the great body of
this system of law as a substratum, we mean of course as
applied to the individual states.

The statute law of England during our provincial day,
or anterior to it, is another great division liable to much the
same sort of counter-argument at the hands of those who

have been charged with the heavy task, at which they
still toil, of rearing up the fabric of American jurisprudence. Next comes the prolific exuberance of our own
statute law superinducting its daily modifications upon the
English code, and giving birth to original systems to meet
the new exigencies of our incessant enterprise, our growing
population, and the genius of all our other institutions.
The statutes and the lawsuits to which steam boats alone
have given rise within the last two or three years would
probably occupy several volumes. Those relative to turn-
pike roads and the contentions they have bred, taking all
the states, would probably fill a dozen, and it would be
difficult to limit the further illustrations we could give.
Patents for new inventions would make an ample not say
curious figure. . . .

Lastly in the structure of our judicature we have a
multitude of different sorts of courts. We have courts of
common law and courts of chancery, admiralty and maritime courts, courts civil and courts criminal, sittings at
nisi prius and full terms in bank, register's courts, orphan's
courts, escheator's courts, justices' courts, with the many
gradations of some of them, and with others that might be
made to swell the catalogue. It may be said, that this is
nothing more than the judicial polity of other countries,
particularly Britain, is liable to; that if you will begin at the
piepoudre and go up to the peers in parliament you will
run through, under some modification or others, as long an
enumeration. This may be true. But the difference is, that
the profession here is not subdivided, in any of the states,
in the ways that it is in England, and the American lawyer
is called upon at one period or other of his life to understand the constitution of each of these forums; to be familiar at least with their principles if not with their forms
as he passes on through the usual stages to the head of his
profession.

It may be supposed that great labor is necessary to
master such a range of knowledge. And such, undoubtedly, is the case. The men among us who reach the vantage

ground of the science, who become as well the safe coun-
selors as the eloquent advocates, are only those who in
their early day explore its ways with repetitions of intense
and, through all its dreadful discouragements to the young
mind, unwearied assiduity; and who are afterwards content to devote their days to business and their nights to
study. Sparing indeed must be their relaxations. If they
stop for repose or turn aside for indulgence, like the son of
Abensina in the affecting oriental tale, they will be reminded when perhaps it is too late of the impossibility of
uniting the gratifications of ease with the rewards of diligence. The true enjoyments to be gathered from the rugged path of the profession, and happily they are at once
animating and refined, are those reflections which come
sweetly over the mind, under the consciousness of
duty successfully performed, and of eminence honorably
achieved. . . .

If mind be the result of external stimuli forcing it into
action, our jurisprudence is surrounded by what must provoke and improve its powers. There are reasons why it
ought not to be expected of us to produce a Lord Byron,
or a Walter Scott, a Dugal Stewart perhaps, or other men
of like stamp with those who enrich the British press with
such a copious and constant flow of profound or elegant
literary and scientific productions. We are yet at some distance, though we trust not very great, from the age that
can feed in any extent the merely classic mind into fullness
and perfection. But we see no reasons at all why we may
not breed Gibbs's, and Garrows, and Saubeys, and Law-
rences, and breed them in abundance.[2] If we have not
gained that stage of our growth when the luxury of the
arts and sciences goes hand in hand with all other luxuries,
we enjoy in a proud degree, to use an expression of the
Edinburgh review, "the luxury of liberty"; and it is not
irrational to suppose that those who officiate so largely at
her altars should arrive at a perfection in their duty.

In throwing out a conjectural sentiment, and one not
altogether hasty, we presume to think, that the law-mind,

if we may so speak, of the United States has, from adequate causes, forerun the general condition of literature, and already been accelerated and matured into as much force and discipline as it is likely to reach in any more distant period of the country's advancement. How it may be in medicine, and in divinity, we do not presume on this occasion to intimate. If there be fit matter for reflection under these heads it must be gone into in some separate disquisition. In painting there might be room to say something, keeping it to the walk of native genius at least. We pass to our proper subject. The profession of the law with us, then, seems to be absorbed by duties as numerous and as commanding at this day, as it is probable that it can be at any more remote epoch of fuller population and greater riches. Those scenes of portentous convulsion which in their occasional visitations rouse the mind of a whole community into temporary and preternatural force, and which more frequently belong to a full than a slender population, and to age than to youth, may indeed form exceptions. But we speak of the settled and ordinary course of things. As our lonely territory continues to be overspread with cultivated fields, and to glitter with the spires of villages and cities, we shall, to be sure, witness a corresponding increase in the professors of this science; but it does not appear to follow that their faculties will be tasked to a higher compass of exertion than the faculties of those who now flourish in the walks of full occupation. There are, doubtless, more men in England at the present day who write well, than there were in the time of Queen Anne or Queen Elizabeth; but it will scarcely be said that they write better than those who were at the head of the list at either of those periods.

As to profound scholarship, as a Wakefield[3] or a Porson[4] might define the term, it is not to be looked for as an adjunct of the profession in any country. But for those classical embellishments which are ancillary, and whose tincture lends its chastening without monopolizing, it is probable that they are as much its concomitants with us at the present as they will be at a more distant era, because as much so we incline to think, taking the profession upon a large scale, as can be made compatible at any time with its unrelaxing and intrinsic toil. The necessity of those preparatory studies which alone can form the taste, and lift up the mind to proper conceptions of eminence, cannot be too anxiously and too constantly impressed upon the youth who is destined for the bar. But when once he has plunged into the profession he will find that, to the precepts of Blackstone's valedictory to his muse, he must submit in the full spirit of obedience. . . .

There is indeed, at the present day in England a judge, perhaps their first, of the volumes containing whose decisions it has been said in the British house of commons, "that they were no less valuable to the classical reader than to the student of law by perpetuating the style in which the judgments of the court were delivered." A man he is of dazzling mind. Born, we believe, a miller's son, he can talk of giving a *rusticum judicium*.[5] Yet, surely no judge upon the face of the earth was farther from having rendered such a one. His intellect is so polished that it has been called transparent. Some of his pages are as if diamond sparks were on them. When he deals in wit, it is like a sunbeam and gone as quick. But so much the worse; we pity the more the suitor, or the poor vice-admiralty judge, it may happen to hit. Abundant learning is also his. We must say of him, that if he wants qualities necessary to consummate the fame of a great judge, he has others which perhaps no judge ever possessed before, or in the same degree. It was said, "How sweet an Ovid was in Murray lost." But the judge we speak of is an Ariel. He holds a judicial wand. Touching the scales with it they at once look even, no matter what preponderance an instant before. How can such a judge be truly great?

One day, in the midst of some of those beautiful little judicial aphorisms the web of which he can weave so fine, he declares "that astutia does not belong to a court." The next "that humanity is but its second virtue, justice being forever the first." The third that it is "monstrous to suppose

that because one nation falls into guilt others are let loose
from the morality of public law." But a frost comes on the
fourth! Certain retaliating orders are laid upon his desk,
that shrine which no foreign touch ought ever to pollute.
Unlike an illustrious British judge who has just returned
from India, the pliant spirit bows obedience. Instead of the
dignity of his mind upholding the independence of justice,
its subtlety is enlisted to show that on her majestic form no
violation was imprinted. In one breath admitting that the
rescript of the throne was the rule of his decision, he strives
in the next to hide the consciousness of judicial obeisance.
In an argument where the utmost attenuation of thought is
drawn out into corresponding exilities of expression, he
labors with abortive yet splendid ingenuity to show, that
justice and such rescripts must ever be in harmonious
union. So spake not the Holts and the Hales! No doubt it
is a keen, and an exquisite, and a supple mind. It can en-
chain its listeners. Leaving its strength, it can disport in its
gambols; it can exhale its sweets. But is it, can it be, great?
Where is the lofty port when it can thus bend? Acknowl-
edging its confinement within royal orders, can it hold in
true keeping, the divine attribute it was sworn to cherish
unsullied? It is impossible.

There graces the first seat of judicial magistracy in this
country a man of another stamp, and exhibiting different
aspects of excellence. Venerable and dignified, laborious
and intuitive, common law, chancery law and admiralty
law each make their demands upon his profound, his discriminating, and his well stored, mind. Universal in his attainments in legal science, prompt and patient, courteous
and firm, he fills up, by a combination of rare endowments,
the measure of his difficult, his extensive and his responsible duties; responsible not to the dictates of an executive,
but, moving in a sphere of true independence, responsible
to his conscience, to his country, and to his God. What a
grand, and to a mind exalted and virtuous, what an awful
sphere? How independent, how responsible! Vain would it
be for us to expect to do justice to the full orbed merit with
which he moves in it. Bred up in a state rich in great

names, counting her Washingtons, her Jeffersons, her Madisons, he long sustained a career of the highest reputation at the bar. Passing to the bench of the Supreme Court of the United States, he carried to its duties a mind matured by experience, and invigorated by long daily and successful toil. In the voluminous state of our jurisprudence, every portion of which is occasionally brought under his review, and in the novelties of our political state, often does it happen that questions are brought before him where the path is untrodden, where neither the book case nor the record exist to guide, and where the elementary writer himself glimmers dimly. It is on such occasions that he pierces what is dark, examines what is remote, separates what is entangled, and draws down analogies from the fountain of first principles. Seizing with a large grasp what few other minds at first see, he embodies his comprehensive and distinct conceptions in language not sarcastic, but suited to the gravity and to the solemnity of the temple around him; thus he is found always with masterly ability, and most frequently with conviction, to lay open and elucidate the difficult subject. If there be any applicable learning, to a mind so formed, so furnished, and so trained, it is reasonable to think that it will be at hand. Where there is none, the fertile deductions of its own independent vigor and clearness stand in the place of learning, and will become learning to those who are to live after him. His country alternately a neutral and a belligerent, again and again is he called upon to expound the volume of national law, to explore its intricate passages, to mark its nicest limitations. Upon such occasions, as well as upon the entire body of commercial law so copiously in the last resort intermingled with his adjudications, his recorded opinions will best make known to the world the penetration of his views, the extent of his knowledge, and the solidity of his judgment. They are a national treasure. Posterity will read in them as well the rule of conduct, as the monuments of a genius that would have done honor to any age or to any country.

Such is the sketch we would attempt of the judicial character of the Chief Justice of our country. That country is on a swift wing to greatness and to glory. To the world at large the early day of her jurisprudence may remain unknown until then; but then it will break into light, and his name, like the Fortesques and the Cokes of the early day of England, fill perhaps even a wider region from the less local foundations upon which it will rest. Let the courts of England boast of Sir William Scott. Those of America will boast of John Marshall.

NOTES

[1] Sir William Scott, Lord Stowell (1745–1836), was judge of the High Court of Admiralty, 1798 to 1820, and particularly outraged the American sense of justice by enforcing what American lawyers believed was an illegitimate standard, the infamous "Rule of the War of 1756."

[2] These were outstanding English judges of the turn of the century, names to conjure with in the America of their time.

[3] Gilbert Wakefield (1756–1801), a learned classical scholar, champion of orthodox Christianity against the Deists.

[4] Richard Porson (1759–1808), foremost Greek scholar of the English eighteenth century.

[5] A rustic judgment—i.e., an opinion of untutored common sense.

DANIEL WEBSTER (1782–1852)

THE DARTMOUTH COLLEGE CASE (1818)[1]

[The career of Daniel Webster is much too variegated to be summarized in a few sentences. I should like simply to remark that the memory of him which most widely obtains today neglects the fact that he was a great lawyer, a man of considerable legal culture. He studied under Christopher Gore in Boston and by the time he was admitted to the bar, 1805, he had read thoroughly most of the massive classics—those books which a half century before John Adams had found so difficult to obtain. He practised law in Portsmouth, New Hampshire; immediately upon his removal to Boston in 1816 he enjoyed a highly remunerative practice.

His defense of the charter of his alma mater before the Supreme Court has long been a classic of American political oratory. While otherwise I have not included in this anthology records of court proceedings, I could hardly leave Webster's peroration out, if only because it has remained our most powerful statement of the sanctity of contract. As such it is the bulwark against any form of public appropriation of a chartered "corporation." Webster's argument would extend as well to common carriers, factories, banks, etc., as to colleges.]

THE DARTMOUTH COLLEGE CASE, 1818[1]

When donations are made, by the legislature or others, to a charity already existing, without any condition, or the specification of any new use, the donation follows the nature of the charity. Hence the doctrine, that all eleemosynary corporations are private bodies. They are founded by private persons, and on private property. The public cannot be charitable in these institutions. It is not the money of the public, but of private persons, which is dispensed. It may be public, that is general, in its uses and advantages; and the State may very laudably add contributions of its own to the funds; but it is still private in the tenure of the property, and in the right of administering the funds.

If the doctrine laid down by Lord Holt,[2] and the House of Lords, in *Phillips v. Bury*, and recognized and established in all the other cases, be correct, the property of this college was private property; it was vested in the trustees by the charter, and to be administered by them, according to the will of the founder and donors, as expressed in the charter. They were also visitors of the charity, in the most ample sense. They had, therefore, as they contend, privileges, property, and immunities, within the true meaning of the Bill of Rights. They had rights, and still have them, which they can assert against the legislature, as well as against other wrongdoers. It makes no difference, that the estate is holden for certain trusts. The legal estate is still theirs. They have a right of visiting and superintending the trust; and this is an object of legal protection, as much as any other right. The charter declares that the powers conferred on the trustees are "privileges, advantages, liberties, and immunities," but by judgment of his peers, or the law of the land. The argument on the other side is, that, although these terms may mean something in the Bill of Rights, they mean nothing in this charter. But they are terms of legal signification, and very properly used in the charter. They are equivalent with *franchises*. Blackstone says that *franchise* and *liberty* are used as synonymous terms. And after enumerating other liberties and franchises, he says: "It is likewise a franchise for a number of persons to be incorporated and subsist as a body politic, with a power to maintain perpetual succession and do other corporate acts; and each individual member of such a corporation is also said to have a franchise or freedom. . . ."

Individuals have a right to use their own property for purposes of benevolence, either towards the public, or towards other individuals. They have a right to exercise this benevolence in such lawful manner as they may choose; and when the government has induced and excited it, by contracting to give perpetuity to the stipulated manner of exercising it, it is not law, but violence, to rescind this contract, and seize on the property. Whether the State will grant these franchises, and under what conditions it will grant them, it decides for itself. But when once granted, the constitution holds them to be sacred, till forfeited for just cause.

That all property, of which the use may be beneficial to the public, belongs therefore to the public, is quite a new doctrine. It has no precedent, and is supported by no known principle. Dr. Wheelock[3] might have answered his purposes, in this case, by executing a private deed of trust. He might have conveyed his property to trustees, for precisely such uses as are described in this charter. Indeed, it appears that he had contemplated the establishing of his school in that manner, and had made his will, and devised the property to the same persons who were afterwards appointed trustees in the charter. Many literary and other charitable institutions are founded in that manner, and the trust is renewed, and conferred on other persons, from time to time, as occasion may require. In such a case, no lawyer would or could say, that the legislature might divest the trustees, constituted by deed or will, seize upon the property, and give it to other persons, for other purposes.

And does the granting of a charter, which is only done to
perpetuate the trust in a more convenient manner, make
any difference? Does or can this change the nature of the
charity, and turn it into a public political corporation? Happily, we are not without authority on this point. It has been
considered and adjudged. Lord Hardwicke[4] says, in so
many words, "The charter of the crown cannot make a
charity more or less public, but only more permanent than
it would otherwise be."

The granting of the corporation is but making the trust
perpetual, and does not alter the nature of the charity. The
very object sought in obtaining such charter, and in giving
property to such a corporation, is to make and keep it private property, and to clothe it with all the security and
inviolability of private property. The intent is, that there
shall be a legal private ownership, and that the legal
owners shall maintain and protect the property, for the
benefit of those for whose use it was designed. Who ever
endowed the public? Who ever appointed a legislature to
administer his charity? Or who ever heard, before, that a
gift to a college, or a hospital, or an asylum, was, in reality,
nothing but a gift to the State? . . .

By the law of the land is most clearly intended the general law; a law which hears before it condemns; which proceeds upon inquiry, and renders judgment only after trial.
The meaning is, that every citizen shall hold his life, liberty, property, and immunities under the protection of the
general rules which govern society. Every thing which may
pass under the form of an enactment is not therefore to be
considered the law of the land. If this were so, acts of at-
tainder, bills of pains and penalties, acts of confiscation,
acts reversing judgments, and acts directly transferring one
man's estate to another, legislative judgments, decrees, and
forfeitures in all possible forms, would be the law of the
land.

Such a strange construction would render constitutional
provisions of the highest importance completely inopera-
tive and void. It would tend directly to establish the union

of all powers in the legislature. There would be no general, permanent law for courts to administer or men to live under. The administration of justice would be an empty form, an idle ceremony. Judges would sit to execute legislative judgments and decrees; not to declare the law or to administer the justice of the country. "Is that the law of the land," said Mr. Burke, "upon which, if a man go to Westminster Hall, and ask counsel by what title or tenure he holds his privilege or estate *according to the law of the land*, he should be told, that the law of the land is not yet known; that no decision or decree has been made in his case; that when a decree shall be passed, he will then know *what the law of the land is?* Will this be said to be the law of the land, by any lawyer who has a rag of a gown left upon his back, or a wig with one tie upon his head? . . ."

There are, in this case, all the essential constituent parts of a contract. There is something to be contracted about, there are parties, and there are plain terms in which the agreement of the parties on the subject of the contract is expressed. There are mutual considerations and inducements. The charter recites, that the founder, on his part, has agreed to establish his seminary in New Hampshire, and to enlarge it beyond its original design, among other things, for the benefit of that Province; and thereupon a charter is given to him and his associates, designated by himself, promising and assuring to them, under the plighted faith of the State, the right of governing the college and administering its concerns in the manner provided in the charter. There is a complete and perfect grant to them of all the power of superintendence, visitation, and government. Is not this a contract? If lands or money had been granted to him and his associates, for the same purposes, such grant could not be rescinded. And is there any difference, in legal contemplation, between a grant of corporate franchises and a grant of tangible property? No such difference is recognized in any decided case, nor does it exist in the common apprehension of mankind.

It is therefore contended, that this case falls within the true meaning of this provision of the Constitution, as expounded in the decisions of this court; that the charter of 1769 is a contract, a stipulation or agreement, mutual in its considerations, express and formal in its terms, and of a most binding and solemn nature. That the acts in question impair this contract, has already been sufficiently shown. They repeal and abrogate its most essential parts.

A single observation may not be improper on the opinion of the court of New Hampshire, which has been published. The learned judges who delivered that opinion have viewed this question in a very different light from that in which the plaintiffs have endeavored to exhibit it. After some general remarks, they assume that this college is a public corporation; and on this basis their judgment rests. Whether all colleges are not regarded as private and eleemosynary corporations, by all law writers and all judicial decisions; whether this college was not founded by Dr. Wheelock; whether the charter was not granted at his request, the better to execute a trust, which he had already created; whether he and his associates did not become visitors, by the charter; and whether Dartmouth College be not, therefore, in the strictest sense, a private charity, are questions which the learned judges do not appear to have discussed.

It is admitted in that opinion, that, if it be a private corporation, its rights stand on the same ground as those of an individual. The great question, therefore, to be decided is, To which class of corporations do colleges thus founded belong? And the plaintiffs have endeavored to satisfy the court, that, according to the well-settled principles and uniform decisions of law, they are private, eleemosynary corporations.

Much has heretofore been said on the necessity of admitting such a power in the legislature as has been assumed in this case. Many cases of possible evil have been imagined, which might otherwise be without remedy. Abuses, it is contended, might arise in the management of such institutions, which the ordinary courts of law would be unable to correct. But this is only another instance of that habit of supposing extreme cases, and then of reasoning from them, which is the constant refuge of those who are obliged to defend a cause, which, upon its merits, is indefensible. It would be sufficient to say in answer, that it is not pretended that there was here any such case of necessity. But a still more satisfactory answer is, that the apprehension of danger is groundless, and therefore the whole argument fails. Experience has not taught us that there is danger of great evils or of great inconvenience from this source. Hitherto, neither in our own country nor elsewhere have such cases of necessity occurred. The judicial establishments of the State are presumed to be competent to prevent abuses and violations of trust, in cases of this kind, as well as in all others. If they be not, they are imperfect, and their amendment would be a most proper subject for legislative wisdom. Under the government and protection of the general laws of the land, these institutions have always been found safe, as well as useful. They go on, with the progress of society, accommodating themselves easily, without sudden change or violence, to the alterations which take place in its condition, and in the knowledge, the habits, and pursuits of men. The English colleges were founded in Catholic ages. Their religion was reformed with the general reformation of the nation; and they are suited perfectly well to the purpose of educating the Protestant youth of modern times. Dartmouth College was established under a charter granted by the Provincial government; but a better constitution for a college, or one more adapted to the condition of things under the present government, in all material respects, could not now be framed. Nothing in it was found to need alteration at the Revolution. The wise men of that day saw in it one of the best hopes of future times, and commended it as it was, with parental care, to the protection and guardianship of the government of the State. A charter of more liberal sentiments, of wiser provisions, drawn with more care, or in a better spirit, could not be expected at any time or from any source. The college needed no change in its organization or government.

That which it did need was the kindness, the patronage, the bounty of the legislature; not a mock elevation to the character of a university, without the solid benefit of a shilling's donation to sustain the character; not the swelling and empty authority of establishing institutes and other colleges. This unsubstantial pageantry would seem to have been in derision of the scanty endowment and limited means of an unobtrusive, but useful and growing seminary. Least of all was there a necessity, or pretence of necessity, to infringe its legal rights, violate its franchises and privileges, and pour upon it these overwhelming streams of litigation.

But this argument from necessity would equally apply in all other cases. If it be well founded, it would prove, that, whenever any inconvenience or evil is experienced from the restrictions imposed on the legislature by the Constitution, these restrictions ought to be disregarded. It is enough to say, that the people have thought otherwise. They have, most wisely, chosen to take the risk of occasional inconvenience from the want of power, in order that there might be a settled limit to its exercise, and a permanent security against its abuse. They have imposed prohibitions and restraints; and they have not rendered these altogether vain and nugatory by conferring the power of dispensation. If inconvenience should arise which the legislature cannot remedy under the power conferred upon it, it is not answerable for such inconvenience. That which it cannot do within the limits prescribed to it, it cannot do at all. No legislature in this country is able, and may the time never come when it shall be able, to apply to itself the memorable expression of a Roman pontiff: *"Licet hoc DE JURE non possumus, volumus tamen DE PLENITUDINE POTESTATIS."*[5]

The case before the court is not of ordinary importance, nor of every-day occurrence. It affects not this college only, but every college, and all the literary institutions of the country. They have flourished hitherto, and have become in a high degree respectable and useful to the community. They have all a common principle of existence, the inviolability of their charters. It will be a dangerous, a most dangerous experiment, to hold these institutions subject to the rise and fall of popular parties, and the fluctuations of political opinions. If the franchise may be at any time taken away, or impaired, the property also may be taken away, or its use perverted. Benefactors will have no certainty of effecting the object of their bounty; and learned men will be deterred from devoting themselves to the service of such institutions, from the precarious title of their offices. Colleges and halls will be deserted by all better spirits, and become a theatre for the contentions of politics. Party and faction will be cherished in the places consecrated to piety and learning. These consequences are neither remote nor possible only. They are certain and immediate.

When the court in North Carolina declared the law of the State, which repealed a grant to its university, unconstitutional and void, the legislature had the candor and the wisdom to repeal the law. This example, so honorable to the State which exhibited it, is most fit to be followed on this occasion. And there is good reason to hope that a State, which has hitherto been so much distinguished for temperate counsels, cautious legislation, and regard to law, will not fail to adopt a course which will accord with her highest and best interests, and in no small degree elevate her reputation.

It was for many and obvious reasons most anxiously desired that the question of the power of the legislature over this charter should have been finally decided in the State court. An earnest hope was entertained that the judges of the court might have viewed the case in a light favorable to the rights of the trustees. That hope has failed. It is here that those rights are now to be maintained, or they are prostrated for ever. *Omnia alia perfugia bonorum, subsidia, consilia, auxilia, jura ceciderunt. Quem enim alium appellem? quem obtester? quem implorem? Nisi hoc loco, nisi apud vos, nisi per vos, judices, salutem nostram, quae spe exigua extremaque pendet, tenuerimus; nihil est praeterea quo confugere possimus.*[6]

NOTES

[1] The technical title of the case is *Trustees of Dartmouth College v. Woodward*. It was first tried before the Supreme Court of New Hampshire in May 1817, where Webster worked jointly with two lawyers then more eminent than he. His plea before the Supreme Court of the United States gained him a place in the front rank of the American bar. The favorable decision of the Court was rendered on February 2, 1819.

[2] Sir John Holt (1642–1710), Lord Chief Justice of the King's Bench.

[3] Eleazar Wheelock (1711–79), founder and first President of Dartmouth College, obtained the charter from Governor John Wentworth in 1769.

[4] Philip Yorke, Earl of Hardwicke (1690–1764), Lord Chancellor.

[5] "It may be that we cannot do this legally, but are willing to do it nevertheless from the fulness of our power."

[6] "Every other refuge and support of good men, wisdom, assistance, law, has failed. Whom else can I call upon? whom supplicate? whom implore? Only in this place, only among you, only through you, judges, can we hold to our safety, which hangs upon a slender and extreme hope; there is nowhere else to which we may flee."

JOSEPH STORY (1779–1845)

ADDRESS DELIVERED BEFORE THE MEMBERS OF THE SUFFOLK BAR, AT THEIR ANNIVERSARY ON THE 4TH SEPTEMBER, 1821, AT BOSTON

[In the persons of Joseph Story and James Kent the dreams of John Adams, the prophecies of Richard Rush, the aspirations of the entire profession seemed, in the eyes of their contemporaries, to be realized. Though Andrew Jackson termed them the "most dangerous" men in the country, their performances as judges and their immense labors in providing American students with native equivalents of Blackstone, marshaled out of an erudition even greater than Blackstone's and apparently the equal of that mastered by any of the British juridical behemoths of the late eighteenth and early nineteenth centuries—these achievements vindicated every boast with which the lawyers had for all the years since the Revolution insulted the mediocrity of the communal intelligence. That both these men were Whigs, that both were in the context of their times what must be called—for lack of a better term— "conservatives," only made the intellectual battlements which they erected around the sacred precinct of the law the more awesome to would-be despoilers. Their writings on the philosophy and theory of law are by now mainly of historical interest, with little or no relevance to modern education and theorizing. Yet out of them more modern legal thinking had to come, if only by reaction. In the retrospect of history, however, it may seem that they both did more for the profession, even granting their gigantic scholarship, by their more casual utterances on the nature, the ideals, the requirements and the satisfactions of legal study. There were a host of other titans who emerged at about the same time, men like William Pinkney, William Wirt, and Horace Binney, who for the time being persuaded themselves and a large portion of the populace that Judge Chipman's call for "genius" had been answered in more than good measure. But supreme among these demigods reigned the two genuine gods of both gentlemanly elegance and scholarly grace, Story and Kent.

Joseph Story was born in Marblehead, Massachusetts, and administered, characteristically, most of his elementary education to himself. He graduated from Harvard in 1798, and read law with two of the leading members of the Massachusetts bar. He read far beyond them, performing prodigies of research which are still legendary in the region and which progressed as far ahead again as Adams earlier had himself advanced. When Story opened his own office, in 1801, he stepped into an assured success. At first he was a Jeffersonian, but the Embargo outraged him as it did his Federalist colleagues, and he became a passionate anti-Democrat. He had a term in the House of Representatives, and in 1811 was appointed, aged only thirty-two, an Associate Justice of the Supreme Court.

Each of the Justices at this time rode—literally—a circuit when not in session in Washington. Story's included all New England except Vermont. Hearing cases in Court was enough of a full-time job for any ordinary man, and following the circuit in New England was enough for another. But Story took on still a third career, in 1829, when he accepted the professorship founded by Nathan Dane at the newly created (1817) Harvard Law School. There he and his colleague, J. H. Ashmun (for a while they were the entire faculty), pioneered in law-school education. Story's prestige was indubitably a principal factor in turning the

Harvard Law School from a provincial academy into a national institution.

As if these three occupations were not enough to kill a man from overwork, Story found time amid them to turn out volume after volume of his massive *Commentaries,* beginning with *Bailments* in 1832 and so on down a list of eight others, ending with *Promissory Notes* in 1845. It is not surprising that in that year even he, with his incredible vitality and his fabulous habits of work, broke down and died. Meanwhile he had written majority opinions in several of the crucial cases tried before the Supreme Court; even his minority opinions are still respected and contribute significantly to our constitutional doctrine.

The lecture of 1821 was delivered when Story was approaching the zenith of his glory. In many ways it ought to serve as the introduction to this volume; I have preferred to some extent to restrict my own commentary thus far in order to let Story tell the full tale now; but out of respect to chronology I have withheld his account until it could be placed in the proper setting. The opening pages of his "Address" recount, better than can any historian, the rise of the profession and enumerate the obstacles with which it had to contend. Story, following in the footsteps of John Adams, had lived intensely through these exhilarating years, and could take comfort that Adams was still alive to read if not to hear him. He could here give full expression to his conception of scholarship, and make an incantation out of the names of the great civilians, of the historic expounders of the Common Law, of the formulators of equity and admiralty, until the imagination of the vulgar was totally routed and the distinction between a real lawyer and a pettifogger was immutably established.

Yet the oration has a further purpose than merely to assert the regal dignity of the law. It is addressed to the American situation, to the problem of constructing, by legal means, a nationalism out of the still loosely joined confederation of states, each jealous of the federal power, the whole riven by sectional competitions. He, of all the

legal thinkers of these years, will be the one most eager to
enumerate the areas of English Common Law which have
no part in American jurisprudence—so that he may cling
the more tenaciously to its substance, which, in spite of
Mr. Jefferson (also still living), he will insist is the law
above and upon the states. By clearing the deck of venerable rubbish, Story is the more prepared to fight for the
great "American" principle of judicial review, and so to
prove himself, though now a "conservative," a liberal
American in the dignified Republican (soon to become
Whig) sense. His whole point is that, as Webster had
demonstrated in the Dartmouth Case, the law is a bulwark against the transitory and ravaging passions of the
mob, but by no means an anti-republican machine. On the
contrary, by serving as defenses against *both* anarchy and
despotism, the courts—primarily those administering the
Common Law in American surroundings, but also those in
equity—are the guardians of democracy, the lions under,
not a throne, but a magnificent Republic.

Thus becomes plausible the terrible burden Story would
lay upon the beginning student of law: that he read not
only Blackstone and then Coke (Story says he himself commenced his study being charmed by Blackstone, but having to go on to Coke, wept)—but, in addition, the dreary
pages of the civilians and decisions in equity—this burden
for the reason that within this maze of erudition is the
magic that will maintain an order of society which in relation to Europe is still "revolutionary" but which in its
own terms is basically conservative.

In the short period from Judge Chipman's *Sketches* of
1793 to Judge Story's "Address" of 1821 this much of the
tendency of the legal mind had been revealed. We think
of those decades as relatively peaceful, affording time for
cogitation. Actually, the pace of the transformation was
breathtaking. Although the great lawyers and judges
dressed with elaborate decorum, read Latin and Greek in
their studies, and drank port ceremoniously, the intellectual
pressures were, to our gaze, tremendous. Story's oration
in 1821 is memorable for its response, in short compass, to
all of these exactions.]

ADDRESS DELIVERED BEFORE THE MEMBERS OF THE SUFFOLK BAR, 1821

Before the American Revolution, from a variety of causes, which it is not difficult to enumerate, our progress in the law was slow, though not slower, perhaps, than in the other departments of science. The resources of the country were small, the population was scattered, the business of the courts was limited, the compensation for professional services was moderate, and the judges were not generally selected from those, who were learned in the law. The colonial system restrained our foreign commerce; and, as the principal trade was to or through the mother country, our most important contracts began or ended there. That there were learned men in the profession in those times, it is not necessary to deny. But the number was small. And from the nature of the business, which occupied the courts, the knowledge required for common use was neither very ample, nor very difficult. The very moderate law libraries, then to be found in the country, would completely establish this fact, if it could be seriously controverted. Our land titles were simple. Our contracts principally sprung up from the ordinary relations of debtor and creditor. Our torts were cast in the common mold of trespasses on lands or to goods, or personal injuries; and the most important discussions grew out of our provincial statutes. Great lawyers do not usually flourish under such auspices, and great judges still more rarely. Why should one accomplish himself in that learning, which is more of curiosity than use? which neither adds to fame nor wealth? which is not publicly sought for or admired? which devotes life to pursuits and refinements, not belonging to our own age or country? The few manuscripts of adjudged cases, which now remain, confirm these remarks. If, here and there, a learned argument appears, it strikes us with surprise, rather from its rarity than its extraordinary authority. In the whole series of our reports, there are very few cases, in which the ante-revolutionary law has either illustrated or settled an adjudication.

The progress of jurisprudence since the termination of the War of Independence, and especially within the last twenty years, has been remarkable throughout all America. More than one hundred and fifty volumes of reports are already published, containing a mass of decisions, which evince uncommon ambition to acquire the highest professional character. The best of our reports scarcely shrink from a comparison with those of England in the corresponding period; and even those of a more provincial cast exhibit researches of no mean extent, and presage future excellence. The danger, indeed, seems to be, not that we shall hereafter want able reports, but that we shall be overwhelmed by their number and variety.

In this respect, our country presents a subject of very serious contemplation and interest to the profession. There are now twenty-four states in the Union, in all of which, except Louisiana, the Common Law is the acknowledged basis of their jurisprudence. Yet this jurisprudence, partly by statute, partly by judicial interpretations, and partly by local usages and peculiarities, is perpetually receding farther and farther from the common standard. While the states retain their independent sovereignties, as they must continue to do under our federative system, it is hopeless to expect, that any greater uniformity will exist in the future than in the past. Nor do I know, that, so far as domestic happiness and political convenience are concerned, a greater uniformity would in most respects be desirable. The task, however, of administering justice in the state as well as national courts, from the new and peculiar relations of our system, must be very laborious and perplexing; and the conflict of opinion upon general questions of law, in the rival jurisdictions of the different states, will not be less distressing to the philosophical jurist, than to the practical lawyer. . . .

In comparing the extent of American jurisprudence with that of England, we shall find, that, if in some respects it is more narrow, in others it is more comprehensive. The whole ecclesiastical law of England, unless so far as it may operate on past cases, is obsolete. The genius of our institutions has universally prohibited any religious establishment, state or national. Nor is there the slightest reason to presume, that the imposition of tithes could ever be successfully introduced here, except by the strong arm of martial law, forcing its way by conquest. It was always resisted during our colonial dependency; and would now be thought at war with all, that we prize in religion or civil freedom. The numerous questions respecting tithes and moduses, quare impedits, and advowsons, and presentations, the fruitful progeny of that establishment, are gone to the same tomb, where the feudal tenures repose, in their robes of state, in dim and ancient majesty. In the next place, the right of progeniture being abolished, and all estates descending in coparceny, and entails being practically changed into fee simple estates, there is no necessity for those intricate conveyances, settlements, and devises, with which the anxiety of parents and friends to provide against the inconveniences of the law has filled all the courts of England. Of this troubled stream of controversy we may indeed say, "It flows, and flows, and flows, and ever will flow on." In the next place, we are rid, not only of the feudal services and tenures, but of all the customary law, of our parent country, the ancient demesnes, the copyholds, the manorial customs and rights, and the customs of gavelkind, and borough English. The cases, in which prerogative or privilege can arise, are few, and limited by law. Long terms, and leases, and annuities, charged on land, are rare among us; and the complicated questions of contract and of rent, which fill the books, are of course scarcely heard of in our courts. We have no game laws to harass our peasantry, or to form an odious distinction for our gentlemen; and the concealed spears, and the man-traps, never cross our paths, or disturb our fancies. The penalties of praemunire cannot be incurred; for we neither court nor fear papal bulls or excommunications. Outlawry, as a civil process, if it have a legal entity, is almost unknown in practice. An appeal of death for robbery never drew its breath among us; nor can it now be brought forth to battle in its dark array of armor, to astonish and confuse us, as it recently did all Westminster Hall. These are no small departments of the Common Law. A few of them, indeed, are almost obsolete in England; but the residue form a body of principles so artificial, and so difficult, that they leave behind them few, which can in these respects justly claim precedency.

With all these abridgments, however, our law is still sufficiently extensive to occupy all the time, and employ all the talents, and exhaust all the learning, of our ablest lawyers and judges. The studies of twenty years leave much behind, that is yet to be grappled with and mastered. And if the law of a single state is enough for a long life of labor and ambition, the task falls still heavier on those, who frequent the national courts, and are obliged to learn other branches of law, which are almost exclusively cognizable there. When it is considered, that the equity jurisprudence of the courts of the United States is like that of England, with the occasional adoption of the peculiar equities of local law; and that their admiralty jurisdiction takes within its circuit, not merely the prize and maritime law, but seizures also for the breach of municipal regulations; when to these are added the interpretation of the treaties and statutes of the United States, and the still more grave discussion of constitutional questions, and the relative rights of states and their citizens, in respect to other states;—it cannot well be doubted, that the administration of justice is there filled with perplexities, that strain the human mind to its utmost bearings.

The most delicate, and, at the same time, the proudest attribute of American jurisprudence is the right of its judicial tribunals to decide questions of constitutional law. In other governments, these questions cannot be entertained or decided by courts of justice; and, therefore, whatever may be the theory of the constitution, the legislative authority is practically omnipotent, and there is no means of contesting the legality or justice of a law, but by an appeal to arms. This can be done only, when oppression weighs heavily and grievously on the whole people, and is then resisted by all, because it is felt by all. But the oppression, that strikes at a humble individual, though it robs him of character, or fortune, or life, is remediless; and, if it becomes the subject of judicial inquiry, judges may lament, but cannot resist, the mandates of the legislature.

Far different is the case in our country; and the privilege of bringing every law to the test of the constitution belongs to the humblest citizen, who owes no obedience to any legislative act, which transcends the constitutional limits. Some visionary statesmen, indeed, who affect to believe, that the legislature can do no wrong, and some zealous leaders, who affect to believe, that popular opinion is the voice of unerring wisdom, have, at times, questioned this authority of courts of justice. If they were correct in their doctrine, we might as well be without a written constitution of government, since the minority would always be in complete subjection to the majority; and it is to be feared, that the experience of mankind has never shown, that the despotism of numbers has been more mild or equitable than that swayed by a single hand. This heresy, as questionable in point of sound policy, as it is unconstitutional in its language, has hitherto made but little progress among us. The wise, and the learned, and the virtuous, have been nearly unanimous in supporting that doctrine, which courts of justice have uniformly asserted, that the constitution is not the law for the legislature only, but is the law, and the supreme law, which is to direct and control all judicial proceedings.

The discussion of constitutional questions throws a lustre round the Bar, and gives a dignity to its functions, which can rarely belong to the profession in any other country. Lawyers are here, emphatically, placed as sentinels upon the outposts of the constitution; and no nobler end can be proposed for their ambition or patriotism, than to stand as faithful guardians of the constitution, ready to defend its legitimate powers, and to stay the arm of legislative, executive, or popular oppression. If their eloquence can charm, when it vindicates the innocent, and the suffering under private wrongs; if their learning and genius can, with almost superhuman witchery, unfold the mazes and intricacies, by which the minute links of title are chained to the adamantine pillars of the law;—how much more glory belongs to them, when this eloquence, this learning, and this genius, are employed in defence of their country; when they breathe forth the purest spirit of morality and virtue in support of the rights of mankind; when they expound the lofty doctrines, which sustain, and connect, and guide, the destinies of nations; when they combat popular delusions at the expense of fame, and friendship, and political honors; when they triumph by arresting the progress of error and the march of power, and drive back the torrent, that threatens destruction equally to public liberty and to private property, to all that delights us in private life, and all that gives grace and authority in public office.

This is a subject, which cannot too deeply engage the most solemn reflections of the profession. Our danger lies in the facility, with which, under the popular cast of our institutions, honest but visionary legislators, and artful leaders may approach to sap the foundations of our government. Other nations have their security against sudden changes, good or bad, in the habits of the people, or the nature of their institutions. They have a monarchy gifted with high prerogatives; or a nobility graced with wealth, and knowledge, and hereditary honors; or a stubborn national spirit, proud of ancient institutions, and obstinate against all reforms. These are obstacles, which resist the progress even of salutary changes; and ages sometimes elapse before such reforms are introduced, and yet more ages before they are sanctioned by public reverence. The youthful vigor of our constitutions of government, and the strong encouragements, held out by free discussion to new inquiries and experiments, expose us to the opposite inconvenience of too little regard for what is established, and too warm a zeal for untried theories. This is our weak point of defence; and it will always be assailed by those, who pant for public favor, and hope for advancement in political struggles.

Under the pressure of temporary evils, or the misguided impulses of party, or plausible alarms for public liberty, it is not difficult to persuade ourselves, that what is established is wrong; that what bounds the popular wishes is oppressive; and that what is untried will give permanent relief and safety. Frame constitutions of government with what wisdom and foresight we may, they must be imperfect, and leave something to discretion, and much to public virtue. It is in vain, that we insert bills of rights in our constitutions, as checks upon legislative power, unless there be firmness in courts, in the hour of trial, to resist the fashionable opinions of the day. The judiciary in itself has little power, except that of protection for others. It operates mainly by an appeal to the understandings of the wise and good; and its chief support is the integrity and independence of an enlightened bar. It possesses no control over the purse or arms of the Government. It can neither enact laws, nor raise armies, nor levy taxes. It stands alone in its functions, without the countenance either of the executive or the legislature to cheer or support it. Nay, its duty sometimes arrays it in hostility to the acts of both. But while, though few, our judges shall be fearless and firm in the discharge of their functions, popular leaders cannot possess a wide range of oppression, but must stand rebuked in their ambitious career for power. And it requires no uncommon spirit of prophecy to foresee, that, whenever the liberties of this country are to be destroyed, the first step in the conspiracy will be to bring courts of justice into odium; and, by overawing the timid, and removing the incorruptible, to break down the last barrier between the people and universal anarchy or despotism.

These are dangers common to all the states of the Union; but there are others, again, not less formidable to the National Government. State jealousies and state excitements, arising from accidental causes, or stimulated by local feelings or political disappointments, will continually create a pressure on the constitution of the United States, or shake those provisions, which are destined to hold the state sovereignties in check. We have lived to see the pointed prohibitions, that no state shall coin money, emit bills of credit, make any thing but gold and silver a tender in payment of debt, pass ex post facto laws, or laws impairing the obligation of contracts, receive, under the guidance of a spirit of over refined speculation, or the pressure of public calamities, a construction, which, if correct, will annihilate their supposed importance; which will make them an unreal mockery; a false and hollow sound; a dead and polluting letter; a letter which killeth, when the spirit would make alive. We have lived to see this constitution, the great bond and bulwark of the Union, subjected to a minute and verbal criticism, which the Common Law repudiated even in its most rigorous construction of the grants of kings; a criticism, which scarcely belonged to the stinted charter of a petty municipality. Attempts have been made, honestly if you please, but in the spirit of over curious jealousy, to cripple its general powers, by denying the means, when the end is required; to interpret a form of government, necessarily dealing in general expressions, if it mean to deal with any thing except legal entities and metaphysical notions, like the grant of a free fishery, or an easement, or franchise against common right; instead of interpreting it, as a constitution to regulate great national concerns, and to protect and sustain the citizens against domestic misrule, as well as foreign aggression. Even its enumerated powers have been strained into a forced and unnatural posture, and tied down upon the uneasy bed of Procrustes. And what, let me ask, with becoming solemnity, what would be the consequence, if these attempts, repudiating the old and settled doctrines of the constitution, should succeed? What but to subject it to the independent and uncontrollable interpretation of twenty-four sovereign states; to give it in no two states the same power and efficiency; to weaken its salutary influences, and subdue its spirit; to increase the discords and rivalries of contending states; to surrender its supreme judicial functions into the hands of those, who feel no permanent interest to exercise or support them; in short to drive us back to the old times, and the old practices under the confederation, when the national powers died away in recommendations, and solemn compacts and pledges were forgotten and contemned, if it did not suit the convenience of states to remember or to redeem them? If the union of the states is to be preserved, (and most earnestly must we all hope, that it may be perpetual,) it can only be by sustaining the powers of the National Government in their full vigor, and holding the judicial jurisdiction, as the constitution holds it, co-extensive with the legislative authority. If, by an adherence to some false and glossy theories of the day, we yield up to its powers, as victims on the altar of public favor, or public necessity, the constitution will sink into a premature and hopeless decline. It will add another, and probably the last, to the long list of experiments to establish a free government, which have alternately illuminated and darkened the annals of other nations, as renowned in arts and arms, as they were for their advancement in literature and jurisprudence.

CHARLES JARED INGERSOLL (1782–1862)

*A DISCOURSE CONCERNING THE IN-
FLUENCE OF AMERICA ON THE MIND;
BEING THE ANNUAL ORATION DELIV-
ERED BEFORE THE AMERICAN PHILO-
SOPHICAL SOCIETY, AT THE UNIVER-
SITY IN PHILADELPHIA, ON THE 18TH
OF OCTOBER, 1823*

[Charles Ingersoll was a son of the Connecticut politician, Jared Ingersoll (1749–1822), who had been a close
friend of Benjamin Franklin. (Ingersoll had, in fact, at
Franklin's recommendation applied for the post of collector
of the revenue under the Stamp Act, and so ultimately became a Tory and was obliged to flee from Connecticut.)
The son was born in Philadelphia, briefly attended the
College of New Jersey (Princeton), was expelled for mis-
conduct, and composed a large amount of bad poetry,
including a verse tragedy which actually achieved a "professional" production in 1801. He read law in the customary fashion, and was admitted to the Philadelphia bar
in 1802.

As the son of a Loyalist, Charles Ingersoll was brought
up in an atmosphere of Federalism. Outraged by British
treatment of American rights—especially that administered
by Sir William Scott, under what he considered a pretense
of legality, against our shipping and our seamen—Ingersoll,
like his fellow Philadelphian, Rush, became a rampant

Jeffersonian, a nationalist, and a highly successful lawyer.
Both men stoutly advocated the American cause in the
War of 1812. He was a widely admired orator, served nine
years in the House of Representatives, favored the annexa-
tion of Texas, opposed the Abolitionists, and was cordially
hated by John Quincy Adams. He was "against" just about
everything proper Philadelphia was for; his *Recollections,*
published in 1861, remains one of those "neglected" American classics in a time when most such negligences are
being remedied. He was a fascinating, often perverse, but
always delightful gentleman.

The "Discourse" of 1823 is one of a number of hortatory
addresses to the genius of America, striving to arouse it to
an intellectual perspective wider than that of mere pioneer-
ing and technological development. As literature, it is the
best of the predecessors of Emerson's "The American
Scholar" of 1837. However, the fame of Emerson's speech
has virtually obliterated the memory of its antecedents,
Ingersoll's "Discourse" among them, despite the efforts of
a few modern researchers to call attention to it.

The whole discourse is worth more space than the present collection allows. I reproduce only the part dealing
with the legal profession. Ingersoll is less sanguine than
Story: he sounds the ominous countertheme which had
taken shape during the Revolution and to which Jesse
Root gave our first utterance. The lawyers of the United
States, he maintains, will never take their destined position in the forefront of the national intellect until they declare their complete independence from English example.

Ingersoll's address gives indication that the opposition to
Story and his school is gathering force. The issue in law as
in literature is that of a persisting "colonial acquiescence."
The apparent rise of the profession would appear here to
be checked by the portent of a civil war within the profession, between legal nationalists and those who would
welcome, as a badge of native maturity, all importations,
not only the Common Law, but also equity and the civil
law. Ingersoll prefigures the position on which later nationalists will take their stand, by exalting the American

genius for "simplicity" over the inherent depravities of
English and "feudal" complexity.]

A DISCOURSE CONCERNING THE IN-
FLUENCE OF AMERICA ON THE MIND,
1823

Annual sessions of five and twenty legislatures multiply
laws, which produce a numerous bar, in all ages the teeming offspring of freedom. Their number in the United
States has been lately computed at six thousand; which is
probably an under estimate. American lawyers and judges
adhere with professional tenacity to the laws of the mother
country. The absolute authority of recent English adjudications is disclaimed: but they are received with a respect
too much bordering on submission. British commercial
law, in many respects, inferior to that of the continent of
Europe, is becoming the law of America. The prize law of
Great Britain was made that of the U. States by judicial
legislation during flagrant war between the two countries.
The homage lately paid by English prime minister to the
neutral doctrines proclaimed by the American government,
in the beginning of the French Revolution, which declares
them worthy the imitation of all neutral nations, may teach
us that the American state papers contain much better
principles of international jurisprudence than the passionate and time-serving, however brilliant, sophisms of the
British admiralty courts. On the other hand, English jurisprudence, while silently availing itself of that of all Europe,
and adopting without owning it, has seldom if ever made
use of an American law book, recommended by the same
language, system, and subject matter. American translations of foreign jurists, on subjects in which the literature
of English law is extremely deficient, appear to be less
known in England than translations of the laws of China.
This veneration on our part, and estrangement on theirs,
are infirmities characteristic of both. Our professional bigotry has been counteracted by penal laws in some of the

States against the quotation of recent British precedents, as it was once a capital offence in Spain to cite the civil law, and as the English Common Law has always repelled that excellent code from its tribunals. I cannot think, with the learned editor of the Law Register, that late English books are a dead expense to the American bar; or that, in his strong phrase, scarcely an important case is furnished by a bale of their reports. But I deplore the colonial acquiescence in which they are adopted, too often without probation or fitness. The use and respect of American jurisprudence in Great Britain will begin only when we cease to prefer their adjudications to our own. By the same means we shall be relieved from disadvantageous restrictions on our use of British wisdom; and our system will acquire that level to which it is entitled by the education, learning, and purity of those by whose administration it is formed.

In their national capacity, the United States have no common law, but all the original States are governed by that of England, with adaptations. In one of the new States, in which the French, Spanish, and English laws, happen to be all naturalised, an attempt at codification from all these stocks is making, under legislative sanction. In others, possibly all of the new States, which have been carved out of the old, a great question is in agitation whether the English Common Law is their inheritance. Being a scheme of traditional precepts and judicial precedents, that Law requires continual adjudications, with their reasons at large, to explain, replenish, and enforce it. Of these reports, as they are termed, no less than sixty-four, consisting of more than two hundred volumes, and a million of pages, have already been uttered in the United States; most of them in the present century; and in a ratio of great increase. The camel's load of cases, which is said to have been necessary to gain a point of law in the decline of the Roman empire, is therefore already insufficient for that purpose in the American. Add to which, an American lawyer's library is incomplete without a thousand volumes of European legists, comprehending the most cele-

brated French, Dutch, Italian, and German treatises on
natural, national, and maritime law, together with all the
English chancery and Common Law. I have heard of an
American lawyer of eminence whose whole property is said
to consist in a large and expensive law library.

Notwithstanding this mass of literature, the law has
been much simplified in transplantation from Europe to
America: and its professional as well as political tendency
is still to further simplicity. The brutal, ferocious, and in-
human laws of the feudists, as they were termed by the
civilians, (I use their own phrase,) the arbitrary rescripts
of the civil law, and the harsh doctrines of the Common
Law, have all been melted down by the genial mildness
of American institutions. Most of the feudal distinctions
between real and personal property, complicated tenures
and primogeniture, the salique exclusion of females, the
unnatural rejection of the half-blood, and ante-nuptial offspring, forfeitures for crimes, the penalties of alienage, and
other vices of European jurisprudence, which nothing but
their existence can defend, and reason must condemn, are
either abolished, or in a course of abrogation here. Cog-
nisance of marriage, divorce, and posthumous administration, taken from ecclesiastical, has been conferred on the
civil tribunals. Voluminous conveyancing and intricate special pleading, among the costliest mysteries of professional
learning in Great Britain, have given place to the plain and
cheap substitutes of the old Common Law. With a like
view to abridge and economise litigation, coercive arbitration, or equivalents for it, have been tried by legislative
provision; jury trial, the great safeguard of personal security, is nearly universal, and ought to be quite so, for its
invaluable political influences. It not only does justice between the litigant parties, but elevates the understanding
and enlightens the rectitude of all the community. Sanguinary and corporal punishments are yielding to the interesting experiment of penitential confinement. Judicial
official tenure is mostly independent of legislative interposition, and completely of executive influence. The jurisdiction of the courts, is far more extensive and elevated than

that of the mother country. They exercise, among other high political functions, the original and remarkable power of invalidating statutes, by declaring them unconstitutional: an ascendancy over politics never before or elsewhere asserted by jurisprudence, which authorises the weakest branch of a popular government to annul the measures of the strongest. If popular indignation sometimes assails this authority, it has seldom if ever been able to crush those who have honestly exercised it; and even if it should, though an individual victim might be immolated, his very martyrdom would corroborate the system for which he suffered. Justice is openly, fairly, and purely administered, freed from the absurd costumes and ceremonies which disfigure it in England. Judicial appointment is less influenced by politics; and judicial proceedings more independent of political considerations.

The education for the bar is less technical, their practice is more intellectual, the vocation is relatively at least more independent in the Untied States, than in Great Britain. Here, as there, it is a much frequented avenue to political honours. All the chief justices of the United States have filled eminent political stations, both abroad and at home. Of the five Presidents of the United States, four were lawyers; of the several candidates at present for that office, most, if not all, are lawyers. But without any public promotion, American society has no superior to the man who is advance in any of the liberal professions. Hence there are more accomplished individuals in professional life here, than where this is not the case. Under other governments, patronage will advance the unworthy, and power will oppress the meritorious. Even in France, where they are, and always have been lawyers of great and just celebrity, we sometimes see that for exerting the noblest, and, in free countries, the most common duties of their profession, for resisting the powerful and defending the weak, they are liable to irresponsible arrest, imprisonment, and degradation, without the succour and sanctuary of a free press, and dauntless public sympathy. In Great Britain, it is true, there is no such apprehension to deter them: and equally true, that professional, as well as political dignities, are free to all candidates. But the ascendancy of rank, the contracted divisions of intellectual labour, the technicality of practice, combine with other causes to render even the English individuals, not perhaps inferior lawyers, but subordinate men.

British jurisprudence itself, too, that sturdy and inveterate Common Law, to which Great Britain owes many of the great popular conservative principles of her constitution —even these have been impaired by long and terrible wars, during which, shut up within their impregnable island, the offspring of Alfred and of Edward, infusing their passions, their politics, and their prejudices into their laws, have wrenched them to their occasions. The distinguishing attributes and merits of the Common Law are, that it is popular and mutable; takes its doctrines from the people, and suits them to their views. While the American judiciary enforces this system of jurisprudence, may it never let wars, or popular passions, or foreign influences, impair its principles.

DAVID HOFFMAN (1784–1854)

A LECTURE, INTRODUCTORY TO A COURSE OF LECTURES, NOW DELIVERING IN THE. UNIVERSITY OF MARYLAND (Baltimore, 1823)

[One of the curious accidents of a nation's memory is that the name of David Hoffman is not so well retained as that of Story and Kent. Both of these men regarded him as a guide and a forerunner, and both paid tribute to him. Probably posterity's neglect is explained by the fact that he never published any monumental volume of "commentaries," as did the two giants, and that his various series of lectures, though immensely influential in their day and still highly readable, were surpassed by later productions.

In the history of legal education, however, Hoffman is a central figure. Born in Baltimore and educated at St. John's College, he immediately became a leader of the Maryland bar; in 1816 he was appointed professor of law at the University of Maryland. He lost considerable income by serving in the school, since he took the post seriously and sacrificed his practice for it. After some twenty-five years of teaching he found the administration of the University not to his liking, resigned, and in 1843 moved to Philadelphia. During his teaching years he published several works on legal science and collections of literary essays. This introduction to his first sequence of lectures, delivered in 1823, epitomizes his generous, noble spirit.

Hoffman still conceives the condition of the profession to be such that it needs, as late as 1823, moral exhortation. He assumes that the great unity is yet to be achieved, and that there is need therefore for concentrated labor, for an acquisition of knowledge beyond any yet imagined in utilitarian America. We should note that Hoffman, like Story and many other partisans of the law, aggressively labels the profession "liberal." This usage is not that of the immense nineteenth-century distinction between liberal and conservative. Here, as throughout our period, the legal mind of America took "liberal" to mean judicious and impartial reasoning within the framework of an assured body of principals. Hoffman, like Kent (see below) and Story, was quite unprepared for the subsequent apparition of Sampson or Rantoul.

The powerful word "science" is for Hoffman the mystery's protection against shysters. He knew about Bentham and the English agitation for codification, but so secure was he in his confidence that a methodical study of the Common Law would prove a forestalling of any theoretical code, this hardly seemed an issue to him. He devoted his life to the search for a methodological treatise, convinced that at the heart of the miscellaneous accretions of the Common Law lay a coherent system of rationality. In his teaching—which all his students remembered with deep affection—he played down the function of memory, and insisted always upon "the general and pervading principles of the science."]

A LECTURE, INTRODUCTORY TO A COURSE OF LECTURES, 1823

A student, who is animated by a just zeal to attain the summits of professional learning and renown, is not to be surprised, or discouraged by the prospect of a thousand nights devoted to research, and a thousand days employed in the practical application of its results. —No eminence, that is worth having, is attainable *per saltum;*[1] nature has included in steady application the seeds both of mental sanity and pleasure; and while, to the pursuit of amusement, she has destined a sickly appetite, inevitably and speedily cloyed, business and study, on the contrary, not only reap a reward in themselves, but quicken the relish of unaccustomed relaxation. Science, if not like the well, which My Lord Coke quaintly describes, is perhaps, like the grotto, or the mine,—to which the access is uninviting and fatiguing, but which often rewards him who is content to grope awhile with pains and patience, with the view of unexpected beauties, wealth and wonders. It is true, indeed, that to taste the pleasures which spring from legal research, we must have entered into the principles, discovered the harmonies, and arranged with method and curiosity the innumerable topicks of the science; as in the caverns of the earth the accomplished and inquisitive mineralogist and geologist reap a satisfaction, and an interest unknown to the uninformed spectators.

With these views of the science, to which you are pledged to devote yourselves, the number and variety of its subjects, instead of alarming your patience, should animate your enterprise.

A profession so liberal and extended, so sublime and important, should be cultivated by those only who are actuated by principles of the purest, and most refined honour. Regarding law as a science equally venerable from its objects, and noble from the ingenuity and mental expansion employed and excited in its acquisition and practice, it should be the ardent desire of its votaries to see its shrine unprofaned by knavery and ignorance, and its retainers not more eminent, from the importance of their functions, than from the honesty and skill with which they discharge them. It is true, we cannot reasonably expect that this can ever be fully accomplished: it is incident to the best things to be the most perverted; and while we may admire and emulate the portraiture which the sincere lovers of this science have been fond to appropriate to its professors, we must be content to see its dignity sometimes debased by the ignorant, and its liberality by the mercenary. We believe that, in most cases, enlarged knowledge, and noble studies exercise, in themselves, a happy influence on those who have pursued them. The very acquisition of liberal knowledge, supposes the acquisition of liberal ideas; so that, in most cases, the possession of intellectual power begets correctness in its application to the purposes of life; and the complexion of its pursuits seems to be, almost necessarily, accompanied by more sound, more enlarged, and more honourable views, than we find in those whose knowledge has been circumscribed. But, if the intrinsick excellence of the profession, and its natural tendency to beget elevated and honest dispositions, be not sufficient to check the wayward proclivity of some men's minds towards vice and dishonour, it is fortunate that our profession has a powerful control over its members, in the authority possessed by courts of justice (whose officers lawyers are, and under whose commission alone, are they competent to act) to suspend them, or wholly to deprive them of the privilege of practice; and, if this be once done, by any court of judicature, all others, by courtesy, would, at once, adjudge them unworthy members, and close every hope of amending their condition, by a change of residence.

You have then, every motive for exerting the utmost assiduity in your studies, and the most sacred honour in the practice of your profession. Respect and influence in society, professional reputation, the highest stations of honour and profit, in a great and enlightened republick, and all the goods of intellectual and worldly wealth are proffered to you. The character of a lawyer who does justice to his profession, and to the important station he holds in life, is, indeed, truly excellent and dignified. He is one, whom early education has imbued with the principles of probity, and habituated to labour and research, in that which enlarges, and refines the mind. He desires to impart lustre to the utility of his learning, by fostering every honourable and amiable affection. The fountains of liberal science and polite letters he has tasted of, before he enters on the pursuit of his more technical studies, and has thus protected himself from pedantry and narrow views. Versed in the sciences most necessary to the purposes of society, he naturally obtains over it a large and legitimate control, which he exercises only that he may become in it a more useful member. He is the asserter of right, the accuser of wrong, the protector of innocence, and the terror of crime. He labours not for those alone who can afford the *honorarium*, but the widow, the fatherless, and the oppressed are ever in his mind. No prospect of gain will ever induce him to advise the pursuit of law against right, or sober judgment; nor will any man's greatness be a shield against the justice due to his client. If he assist in the enaction of laws, which he may afterwards be called on to vindicate, it is done with an eye solely to his country's good, and whilst he respects its legislature and judiciary, he learns to reverence the constitution more than either. —History is his field, as he learns in it the rudiments and revolutions of his science. Rhetorick and logic are the weapons by which he imparts to his oratory warmth and grace, force and clearness. From his knowledge of man he learns truth, and he cultivates rectitude for the more useful exercise of his powers. Destitute of these, he is either unprofitable, or mischievous to society, and endued with them, he is one of its *chiefest ornaments* and *firmest safeguards.* . . .

The tendency of science, as she enlarges her acquisitions, is to methodize and arrange them. As want is the obstacle to the first steps of her progress, so abundance is that of her later stages. If in the gradual accessions to human learning, the base could be accurately separated from the precious—the certain from the obscure and the impenetrable, the task of the modern scholar were comparatively easy; and if his *memory* were burdened, his *judgment* would be relieved and anticipated. Such, however, are the revolutions of human opinion, such the motive for reverting often to systems and doctrines deemed to be exploded —that scarcely any thing which has been written can be thrown entirely aside, as having been tested to be false, or unfit for the purposes of instruction. Scarcely any, so to

speak, of the *old furniture of the mind,* is to be thrown
entirely out of doors.

If such is the case in regard to the sciences more metaphysical and theoritick, it is manifestly more so in such as
are positive and arbitrary. In them, as in municipal law,
for example, it is not sufficient to establish only general
principles, whose application is left for the individual, in
each particular case as it occurs. As these principles are
continually compared with the emergencies of life, as their
seeming collision, in particular cases, is explained and reconciled, and as it is important to know distinctly their
operation on our interests and conduct, cases decided on
analogous principles are carefully sought; the records of
expository jurisprudence are perpetually swelled, and the
general maxim comes attended in the books by a host of
corroborative instances of its application. Hence the voluminous books of reports, from which the inquirer is to seek
his principles, his maxims, his precedents—scarcely more
from the cases which have *established,* than from those
which have sought to *impeach* them.

Hence too the importance, nay, necessity, as adjudicated
cases multiply, of arranging them in classes, and extracting
their spirit in treatises. This method subserves a double
purpose: it gives the student a comprehensive view of the
subject, and collects under his eye the cases from which it
has been extracted, to which he may, and often should refer for confirmation or correction. It is true, that while a
student has the power to inquire at the fountains themselves; while the amount of collected knowledge is not yet
so great but that within the usual legal novitiate, he may
himself survey the whole ground, it is all important, for correct and certain knowledge, that he mark, learn, and digest
for himself. Such, however, is the vast extent of most of the
branches of *legal* science, that such a mode of study would
be nearly impossible. But should he pursue this course to
the greatest extent, the methodized treatises, especially of
our own time, are of infinite use: they give the natural
order of inquiry, they show what is to be sought, and
where it is to be found—with such aids, if we inquire for

ourselves, it is of little importance that our conclusion shall be exactly the same.

The Common Law has in it a feature somewhat peculiar; or at least it has this in a peculiar degree. We find that it has survived many ages, and many revolutions of manners, and has yet been accommodated to them all. Hence, in many cases, it has retained its *form*, while it has altered its *spirit*, and the student, astonished sometimes at the principles, and more frequently at the forms which it presents, can only discover their reason in an antiquated system. It is scarcely necessary to say how valuable is a guide through these mazes of blackletter learning, where so much is dark, some is useless, and some perhaps, even absurd. How, necessary, if not brilliant, the *industry*, which, content to groupe, like a Belzoni among the catacombs, brings from amidst dust, oblivion, and darkness, some scattered but valuable relicks! . . .

It may be laid down as a fundamental truth, that all sound legislation must have relation both to the moral and physical nature and condition of man. Such is the intimate relation between *mind* and *matter* as to render it impossible to proceed far in the philosophy of natural and political jurisprudence, without some acquaintance even with man's physical nature, and certainly with the phenomena of mental philosophy. Hence was it that the great German metaphysicians, Leibnitz and Kant, were not content to study the georgicks of the mind—they cultivated the laws of *matter* with equal zeal—so Descartes, Clarke, Cudworth, Locke, Reid, Stewart, and others, have acknowledged the intimate connexion between physicks and metaphysicks, on the one hand, and ethicks and jurisprudence, on the other. The judicious remarks of Dugald Stewart[2] on the aid which metaphysicks have lent to inquirers into sciences, seemingly remote from its pursuits, have a particular force as regards the jurisprudent. To the lawyer the ready perception of distinctions, the scrupulous and determined definition of terms, the analytical powers, and the habit of sifting the combinations established in the fancy, and the

casual associations which warp *common* understandings,
are of utility every day, and must be made *habits* of the
mind, because their exercise is for the most part extem-
porary. —"The connexion between metaphysicks and ethicks," says Stewart, "is more particularly close, the theory of
morals having furnished several of the most abstruse questions which have been agitated concerning the general
principles (both intellectual and active) of the human
frame,"—and, we may add, what is ethicks, moral philosophy, and natural jurisprudence, but different *names* for
essentially the same system of rules, all dependent on the
laws of the human mind? But, without pressing further
this alliance between the laws of matter and of mind, and
the close connexion between Ethicks and Natural Law, it
must be admitted that ethical and political considerations
are nearly akin to the proper studies of the accomplished
lawyer. Even municipal law (in its most restricted signification) is not a system of merely positive and arbitrary
rules. It has its deep foundations in the universal laws of
our moral nature, and, all its positive enactments, proceeding on these, must receive their just interpretation with
a reference to them. Would it be possible (for instance)
to interpret justly a law, or explain a contract, without
knowledge of the general principles on which they are
promulgated or entered into? Whence proceeds the rule
that laws should not be retrospective, but from the principle of natural law, or ethicks, that associations are bound
only by rules to which they may be supposed to have con-
sented? What are the rules of evidence, but metaphysical
and ethical modes of investigating truth on the one hand,
and limiting our deductions by a regard to human rights
and feelings, and to our moral constitution, on the other?
How else is the great point of expatriation (on which
there have been so many positive enactments) to be settled
but by reference to the universal principles on which political association at first arose? In these and infinite other
cases, nay, in all modifications of positive institutions, there
can be no just design on the part of legislators, nor correct
interpretation on those who administer their provisions,

without knowledge of the true principles of moral and political philosophy. Nay, the very obedience of the governed proceeds, doubtless, from an apprehension, however imperfect, of the great and obvious principles of moral justice. As in the construction of the most elaborate machine, no law of physical nature can possibly be transgressed, so in the great scheme of government, provisions seemingly the most arbitrary, and the most connected with an artificial state of society, cannot violate, with impunity, the great moral law—and therefore, whether as legislators or expounders of legislative institutions, you must be sure that you understand justly their true principles. Metaphysicks, ethicks, and politicks, then, are the appropriate studies of the jurisprudent—on these repose, as solid foundations, all sound legislative enactments; and, as these apply to the conduct of a being composed of body, as well as soul or mind, the physical and moral nature of this being should be known to those who presume to minister, in any way, in the temple of justice. I have deemed these observations proper for those (should there be any such) who may erroneously incline to regard with indifference the ethicks and metaphysicks of the law, and would wish to vindicate the propriety of bestowing much attention on these too much neglected portions of our science.

NOTES

[1] At a bound.

[2] Dugald Stewart (1753–1828), Scottish philosopher of the "common sense" school.

JAMES KENT (1763–1847)

A LECTURE, INTRODUCTORY TO A COURSE OF LAW LECTURES IN COLUMBIA COLLEGE. DELIVERED FEBRUARY 2, 1824

[James Kent dominated what I may term the "orthodox" conception of legal thinking in this country. He did so by his decisions but chiefly through his *Commentaries on American Law,* first published in four volumes, 1826–30. Five more editions appeared before his death, all revised by him. Since his death, eight editions have come out, the last one in 1873, edited by Oliver Wendell Holmes, Junior. Although Story might be more voluminous and more detailed, the prevailing assumption throughout the middle decades of the nineteenth century was that Kent, for vastness of comprehension and for elegance of style, stood as *the* American equivalent of Blackstone.

In the present century, students of law find Kent even more of a bore than Story. They do not see much charm in Kent's stiffly neoclassical rhetoric—which utterly seduced his younger contemporaries—and they find his treatment of almost all areas platitudinous. Some historians insist that he was a much greater judge than commentator, and assuredly, several of his opinions have become as much a part of the law of the land as any of Marshall's or Story's. I confess that I found no single section of the *Commentaries* suitable for excision to represent him in this volume. He was meticulous, rational, but not given to generalization. Wherefore he was not a successful teacher, as was his friend Story; yet from one of his few attempts to be one I select a passage that reveals, in short compass, the quality of mind which made him the most revered, the most reviled, the most feared member of the American bar of his time.

Kent was born in Dutchess County, New York, of New England stock. He graduated from Yale in 1781, read Blackstone at the age of fifteen, and was admitted to the New York bar in 1785. He passionately admired and strove to imitate Alexander Hamilton. Columbia College attempted to institute instruction in the law, but Kent's course in 1794–95 seems to have dismayed the students, and the venture expired. In 1798 he was made a judge of the New York Supreme Court, in 1804 Chief Justice. In 1814 he was removed to the newly established Court of Chancery, where he served with distinction until in 1823 the constitutional convention, by fixing the age of retirement at sixty, obliged him to retire. He devoted his remaining years to the *Commentaries,* fighting for the reputation of the Common Law and expending his considerable venom upon all advocates of codification.

After his enforced retirement, he moved from Albany to New York City, where he endeavored to revive at Columbia the professorship he had let languish in 1798. He had no success, but before he again gave up he delivered and printed this "Lecture," in which the substance of his mentality is revealed.

The "Lecture" forecasts the structure of the *Commentaries,* which were also to commence with an extended argument for the law of nations and for the importance of American study of the "civilians" in the terms here briefly put forth. By the 1820s exponents of the "doctrinal" conception of American jurisprudence had perfected a technique which served not only to resist the critics and enemies of their science, but so to baffle them that they hardly knew where to strike. Kent, Story, Hoffman, and their ilk stoutly defended the Common Law as being an accretion

of reasonable decisions, and so—once divested of its peculiarly English quirks—already at one with the Law of
Nature and *therefore* not requiring codification. At the
same time, however, they held up for the admiration of
provincial America the civil law of the continent, with its
heritage of the Roman Law, the code of Justinian, and
the learned endeavors of Grotius and his followers to construct a systematic body of regulation for international behavior. Thus they further reduced the simple-minded back-
country lawyer to a realization of his ignorance, and simul-
taneously enhanced the glamour of those who could recite,
as Kent here does, an incantation of the names of the
great civilians, of whom the ordinary neophyte had never
even heard.

Perhaps the most astonishing aspect of these scholars of
the Common Law and the civil, considering especially the
temper of the America of the period, is that they all un-
abashedly admitted to their students that the civil law
would be of no immediately utilitarian value in practice,
yet insisted that aspirants should learn it in order to demonstrate that they belonged to a "liberal" calling. The fact
that those who most paraded their competence in the two
disciplines, from Theophilus Parsons and John Adams down
through Kent and Story, were Federalists and Whigs—and
so in our terminology "conservatives"—that they were hostile to Jefferson and hated Andrew Jackson, goes far to explain the motives behind such a presentation of the civilians as Kent here makes. By the close of our period, in the
1850s, we will see that the doctrinal faction will apparently
have triumphed—that Americans will have made an end,
as one jurist put it, of "that narrow-minded and petty
bickering about the superiority of one system over the
other," because they will have recognized that "sectarian-
ism can find no permanent place in the science of jurisprudence." Ironically enough, those, like Kent, who in the
1820s were most confident that they had achieved that
union, were those most violently opposed to the movement
toward "codification."]

A LECTURE, INTRODUCTORY TO A COURSE OF LAW LECTURES, 1824

There is no science that excels that of law, in the variety and importance of its application to the business and duties of civil life. The whole machinery of government consists of a combination of institutions and laws, for protecting the rights, securing the property, and promoting the happiness of the people. When we reflect, for a moment, upon the complicated nature of our political systems, and the vast demand that is constantly made upon the profession, to supply the numerous offices of public trust; when we advert to the diversified character and powers of our courts of justice, and the active and inquisitive genius of our people, pressing with daring enterprise and animated competition into every business and calling, we shall be forcibly struck with the efficacy and eminent value of legal learning. Our private rights depend upon the enlightened and faithful administration of justice; and the political liberties of the people are essentially concerned in the character of our laws, and the skill and judgment of those who make them. But we are not to expect either wisdom in the law, or intelligence and integrity in the administration of it, if that part of the rising generation, who are destined by their education and genius to act a distinguished part on the theatre of public action, be not duly qualified, by a thorough acquaintance with the principles of our governments, and the spirit of our laws, to supply the wants and fulfil the expectations of their country. Whoever looks forward to the duties of any great public trust, either in the legislative, executive, or judicial departments, and means to perform those duties with usefulness and reputation, must have the essential qualifications of a lawyer, as well as of a general scholar. He must not only be properly instructed in moral science, and adorned with the accomplishments of various learning; he must not only have his passions controlled by the discipline of Christian truth, and his mind deeply initiated in the elementary doctrines of natural and public law, but he must be accurately taught in every great leading branch of our own domestic jurisprudence.

If knowledge be power, it must be so emphatically, when it is law knowledge in constant action, in the midst of a community being under the government of laws. The history of the *American* republics is already replete with illustrations of this truth. *England* affords memorable instances of the commanding authority of legal learning; and the histories of *France, Holland,* and *Germany,* abound with illustrious examples, drawn from the character of their civilians and public jurists, of the moral influence of this power, when directed by sound sense, and inspired with pure and benevolent intentions.

But my purpose is not to pronounce an eulogy upon the profession. It is merely to remind the student, as well as the lawyer, of the gravity of his pursuit, and the dignity of the trust. Knowledge is of slow acquisition, the fruit of steady, close, and habitual application. It appears to be the general order and design of Providence, manifested in the constitution of our nature, that every thing valuable in human acquisition, should be the result of toil and labour. Life itself is a state of mental discipline for a being destined for immortality; and the formation of any character which is to command the homage of its own age, and to descend with honour to posterity, by means of its moral power and intellectual greatness, can only be the result of hard and inflexible endurance in duty. Knowledge alone is not sufficient for pure and lasting fame. It is mischievous, and even dangerous, unless it be regulated by moral principle. If the young lawyer intends to render himself truly useful to mankind, if he expects to be a blessing and not a scourge to his fellow citizens, he must cherish in his own bosom, and inculcate by precept and practice, a firm and animated zeal for justice. It must follow him in all his practical pursuits, as a living and invigorating principle of action. He must likewise cultivate throughout all his forensic concerns, and vexatious details of business, and habitual candour, and a sacred reverence for truth. The consequences will be most benign, both to his temper and character. No man can preserve in his own breast a constant and lively sense of justice, without being insensibly led to cherish the benevolent affections. Those affections sharpen the perceptions of the moral sense, and give energy and a proper direction to all the noble powers of the understanding. The observation which I have somewhere met with, is no less profound than striking, that wisdom is as much the offspring of the heart as of the head.

It will be readily admitted, that a sound law education is as important in this country, as in any other, where order and justice have established their dominion. If I do not deceive myself, it is even more so, owing to the very popular character of our governments; and yet the science of law is not made the business of education here, to the extent that it is in many parts of *Europe*. On the *European* continent, the municipal law of each country is academically taught. Their universities are professional schools, where the students who have finished their course of classical studies, resort for particular instruction in the elementary learning of the profession to which they are destined. In *England,* law is regularly taught in the two universities as a necessary branch of a finished education; and there is an ancient and venerable collegiate law establishment at *Westminster,* which Lord *Coke* considered to be, in his day, the most famous university in the world, where any human science was taught. A series of juridical lectures was delivered there not long since, which gave to that foundation a portion of renovated lustre. And in our own country, the law is taught in a classical manner in public schools, and in some of the universities out of this state, with great credit and success. Why, then, it may be asked, should not this state, and even this city, be capable of supporting a collegiate law institution, upon a large and liberal plan? There is so much business of every kind and degree, such a rapid circulation of property from hand to hand, such a dense, active and diversified population, in this great and growing emporium of *American* commerce, that there must be constant need of the protection, and aid, and light, and learning of the law. And surely it is most desirable, and of very great importance, that the principles of a science which protects every interest, and binds every relation in civil society, which comes "home to men's business and bosoms," and touches every cord of human sympathy, should be thoroughly studied, and diffusively known. The end and design of a course of academical lectures, is to give to the law the attraction and cultivation of a liberal science. It is to direct the researches of the student; to inspire him with a thirst for knowledge, and a noble emulation to excel; to raise the standard of merit, and to cast contempt upon ignorance, and idleness, and dissipation. The sure and certain consequence of a well-digested course of juridical instruction, will be to give elevation and dignity to the character of the profession.

I had thoughts, in the first instance, of attempting a course of lectures in a more retired and private capacity; but upon further reflection, it appeared to me to be equally beneficial, and more convenient, to teach law within the precincts, and under the patronage of this highly eminent literary institution. Public academical lectures have been used in most countries and ages, to teach the elements of learning. The law by this means takes her station by the side of the other liberal arts and sciences, is cheered by their friendship, and borrows help from their resources. We cannot be altogether insensible to the inspiration of local enthusiasm. The science I am now to teach, may possibly imbibe some small portion of that matchless vigour and classical taste, which are felt or taught within these walls, by the perusal and study of the admired compositions of the ancients. There is justness and force in the remark, that the sciences have always flourished best in the neighbourhood of each other. The reason may be, which *Cicero* assigns, that there is a common connexion between them, and a general knowledge of the whole, illustrates and adorns the particular science in which we may excel. Perhaps I may add, that I have been not entirely indifferent to the fact, that we are here placed in the immediate vicinity of that magnificent hall of justice, which is the seat of professional business, the busy forum of litigation, the centre of a thousand anxious inquiries; and, with me in particular, who have been so long accustomed to pass its vestibule, it is associated with many tender recollections, not only of living worth, but of departed genius, eloquence, and virtue.

A course of lectures on the science of law ought to comprehend:

1. A general outline of the principles and usages of the law of nations.

2. A full and accurate view of what may be termed the constitutional law of the *United States*.

3. The municipal law of this state, or its domestic jurisprudence. This ought to be examined with full and minute illustration, not only as to its general principles, but in all its extensive and practical details.

It would be improper in this introductory discourse, to enter upon any consideration of our local law. Time will only permit me to add a few observations, showing the importance of a knowledge of the law of nations, and of constitutional law, to the professed lawyer, and to gentlemen of every rank and occupation in life, who may wish to understand the great interests of the nation, or to take a share in its concerns.

The law of nations defines the relations and regulates the intercourse between independent states. It is founded partly on the fundamental principles of morality and justice; and in that view, it is the science of ethics applied to the conduct of nations in their collective capacity. But it is founded principally upon usages, customs, and conventions, prevailing among the civilized powers of *Europe*, and adopted for the better regulation of their intercourse with each other.

The law of nations has received its cultivation, and almost its existence as a science, in modern times. It is the law of the Christian world, and assumes the precision and certainty, and binding force of positive institution. It connects the nations together by the ties of mutual intercourse and mutual dependence, and a sense of common duty.

Nations now appeal to it in support of their claims and of their complaints, as to a code of moral and political obligation. It is every where admitted by the writers on general jurisprudence, that nations are bound by the same obligations of truth, and justice, and humanity, and compact, which bind individuals in private life; and they cannot violate those obligations without being subjected to the penal sanction of reproach and disgrace, and without incurring the hazard of punishment to be inflicted in open and solemn war by the injured nation. And when the *United States* became independent, and took their separate and equal station among the powers of the earth, they acceded to this same system of public law, and became a voluntary member of the community of *European* nations, by whom alone this modern science of international law had been cultivated and adopted. Our government has constantly acknowledged the binding obligation of this code, and appealed to it as the common standard of right and duty, in their intercourse with other powers, whether in peace or war, and whether they acted in the capacity of a neutral or a belligerent nation.

This science ought, therefore, to be studied with profound attention. Its general principles ought to be understood by every person who may hereafter be called to take a share, either in the legislative councils of the nation, or in any part of the administration of the government. No one can presume to be an accomplished statesman, without this knowledge. It is to be learned by the study of public treaties, which are replete with provisions in affirmance of the general law of nations, and afford the most authentic evidence of universal usage and practice. But it is especially to be acquired by becoming familiar with the doctrines of those great masters of public law, who are consulted by all nations as oracles of wisdom; and who have attained, by the mere force of written reason, the majestic character, and almost the authority of universal lawgivers, controlling by their writings the conduct of rulers, and laying down precepts for the government of mankind. I place at the head of these illustrious jurists the learned *Grotius*.[1] He found the law of nations, as *Barbeyrac* has observed, in a frightful chaos, and he undertook the necessary task of recovering it from the darkness of feudal barbarism. He digested into one systematic code, the principles of public right, and showed, by the abundance of his learning, that its foundations were laid deep in natural justice, and in the moral sense of all antiquity. He explained his principles to the Christian powers, and exhorted them to the observance of the duty of preserving faith and cultivating peace. His great work *on the law of war and peace*, made a sudden and surprising impression on the spirit of his age, and the social system of *Europe*. It enlightened mankind on the subject of national right. It humanized their manners, and tended, in a very considerable degree, to lessen the violence of war. *Puffendorf, Barbeyrac, Bynkershoeck, Burlemaqui, Wolfius, Vattel, Heineccius, Montesquieu, Rutherforth,* and *Martens*,[2] may be selected as his most illustrious disciples in the school of public law. Their works have stood the piercing investigation of statesmen, and the philosophical spirit of inquiry. They have methodized the system, enlarged it by their genius, confirmed it by their authority, and rendered its principles applicable to all the complicated relations of peace and war. These writers are principally appealed to in the negotiations and diplomatic discussions between the Christian powers, as decisive authorities in cases not controlled by positive stipulation.

The law of nations is likewise to be studied in the body of the civil law, and on which, owing to its equity and justice, much of the public law of *Europe* is founded. It is the embodied wisdom of the ancient *Romans*, which has survived the ruins of their empire, and has transfused its influence into the domestic institutions of every civilized people, by the mere force of its intrinsic excellence. But much more is this law to be sought and studied in the judicial decrees of the higher courts of justice, in this and in other countries, where we shall find the usages and the duties of nations well understood, and frequently explained both upon authority and principle, and with that depth of

Lincoln Christian College

research, and that liberal and enlarged inquiry, which strengthens and embellishes the conclusions of reason.

It may, perhaps, be objected to this branch of law, that it is a system without any efficient sanction, a code of mere elementary speculation, and destitute of any real influence on the fortunes of the human race. There are, no doubt, awful precedents within time of memory, which give colour to this desponding conclusion. But the principles of the system are founded in the maxims of eternal truth, in the immutable law of moral obligation, in the suggestions of an enlightened public interest; and they maintain a steady influence, notwithstanding the occasional violence by which that influence is disturbed. It is a maxim derived from the best authority in all antiquity, from *Cicero* himself, that justice is the great standing policy of civil society, and no state can be well governed without it. The law of nations continues to be appealed to by the tribunals and statesmen of every country, as a code of present, subsisting, active, durable, and binding force. In the language which has been recently and beautifully applied to it by one of the first lawyers and statesmen of our own country, it is "the world's collected will, and o'er thrones and globes elate, sits empress." Its authority can no more be weakened or abrogated by the ordinances of any particular people, or the violence of any particular power, than the law of the land can be repealed by the resolution or practice of a single individual. Its adoption is founded upon common consent, and it requires common consent to annul it. Public opinion is at this moment silently corroding the fabrics of despotism, condemning the violations of public law, and setting limits to power by the influence of the cultivated reason of the age. The efforts that are now making to abolish the slave trade, to suppress piracy, to enlarge the boundaries of commerce, and to diffuse much more extensively the benefits of civilization and the blessings of independence, are grounded upon the principles of public law.

It has appeared to me, therefore, that every well educated gentleman and scholar, and especially every lawyer and statesman, ought to be early and perfectly instructed in the doctrines of this national jurisprudence.

The other head of the course on which I proposed to make a few preliminary remarks, for the purpose of recommending it to more general attention, is the constitutional law of this country. This branch of law relates to the powers and duties of the national, and of the state governments, in their organized character, in relation to each other; and it presents many delicate and difficult questions, arising upon the conflicting powers, and interfering movements of the two systems.

In the consideration of this subject, we must investigate thoroughly the principles of the union of this great assemblage of communities, as they appear in the constitution of the *United States*. The true construction of that instrument in doubtful cases, and the exact extent and circumscribed limits of the residuary authorities of the states, are to be ascertained from the declared sense and practice of the governments respectively, when there is no collision; and in cases of difficulty, if the question be of a judicial nature, from the final determination of the Supreme Court of the *United States*. The *American* union acts as one single consolidated government, in its intercourse with foreign states. It is known to them only in its national capacity. The interior structure must present to the eye of a stranger, a system exceedingly complex in its plan, difficult to be accurately understood, and hazardous in its movements to the harmony and tranquillity of the union. It has no adequate model in the establishments of other nations, and, I should apprehend it would be very liable to disorder, in the possession of any people, who had not been educated in the discipline of free institutions, and habitually taught to obey law, and respect the judicial authorities. With us, however, it has proved admirable in practice, and has been eminently conducive to the freedom, the security, the prosperity, and the glory of our country.

The judicial power of the union is the ultimate expounder of the constitution, for it has cognizance of all cases in law and equity arising under the constitution, laws, and treaties of the union, and consequently, of all cases of a judicial nature arising upon the adverse claims and laws of the state governments. And when we reflect for a moment on the many cases in which the powers of the federal and state governments may be brought in collision with each other, or within the influence of each others' movements, the magnitude of the trust confided to the judicial of the union will be apparent. And the delicacy of it is infinitely increased in our view, when it is considered that the governments of the individual states are regularly organized communities, with much of the power, and more of the *insignia* of sovereign authority.

The decision of the federal courts ought therefore to be studied, digested, explained, and universally understood, in respect to all the leading questions of constitutional law. The authorities of every state, as well as the people at large, are interested in that knowledge. The harmony, and perhaps the stability of the union, depends in a very material degree, upon the just and discreet exercise of the judicial power. I am no votary of the infallibility of any human tribunal; but it is no more than a just tribute to truth and candour to acknowledge, that the Supreme Court of the *United States* has hitherto discharged its high duties with such ability, firmness, and moderation, as to command the respect, and retain the confidence of the nation. I have always been much impressed with the immensity of the weight and value of its trust, and with the severe and majestic simplicity of its character. It may be said of that Court, and certainly with as much propriety as it has been said in reference to the *Roman sages,* that justice has there unveiled her mysteries and erected her temple.

NOTES

[1] Hugo Grotius (1583–1645), Dutch publicist and statesman, of whose *De Jure Bellie et Pacis,* Paris, 1625, Kent's description is entirely accurate.

[2] This array of the great names in the development of the civil law in Europe is a characteristic flourish of erudition by which such scholars as Kent and Story impressed upon the ordinary practitioner a sense of his inferiority; to annotate each of them in this context would be a work of pedantry, but we must remember that Kent knew them not only in name but in the substance of their ponderous treatises.

PETER DU PONCEAU (1760–1844)

*A DISSERTATION ON THE NATURE AND
EXTENT OF THE JURISDICTION OF THE
COURTS OF THE UNITED STATES, BE-
ING A VALEDICTORY ADDRESS DELIV-
ERED TO THE STUDENTS OF THE LAW
ACADEMY OF PHILADELPHIA, AT THE
CLOSE OF THE ACADEMIC YEAR, ON
THE 22nd APRIL, 1824*

[The son of Joseph Story, in a filio-pietistic tribute to
his father, was proud to say that "as America takes to itself
and naturalizes the people of all nations, who seek its protection, thereby creating a composite people," so the justice "thought it should be cosmopolitan in its jurisprudence,
and embody into its law all good rules and principles,
whatever might be their birthplace." However, the endeavors of Story, Kent, and Hoffman to "blend and combine"
suffered embarrassment more often than encouragement
from one who professed to be an ally but who was the one
theorist of distinction in the country actually educated in
the civil law. Peter du Ponceau had a habit of exhibiting
polite respect for the Common Law, but he held as well
the ingrained conviction of the continental lawyer that the
Common Law is an English mystery, concocted out of stupidity and compromise. However much he might favor the
"blending," he could not muster enough respect for the
Common Law to make himself a partner in the great en-

terprise. Yet he did in the end supply invaluable assistance to it because he, the only one actually bred in the civil law, came out firmly against an American codification, and showed the Common Lawyers how to resist even the Code Napoleon.

He was born Pierre Etienne du Ponceau at St. Martin on the Île de Ré. He learned his English from soldiers quartered on the town. He studied for clerical orders but lost his faith; he became secretary (because of his ability to use English) to Baron Steuben, and sailed with him to America, arriving at Portsmouth, New Hampshire, in 1777. He was immediately appointed a captain in the Continental Army and served Steuben as aide-de-camp. In 1781 Du Ponceau became a citizen of Pennsylvania; while secretary to Robert Livingston he studied law, and in 1785 was admitted to the Philadelphia bar. In the post-Revolutionary years he rapidly acquired a large practice because he was the only man in the area, or indeed in the new states, who had such a mastery of civil and foreign law as to be of great usefulness in the intricate problems of commercial adjudication. He was a passionate student, with a delightful avocation for philology. His teaching in the "Law Academy" was in effect instruction at the University of Pennsylvania, since the university's Law School grew out of the academy. A man of broad culture, and throughout his life in this country full of admiration for the American scheme of federal union—which to his European intellect seemed utterly illogical but miraculously effective—he has been curiously neglected by historians of American law. He deserves much more recognition than this short excerpt provides.]

A DISSERTATION ON THE NATURE AND EXTENT OF THE JURISDICTION OF THE COURTS OF THE UNITED STATES, 1824

That there are implied, as well as express, powers granted by the Constitution of the United States to the national government, is what it is at this day impossible to deny or even to doubt. Some of those have already been acted upon, and are in the full course of actual exercise; others are preparing to be carried into execution. It is too late now to controvert the doctrine of implied constitutional authority.

But while these implied powers are admitted on all hands to exist in the federal government to a greater or lesser extent, a question has arisen, whether it is competent for the judicial department, whose sphere of action the Constitution has been peculiarly careful to limit and define, to assume rights to themselves by their decisions *a priori,* and to carry them *provisionally,* as it were, into effect, before the legislature has made any law upon the subject, or has given them the special authority which seems to be required. In other words, the inquiry is, whether the Federal Courts have a right independent of the people of the United States or their representatives, by virtue of some occult power supposed to be derived from the *Common Law,* to mould the Constitution as they please, and to extend their own jurisdiction beyond the limits prescribed by the national compact?

There would have been but little difficulty in solving this simple question, if, by a carelessness of expression unfortunately too common in our legal language, it had not been clothed in the ambiguous words *Common Law jurisdiction,* which have been the source of all the doubts and all the hesitation that it has produced, because it was not considered that these words are susceptible of a double interpretation, implying in the one sense, a jurisdiction perfectly lawful, and in the other a power in direct opposition to the letter and spirit of our national charter; so that the controversy has been to maintain or reject altogether, and in every sense, this *Common Law jurisdiction,* while a proper distinction would probably have reconciled all conflicting opinions upon the subject.

In order that this may be clearly understood, it is necessary to enter into some preliminary explanations. In England, the country from whence we have derived, not only our system of jurisprudence, but most of our civil and political institutions, there is a metaphysical being called *Common Law,* which originally was a code of feudal customs, similar to the *coutumes* which, until lately, governed the different provinces of the neighbouring kingdom of France, but which, by gradual steps, and by the force of circumstances has become incorporated and in a manner identified not only with the national jurisprudence, but, under the name of *Constitution,* with the political government of the country. The king's prerogative and the rights of the subject are alike defined and limited by the *Common Law.* The various and often conflicting jurisdictions of the different tribunals in which justice is administered are also said to be derived from it, although in many instances they are known to be founded on gradual and successive assumptions of power; but those having been established and consolidated by time are now become *Common Law.* This *ens rationis*[1] is a part of every civil and political institution, and every thing connected with the government of the country, is said to be a part of it. Thus the law of nations, the law merchant, the maritime law, the constitution and even the religion of the kingdom, are considered to be parts and parcels of the *Common Law.* It pervades everything, and every thing is interwoven with it. Its extent is unlimited, its bounds are unknown; it varies with the successions of ages, and takes its colour from the spirit of the times, the learning of the age, and the temper and disposition of the Judges. It has experienced great changes at different periods, and is destined to experience more. It is from its very nature uncertain and fluctuating; while to vulgar eyes it appears fixed and stationary. Under the Tudors and the first Stuarts forced loans, wardships, purveyance, monopolies, legislation by royal proclamations, and even the Star Chamber and High Commission Courts, and slavery itself, under the name of *villenage,* were parts of the *Common Law.* At the revolution it shook off those unworthy fetters, and assumed the character of manly freedom for which it is now so eminently distinguished.

Twelve Judges, who hold their offices during good behavior, are the oracles of this mystical science. In a monarchy like England, which has no written constitution, but in which all the rights of the sovereign as well as the privileges of the people are to be deduced from the *Common Law*, those Judges are an useful check against the encroachments of the monarch or his ministers; hence the common law and the judicial power are in that country almost objects of idolatrous worship. While the United States were colonies, they partook of this national feeling. The grievances which induced them to separate from the mother country were considered as violations of the *Common Law*, and at the very moment when independence was declared, the *Common Law* was claimed by an unanimous voice as the *birth right* of American citizens; for it was then considered as synonymous to the British Constitution, with which their political rights and civil liberties were considered to be identified. In the dissentions that arose between the colonies and Great Britain, the *Constitution*, or the *Common Law*, which was the same thing, was appealed to in favour of the doctrines which the contending parties respectively maintained. It was, therefore, held by all in equal veneration, and by all cherished as their most precious inheritance.

The revolution has produced a different state of things in this country. Our political institutions no longer depend on uncertain traditions, but on the more solid foundation of express written compacts; the Common Law is only occasionally referred to for the interpretation of passages in our textual constitutions and the statutes made in aid of them, which have been expressed in its well known phraseology; but there ends its political empire: it is no longer to it that our constituted authorities look to for the *source* of their delegated powers, which are only to be found in the letter or spirit of the instruments by which they have been granted.

The Common Law, therefore, is to be considered in the United States in no other light than that of a system of jurisprudence, venerable, indeed, for its antiquity, valuable for the principles of freedom which it cherishes and inculcates, and justly dear to us for the benefits that we have received from it; but still in the happier state to which the revolution has raised us, it is a SYSTEM OF JURIS-PRUDENCE and nothing more. It is no longer the *source* of power or jurisdiction, but the *means* or instrument through which it is exercised. Therefore, whatever meaning the words *Common Law jurisdiction* may have in England, with us they have none; in our legal phraseology they may be said to be *insensible*. To them may be applied the language in which the common lawyer of old spoke of a title of the civil law: *"In ceulx parolx n'y ad pas entendment. . . ."*[2]

I am well aware that this doctrine of the nationality of the Common Law will meet with many opponents. There is a spirit of hostility abroad against this system which cannot escape the eye of the most superficial observer. It began in Virginia in the year 1799 or 1800, in consequence of an opposition to the Alien and Sedition Acts. A committee of the legislative body made a report against those laws which was accepted by the house, in which it was broadly laid down that the Common Law is not the law of the United States. Not long afterwards, the flame caught in Pennsylvania, and it was for some time believed that the Legislature would abolish the common law altogether. Violent pamphlets were published to instigate them to that measure. The whole, however, ended in a law for determining all suits by arbitration in the first instance, at the will of either party, and another prohibiting the reading and quoting in Courts of Justice of British authorities of a date posterior to the revolution. Both these statutes, as you well know, are still in force.

It was not long before this inimical disposition towards the common law made its way into the State of Ohio. In the year 1819, a learned and elaborate work was published in that State,[3] in which it was endeavoured to prove not only that the Common Law was not the law of the United States, but that it had no authority in any of the States that had been formed out of the old north western territory. But few copies of his work have been printed; nevertheless as it is learnedly and elaborately written, it cannot but have had a considerable degree of influence.

In other States, attacks upon the Common Law, more or less direct, have appeared from time to time. Its faults (for it is not free from them) are laid hold of and exhibited in the most glaring light; its ancient abuses, its uncertainty, the immense number of volumes in which its doctrines are to be sought for, its various and daily increasing modifications in the different States, the contradictory decisions which occur among so many independent tribunals, and above all the supposed danger to our institutions from its being still the law of a monarchical country, the opinions of whose Judges long habit has taught us to respect, which opinions are received from year to year, and admitted in our Courts of justice if not as rules, at least, as guides for their decisions; these are the topics which are in general selected for the animadversions of those who hold the contrary opinion to mine, and there is enough of plausibility in them to make us presume that they are not without effect on the public mind.

That there are real and serious inconveniences in our actual system of jurisprudence, is what no candid man will deny; but none of them is, nor are all of them sufficient to induce the abolition of the Common Law. Were it abolished, a still greater difficulty must arise, to fill up the immense chasm which would be produced by its absence. Not all the codes of all the Benthams would be capable of producing that effect.

The task of legislation is not so easy a one as some people seem to imagine. The immortal Bacon was of opinion that neither lawyers nor philosophers were fit for it; the former because their notions were too narrow, the latter because theirs were too enlarged. He thought that this business could only be safely confided to statesmen, as being best acquainted with mankind. For my part, I am inclined to think that a good legislator ought to possess the combined knowledge and talents of the lawyer, the philosopher, and the statesman. I need not say how few there are of those in any age or in any country.

But admitting that this country possesses superior legislative talents to any other, I assert, without the fear of contradiction, that it is impossible to abolish the Common Law. Make as many codes as you will, this second nature will still force itself upon you:

Expellas furca tamen usque recurret.[4]

In proof of this, I shall adduce a very recent and very striking instance. The emperor Napoleon gave to the French a new and uniform code of laws, which has been now in force about twenty years. It is admitted to be as complete as a work of this kind can be, and well suited to the nation for whom it was made. But I can assure you, that, as far as I have been able to observe, the digests and code of Justinian, the former laws and ordinances of the kingdom, and the immense collection of the works of the civilians and French jurists are not less quoted at present in the lawyers' pleadings than they formerly were, and so it would be with us if we were to abolish the Common Law. We should still recur to it for principles and illustrations, and it would rise triumphant above its own ruins, deriding and defying its impotent enemies. . . .

General jurisprudence is a part of the common law, but its rules and principles are not exclusively to be found in Common Law writers. That science ought to be studied, particularly in this country, where a light is to be held to the judiciaries of twenty-four different States. Whence is this light to proceed, but from the writings and discussions of liberal and learned jurists? The conflict of opinions will produce truth, and truth at last will find its way every where. The law should be treated as every other science; its theories should be scanned, and its defects pointed out; the excellent principles with which it abounds should be confronted with the decisions in which they have been either forgotten or misapplied, and this course should be pursued until the whole system at last shall be founded on

the basis of universal justice. For justice, not in form merely,
but in substance is a debt which is due by every government to its citizens.

Sir William Jones,[5] in England, endeavoured to point
out this noble path to his country men, and with that
view published his excellent treatise on the law of bailments. But the age was not prepared for his doctrines, the
lights that he shed on our science were too strong for the
eyes of his cotemporaries; he was sent to India in honourable exile, there to waste his gigantic powers in curious,
indeed, but fruitless disquisitions on oriental languages and
antiquities. Romilly[6] did much while he lived. Mackintosh[7]
is still alive for the good of his country and of mankind.[8]

Those who wish to see uniformity of jurisprudence in
this widely extended union, ought to remember that nothing is uniform but sound principles, and that false theories
and false logic lead inevitably to contradictory decisions.
In England, there is in fact but one great judicature, sitting
at Westminster. Although divided into different tribunals,
the same spirit pervades them all, and in important cases
the twelve Judges meet together to decide. Above them is
the House of Lords, whose judgments are final and conclusive. Here we have, on the contrary, twenty-four different supreme judicatures, with a countless number of inferior tribunals, dispersed over an immense extent of territory.
Beyond them there is no authority whose decisions are
binding in all cases. The Supreme Court of the United
States is limited in its jurisdiction and powers, and except
in certain matters of national concern, State Judges do not
conceive themselves bound to conform to their opinions.
In short, there is no polar star to direct our uncertain wan-
derings. We must then either tacitly submit to receive
the law from a foreign country, by adopting the opinions
of the English Judges, however they may vary from our
own, or even from those which they formerly entertained,
or we must find some expedient to preserve our national
independence, and at the same time to prevent our national law from falling into that state of confusion which
will inevitably follow from the discordant judgments of so

many co-ordinate judicial authorities. Already the evil is felt in a considerable degree; it will be more so in process of time, and it is to be feared, that in the course of fifty years the chaos will become inextricable, unless a speedy remedy is applied.

The only remedy that I can think of is to encourage the study of general jurisprudence, and of the eternal and immutable principles of right and wrong; of that science by which Cicero enlightened, not only the praetors of his days, but the Judges of succeeding ages, and which, I am sorry to say, has fallen too much into neglect. When the principles of that science are sufficiently disseminated, they will fructify, and statutes and judicial decisions will gradually take their colour from them. System will be introduced where it is wanted. Sound theories will take the place of false ones, and the rules of genuine logic will direct their application to particular cases. All this will be done gradually and insensibly, and the benefit of it will be felt by our remotest posterity. Otherwise, it is to be feared, that other and worse remedies will be applied; for every one of us must be sensible that the evils which I have mentioned are generally felt, and that the spirit of innovation is abroad; a spirit which manifests itself by rash and undigested experiments, and sometimes by demolishing without re-building, so that at last we shall be reduced to a state of confusion worse confounded.

It is therefore incumbent on the rising generation to apply themselves to the study of those general principles, which, if that spirit should continue to exist, will enable them at least to direct it into its proper channel, and prevent the axe from being applied at last to the root of the tree.

Those who may think that there is an advantage in the science of the law being involved in mysteries and artificial theories, are egregiously mistaken. The science of medicine was so once, when genius lashed it with the pen of Molière. Since it has abandoned its senseless nostrums and formulas, and fixed itself firmly on the basis of fact and experiment, it has considerably gained in respect,

honour, and emolument. By pursuing a similar course, the
legal profession will receive similar rewards.

I do not mean to say that theory should at once supersede established rules, or that the student should erect
himself into a legislator. I have no such preposterous ideas.
Your studies are principally to be directed to the law, as
it is, and with a view to its regular practice: hence in our
ordinary exercises I have avoided touching upon such subjects as this, and I have explained the laws to you as they
are found in our books and in the decisions of our tribunals.
But on this occasion, I cannot forget that there are some
of you who are destined to be one day the Judges and
legislators of our country. To those who are fired with this
noble ambition, I have particularly addressed the preceding
observations, not to diminish the respect which they owe to
the laws by which we are governed, but to shew the utility
of the principles of general jurisprudence, and what benefits may be derived from them.

Nor must it be believed that I am a friend to rash and
sudden innovation; on the contrary, I am well convinced
that amendments in the laws ought to be gradual and
almost insensible, and that the delicate chisel, and not the
rough axe, is the instrument to be employed; but the
delicate chisel can only be skilfully used by the masters of
the art. I would compare our system of laws in this respect to one of those ancient statues of Phidias or Praxite-
les, which have been in part mutilated or defaced by the
hand of time: an able sculptor, and not a stone mason,
should be called upon to repair it.

The true principles of jurisprudence, in order to fructify,
ought first to take root in the minds of the members of the
legal profession. Then, and not till then, will false principles gradually give way, as the ripe fruit falls from the
tree. But in order to produce that effect, we ought to invite each other to reflection on these important subjects
by learned treatises and free discussions, and the labours
of the jurist ought not to be confined to mere compilations.
In short, jurisprudence ought to be treated as a philosophical science. If Montesquieu[9] had not written, the distinc-

tion between the three powers of government would be yet unknown, and their limits undefined. If Beccaria[10] had not written, the torture and its horrid concomitants would not have disappeared from the face of Europe, and sanguinary codes would not almost everywhere have given way to mild punishments. All the amendments which Blackstone in his Commentaries suggested to be made in the Common Law, have been adopted, and some of them improved upon in this country, and it is only to be regretted that he did not suggest more.

But as I have observed, these suggestions ought to come from those who have made legislation their peculiar study, and ought to be made in the grave and solemn manner which the subject requires. They ought to be addressed to the understanding of those who are best able to judge of them.

Therefore, I address myself exclusively to the profession, by whom I expect to be understood and appreciated. To their tribunal I submit the observations I have ventured to make, soliciting only brotherly indulgence.

The Common Law is destined to acquire in this country the highest degree of perfection of which it is susceptible, and which will raise it in all respects above every other system of laws, ancient or modern. But it will not have fully reached that towering height, until the maxim shall be completely established in practice as well as in theory,

THAT PURE ETHICS AND SOUND LOGIC ARE ALSO PARTS OF THE COMMON LAW.

NOTES

[1] Essence of reason.

[2] "In these words there is nothing to be heeded."

[3] *Historical Sketches of the Principles and Maxims of American Jurisprudence, in Contrast with the Doctrines of the English Common Law on the Subject of Crimes and Punishments.*—By John Milton Goodenow, 428 pp. 8 vo. Steubenville, 1819 [Du Ponceau's note]. As Du Ponceau notices, the limited circulation of Goodenow's volume circumscribed its effect, but it is a fine

expression of that post-Revolutionary hatred of the Common Law which, despite the conjurations of Kent and Story, was transported across the mountains and for several decades flourished in the Mississippi Valley.

[4] "Expel it with a pitchfork, nevertheless it will forever rush back."

[5] Sir William Jones (1746–94) published his classic *On the Law of Bailments* in London, 1781.

[6] Sir Samuel Romilly (1757–1818), a voluminous and vigorous advocate of the reform of English law.

[7] Sir James Mackintosh (1765–1832), lawyer, philosopher, and historian.

[8] In this country we have to regret that Chancellor KENT, one of the greatest luminaries of our science, by the effect of an impolitic provision in the Constitution of his own State, has been displaced from the office which he so many years filled with honour, because he was—sixty years old [Du Ponceau's note].

[9] Montesquieu (1689–1755), the French philosopher, published *L'Esprit des Lois* in Geneva, 1748.

[10] Cesare Beccaria-Bonesana (1735–94) published *Dei Delitti e della Pene (On Crimes and Punishments)* in 1764.

WILLIAM SAMPSON (1764–1836)

*AN ANNIVERSARY DISCOURSE, DELIV-
ERED BEFORE THE HISTORICAL SO-
CIETY OF NEW-YORK, ON SATURDAY,
DECEMBER 6, 1823: SHOWING THE ORI-
GIN, PROGRESS, ANTIQUITIES, CURIOS-
ITIES, AND THE NATURE OF THE COM-
MON LAW* (New York, 1824)

[Any passing, external observer of American society in the 1830s would have concluded (as did Tocqueville) that the lawyers had won their triple campaign: they had cowed the populace into a respect for law as such; they had subdued the native suspicion of the Common Law; they had vindicated the intellectual superiority of the profession by their deft combination of the Common Law with the civil. Through this elaborate strategy, never quite directed by any central command but nevertheless guided by the powerful figures of Kent, Story, Hoffman, Webster, Binney, et al., the snake of Americanization had been scotched, if not killed. The tentative, half-distrustful pleas of a Jesse Root, back in 1798, for a fresh codification of American law, without regard to the Common Law or even to Blackstone, had supposedly been stifled forever, especially with the help of a French Du Ponceau.

Yet all the literature of the period after 1789 shows that the lawyers knew they could only scotch the snake and never quite eradicate it. The people's hatred of the

law persisted, even while they were all "going to law."
And their deep distrust of whatever was told them about
the Common Law became a constantly exacerbated conviction that they were being hoodwinked by such master
prestidigitators as Kent and Story. Still, out of the grum-
blings of frontier lawyers and Jacksonian politicians came
no effective resistance—even though in Ohio one counsel
is reputed to have demanded of the judge whether the
commentaries of Kent and Story were portions of the Constitution!

We should not be surprised that the first voice to be
raised in articulate protest against this triumphal march of
the "orthodox" lawyers should be that of a recalcitrant
Irish patriot, forcibly exiled to the United States by a Tory
government of Britain. Whereas Du Ponceau, coming from
France, was sweetly determined to make his peace with
the Common Law, William Sampson came in a huff, resolved to root out the mental tyranny of the English Common Law from the jurisprudence of his violently adopted
country. With the delivery of his speech in 1823 (first
published in 1824) before so august an assembly as the
New-York Historical Society, the Kents and the Storys
realized that they did indeed have a fight on their hands,
that the conquest of the Republic by their sophisticated,
cosmopolitan ideal of law would not be so easy as it at
first appeared, and that a nativist reaction—even though led
by such an immigrant as Sampson—would not be subdued merely by further display of erudition.

William Sampson was born in Londonderry, Ireland,
to a family of culture and position. He studied at Lincoln's
Inn, so that when he berates the Common Law he knows
whereof he speaks. By becoming an Irish patriot he sacrificed a lucrative practice in Ireland. The British Government deported him at its own expense, but the New York
bar welcomed him. He served notice as to what it might
expect of him by taking on the defense in 1810 of the
Journeymen Cordwainers, the first trial in which the legality of a trade union was tested. Thus he was a pioneer
champion of organized labor and also a devout Catholic

—a configuration which would persist in American society. In 1813, with *The Catholic Question in America,* he stoutly defended the legal sanctity of the confessional—not a popular position among a predominantly Protestant and actively anti-Catholic people. Yet because he was ferociously anti-English, much was forgiven him. He argued several crucial cases before the Supreme Court.

In his "Anniversary Discourse," Sampson demonstrates, as though inspired by a supernatural instinct, just how the cry for codification would be identified with a nationalistic spirit which regarded England itself and the veneration in this country for English exemplars as the enemies of native virtue. That he as an immigrant should take up the two causes of codification and of nationalism with such fervor betrays the manner in which they had been already coalescing under the ground on which Kent and Story appeared to walk with serene confidence. Actually, these jurists knew that the ground was not firm, that the eruption might come at any moment—much of their massive publication was an effort to forestall the eruption of such a geyser as Sampson.]

AN ANNIVERSARY DISCOURSE, 1824

The law has, indeed, been too long banished from the communion of the liberal sciences, proscribed as a dry and crabbed art, interesting only to those who practise it for gain; as though its spirit were all disingenuous mystery, its language a barbarous jargon, its root in savage antiquity, its growth through ages of darkness, its fruits but bitterness and vexation: and this in despite of the high and lofty panegyrics hourly bestowed upon it by its admirers.

It is time that these differences should be reconciled. The well-being of society requires that a subject of such vital importance, should be brought to the test of reason in the open light of day. The law of a free people should never be a matter of indifference. It is supposed to be the public reason, uttered by the public voice; and in proportion to its wisdom, will be the dignity of the people. It is the school of public morals; and next to religion, that which has most influence on the manners and happiness of a nation. It is the guide of all our actions, and the rule of all our conduct. It is the part of a good citizen to love the laws, and the duty of every one to obey them; but that love should be without bigotry, and that obedience without servility. The efficacy of the law depends on the confidence it creates, and it never will inspire so much confidence, as when it lays aside the veil of mystery, and presents itself in all the simple majesty of truth. Appearing as a human, not a preternatural institution, its defects will be excused, its excellencies acknowledged, and what is most desirable, it will advance with a free and unimpeded step towards perfection. Its stubborn forms will be taught to bend to the convenience and exigencies of the people for whose use it subsists. It will be separated from the rubbish and decay of time, and stripped of the parasitical growths that darken and disfigure it.

It is perhaps to be regretted, that the youth who dedicate themselves to the study of our legal constitutions, should be greeted on the threshold with phrases strange to the ears of freedom: that they cannot enter the vestibule without paying constrained devotion to idols which their fathers have levelled in the dust. The *Commentaries* of Sir William Blackstone are still the only clue where by to tread the mazy labyrinth through which they have to pass; and the fascinating eloquence of that author, conceals a thousand sophistries dangerous to the principles which every citizen of our free republic ought, and every professor of our laws is sworn, to maintain. Impressions thus stamped on young minds, are not quickly eradicated, and if once taught to believe, that excellence is only to be found abroad, they will not care to seek for it at home. The *Commentaries*, it is true, deserve our admiration, and we owe some gratitude to the author, who has rendered the complicated and perplexed code upon which our wiser, though yet imperfect system, has been engrafted, accessible and tangible. What it was before he wrote, may be gathered from this, that the benefactor and founder whose intentions he was appointed to carry into effect, spent half a century in compiling in the most condensed form, four and twenty elephantine folios, to serve as a brief index to the books which even then composed the lawyers' libraries, but are tenfold increased with us, and continue to increase in the like accumulated ratio. Various amendments also, first suggested by Blackstone, have been carried into execution with us, and from the able manner in which he has laid bare many defects and anomalies of the English law, though its professed apologist, we may imagine how he would have written and taught, had it been his fortune to witness, as we do, the wonderful effects of true liberty upon human prosperity and happiness: how a people without hierarchy, nobility, monarchy, distinction of condition, rank, or privilege, can govern themselves, and flourish beyond what hope or fancy could predict. Had he experienced this, and been endowed and appointed to eulogize our laws and constitutions, how ingeniously, how impressively, would he have contrasted them with the decayed and vicious institutions which he has so extolled. . . .

Let us keep in mind, that we too must become ancestors and be judged by posterity. We cannot altogether foresee what may be said of us, but part we may imagine. These people, (it may be said) long after they had set the great example of self-government upon principles of perfect equality, had reduced the practice of religion to its purest principles, executed mighty works, and acquired renown in arts and arms, had still one pagan idol to which they daily offered up much smoky incense. They called it by the mystical and cabalistic name of Common Law. A mysterious essence. Like the Dalai Lama, not to be seen or visited in open day; of most indefinite antiquity; sometimes in the decrepitude of age, and sometimes in the bloom of infancy, yet still the same that was, and was to be, and evermore to sit cross-legged and motionless upon its antique altar, for no use or purpose, but to be praised and worshipped by ignorant and superstitious votaries. Its attributes were all negative, its properties all enigmatical, and its name a metaphor. Taken in many senses, it had truly none. It was oral tradition opposed to written law; it was written law, but presuming the writing lost; it was that of whose origin there was no record or memory, but of which the evidence was both in books and records. It was opposed to statute law, to civil law, to ecclesiastical law, to military law, to maritime and mercantile law, to the law of nations; but most frequently contrasted with equity itself. It was common sense, but of an artificial kind, such as is not the sense of any common man; it was the perfection of reason, but that meant artificial reason. And as to its growth and progress there is as little agreement amongst its panygerists at this hour. Some tell us it was perfect in its inception, and became corrupt through time; others that it had a barbarous origin, but gradually grew to perfection. Some that it was anciently wise, and then grew foolish, and from thence has been in a state of convalescence. One speaks of it in his day, as being the perfection of human reason; another shows it to have been at that very period under a dark and fearful inumbration. With false theories it must ever be so; for there is but one thing uniform, and that is truth, one thing wise, and that is simplicity. . . .

It was my intention here to have pointed out some of the most curious and interesting subjects, connected with the history of our law, but time will not permit. They will present themselves readily to the historian who shall devote his labours to the useful and honourable task of exploring, with a view to future improvement, the true foundations of our law. And let none be deterred, by the supposed dryness of the subject. The historic muse is not austere, except when dulness woos her; invoked by genius, she gives to the coldest subjects warmth and animation. And as the geographical historian is not content to determine the depth of the valley, or the height of the mountain, but enriches his works with moral instruction, by the history of the human beings who lived and roved, and worshipped and fought, and flourished and fell, by the mountain's side, upon the verdant plain, by the river's bank, or the wide ocean wave: so the historian of our law, derived as it is from such an ancient and a distant source, will find his subject abounding in those changeful events, metamorphoses and transitions, which will impart to real and most important history, all the high charms of poetry and fiction. Whilst fancy roams at large, through time and space, and "distance lends enchantment to the view," reason will knit the chain that binds effect with cause, and judgment will approve the generous design. This discourse is but a short prelude, to challenge into the noblest field of exertion the talent and genius of our country, much of which is now lost in barren erudition. If the hundredth part of that painful industry and acknowledged talent, which is wasted upon vain and ever baffled efforts to reconcile the irregularities, explain the anomalies, sustain the paradoxes, and solve the riddles of our entangled jurisprudence, was bestowed upon a science capable of improvement or advancement, what glorious fruits would it not, e'er now, have brought forth, instead of that sickly and exotic growth, that has no sap or freshness; upon whose withering branches some faint pale blossoms may appear, but rich fruit cannot ripen. We should have had laws suited to our condition and high destinies; and our lawyers would have been the ornaments of our country. No longer forced into the degrading paths of Norman subtleties, nor to copy from models of Saxon barbarity, but taught to resolve every argument into principles of natural reason, universal justice, and present convenience, truth would have been the constant object of their search; chicane and pettifogging would have found no dark crevices to lurk in; bad faith would have been banished from the temple of Justice; good sense would not be shocked with the failures of right, upon exception of idle and unmeaning form; and Justice would not be seen for ever travelling upon by-paths, such as necessity enforces by the sides of a broken road.

And what subject can be at once so important, and so amusing, as to trace our law through all its various and progressive changes, from its first rude origin in the wilds of Gaul and Germany, and its first crossing the salt wave, till after a long sojourn of troubled ages, it again passed the wider expanses of ocean, and arrived at this western continent. Here, "like a tree set by the water side, it will spread its roots towards the moisture, and will not fear the heat when it cometh, for its leaf shall be green, and it will not cease to bring forth its fruit."

To realize this boast, we have but to put our hands to the good work of reformation which cannot be long delayed, and which alone can satisfy the determined will of the people. Having adopted the Common Law of England so far as it is not repugnant to our constitutions, we have a mighty interest to know clearly what it is, and from what stock it comes. We must either be governed by laws made for us, or made by us. If we do not credit the stories of King Brutus, or King Lucius, or Doctors Faganus or Divanus, or of the Graeco-Trojan code, translated by the great-grandson of Aeneas, who after slaying the giants and their King Gog Magog, took possession of Britain, and dying divided it among his three sons: so neither should we believe that we can be governed, at this day, by the oral traditions of semi-savage Saxons who could have no knowledge nor conception of the objects with which our law is conversant. We cannot believe that those vast importations, which come wet from the press, or new bound in calves' skin, treating of bills of exchange, promissory notes, policies of insurance, charter-parties, banks, steamboats, patent-rights, and such learning, can be rationally connected with the oral traditions, or ancient common laws, *of which our Saxon ancestors were so unjustly deprived, by the chicaning and finessing Norman clergy.*

If this Common Law is but oral tradition, how comes it to fall about our ears in overwhelming showers of printing? How came these ancestors by traditions touching what they could have neither known nor contemplated? Had they possessed the arts and sciences which time has since brought to light, we might be justified in looking back to their times, their manners, and their usages for instruction.

Instead of their judicial astrology, had they known the true theory of the heavenly bodies, so as to interrogate them with certainty as to their course and position in remote and trackless oceans; had they understood the virtues of the magnetic needle, and by its guidance to explore all earthly regions, habitable and inhabitable; had any of their sages commanded the fleeting clouds to discharge their latent fire; had any of their artists yoked that fierce consuming element to the peaceful car of commerce, or thundering engine of defensive war; had they, for the cure of diseases, instead of magical incantations, and impious consultations with the dead, discovered the circulation of the blood, the structure of the human frame, and its wonderful and delicate organization, and by accurate experiment been taught to heal, to succour, or to cure; had they been acquainted with that wonderful instrument, which multiplies intelligence, and renders ancient and foreign learning familiar and vernacular; had the use of letters, instead of being unknown, or if known, confined to cloisters or to subjects of scholastic and theological disputation, been cultivated and extended to all ranks, and all useful purposes, we might look back to them for wisdom. If, instead of the skin-covered baskets, in which our Celtic ancestors carried on their trade and navigation, or the barks in which our Saxon and Scandinavian ancestors coasted along in their piratical excursions, their merchant sitting at his desk, by the simple agency of his pen, could have given impulse and direction to ships of mighty magnitude and wonderful construction, rare and curious combinations of art and elegance, preordain what seas they were to traverse, what climes to visit, what ports to enter, what delays to make, when to return, and by what route, with all the thousand details that the refinement of commerce has produced, and the free use of letters can express; then we might derive from them wise laws and ordinances of commercial intercourse. Had their landed possessions been unfettered by feudal rules, and free to circulate for the purposes of peaceful life, and had their personal possessions been any thing more than their cattle and their arms, their modes of contract and conveyance, whether expressed in Greek, in Latin, in Erse, in Danish, in Saxon, in Norman, or in forensic English mixed and compounded of them all, might govern us in that variety of transfers and modifications which refinement in commerce and civilization renders necessary. And time and labour would be better bestowed in searching for such precious antiquities, as models of our legal forms and institutions, than in digging in subterraneous ruins for vases, and torses, and columns, and sculptured ornaments, wherewith to embellish the arts of luxury and pride.

It is the meagreness and insufficiency of this ancient stock, that has obliged judges to legislate *pro re nata*,[1] upon every new point. It is the complication of these stinted usages with the perverse intricacies of the Norman jurisprudence, that has made decisions less wise than if their authors had been more free to follow the dictates of their own good sense, or less restrained by the antisocial spirit of the Common Law, from resorting to universal principles, and to codes of approved and written reason. The colonial laws, and the constitution and statutes of the state, have successively pruned the exorbitances and strange peculiarities of the English jurisprudence: and it is therefore that the decisions of our judges, due regard had to their personal merits, stand so far above those which we import. It is for that reason also, that we should import no more; for with every deference due to the learning, wisdom, and integrity of English judges, they are not fit persons to legislate for us. If we are indebted to them for much good learning, it is more becoming to pay them back with interest, than run deeper in their debt. Dependence can never cease if one nation is always to teach, and the other always to learn. Our condition is essentially different from theirs. They are appointed by a king, and he is the fountain of their justice and its administration. Some of them are stationed at Westminster, and some are supposed to follow this moveable fountain wherever it shall be. Must we too follow? Must we tread always in their steps, go where they go, be what they are, do what they do, and say what they say? Too much of this sympathy may endanger our very being. If we can only be wise when they are wise, we must also be foolish if they are foolish, doat when they doat, and die when they die; and then, if I may borrow for illustration the witty conceit of the author of *Hudibras*, we shall be like him whose nose being made of the porter's brawn, could not outlive the parent substance,

> And when the date of knock was out,
> Off dropped the sympathetic snout.

In despotic countries the will of the sovereign is the law, and his glory the sole end: earth, air, and sea, are referred to his dominion: time is measured by the years of his reign: and his subjects are quantities to estimate his grandeur. His vices or his virtues, his battles and his sieges, his intrigues, usurpations, and alliances, his pleasures and amours, absorb all other interests; and the servile pen of the historian and the poet, is ever ready to pay divine honours to successful crime. In a free country, triumphs and victories, are only valued as the means of peace and safety; and the glory of the hero, is to have fought in the defence of his country's liberty and laws. So thought the ever honoured patriot, who in that farewell address, which breathes the spirit of his wisdom and his virtues, anticipates as the great reward of all his services, to enjoy in the midst of his fellow citizens, the benign influence of good laws, under a free government.

There is one country then, whose history is yet unstained with crime or usurpation, where the faithful chronicler of its short but bright career, may invoke both liberty and truth to bear him company. Need I name it? No, for before I spoke the exulting heart of every hearer had already answered, It is ours—it is our own.

It may be asked, Why this censure upon our ancestors and upon their usages, and whether there is any code for which we would exchange our law. I answer: as to our ancestors I hold them all in equal honour, and treat them better than they have done each other. I would not ruffle a feather in the cap of any of them: but it is no disparagement to say, that they were barbarous in times of universal darkness. And as to our laws, it is one thing to change, and another to reform them with a tender, patient, kindly, and experienced hand; and God forbid they should be touched or meddled with, by any other than the wise and honest.

Our law is justly dear to us—and why? because it is the law of a free people, and has freedom for its end, and under it we live both free and happy. When we go forth, it walks silent and unobtrusive by our side, covering us with its invisible shield from violence and wrong. Beneath our own roof, or by our own fireside, it makes our home our castle. All ages, sexes, and conditions, share its protecting influence. It shadows with its wing the infant's cradle, and with its arm upholds the tottering steps of age. Do the smiles of the babe give gladness to the mother's heart, her joy is perfect in the consciousness that no tyrant's power dare snatch it from her arms; that when she consigns it to repose, its innocent slumbers are guarded by a nation's strength, and that it sleeps more free from danger than kings amidst their armed myrmidons. And when life's close draws near, we feel the cheering certitude, that those we love and leave shall possess the goods that we possessed, and enjoy the same security in which we lived and died. But that we are indebted for this, to Saxon, Scandinavian, Gaul, Greek, or Trojan, is what unsophisticated reason will not endure. We owe it to the growth of knowledge, and to the struggles of virtuous patriots, many of whom have bled and died for it: we owe it to fortunate occasion and favouring providence. But even this part of our law which thus secures our rights and liberties, is not untainted with pedantry, nor free from all absurdity. A sister state has already set on foot the experiment of a penal code, and committed its execution to the hands of one of its most capable citizens.[2] Let us hail the happy augury and prepare for a still nobler effort, which imperious necessity will force upon us, and which cannot and ought not to be long delayed.

If the experiment had never before been made of a judicial code, substituted in the place of antiquated legends, usages, and customs, we might fear to engage in an untried and hazardous undertaking. If no attempt had ever yet been made, to reduce to a body of written reason, the scattered fragments of a nation's laws or usages, or if when such attempts were made, disorder and mischief had constantly ensued, we might take warning from such examples. If no wise jurists had ever recommended the digesting and new ordering of the law, there might be temerity in the proposal, but Hale and Bacon have not only approved, but offered their views and plans. And are not our own written statutes periodically revised; why not that part of our laws that rests upon less solid evidence? It has been the first glory of the greatest sovereigns and the best policy of the wisest people. The most celebrated lawgivers have travelled into all regions where early civilization had left its luminous traces, to gather the chosen flowers and fruits of every clime. If the fathers of our revolution at the peril of much more than life, of all the vengeance that offended power can visit on the unsuccessful patriot, dared to uproot the three great pillars of the Common Law—the monarchy, the hierarchy, and privileged orders—shall we stand in superstitious awe of unlaid spectres, shall we still be amused by nursery tales, and tremble at the thoughts of innovations upon institutions which their admirers themselves assimilate to the practices of the Gentoos, the Mexicans, and the children of the Sun; which have not half the imposing dignity of those of our ancestors, the red men of the five nations, as may be seen by any one who will read the account of them by Mr. Colden,[3] and compare it with the uncouth manners of the Saxon Heptarchists. It is true, at the same time, that the English reports contain amidst a world of rubbish, rich treasures of experience, and that those of our own courts contain materials of inestimable worth, and require little more than regulation and systematic order. This with fixing and determining the principles on which they ought to depend, and settling by positive enactments all doubts that hang upon them, abolishing for ever all forms that impede the march of justice, and firmly establishing those which are needful to its ends, and translating into plain and intelligible language, those borrowed, ill-penned statutes, of which every word gives rise to endless commentaries, will complete the wished for object. Particular cases will not then be resorted to instead of general law. The law will govern the decisions of judges, and not the decisions the law. Judgments will be *legibus non exemplis*.[4] And it will not be necessary that at least one victim should be sacrificed to the making of every new rule, which without such immolation would have no existence.

Our jurisprudence then will be no longer intricate and thorny; nor will it need those fictions, which give it the air of occult magic, or those queer and awkward contrivances, which, by rendering it ridiculous, greatly diminish its dignity and efficacy. We shall be delivered from those odious volumes of special pleading, which cannot be used without degrading and lowering the tone of moral sentiment: which destroy by their verbose jargon, the very end of logical precision at which they profess to aim: where the suitor's story is told in twenty different ways, and answered in as many, and must be hunted for with fear and trembling in printed books, (but, oh! such books!) and made conformable to precedents composed before the party was in being, and which, in no one single instance, conform to the truth: insomuch, that he who dares to tell his case according to the simple and honest truth, will for that very reason, if for no other, fail in his suit. We shall be delivered too from those ever increasing swarms of foreign reports and treatises, which darken the very atmosphere by their multitude, and generate their kind amongst us, and against which we must either rise in arms, as certain oriental nations are said to do against the flights of locusts, or else abandon our own fair fields, and the fruits of our own genial soil, to their pernicious action.

Sir Edward Coke, complains, in the words of Solomon, that of writing of books there is no end. He however wrote, and not sparingly. He also says, quoting Seneca, "it matters not how many books thou hast, but how good: multitude of books do rather burden than instruct, and it is far better, thoroughly to acquaint thyself with a few authors, than to wander through many." "The ancient order of argument," he says, "was altered, for formerly the citing was general, but always true in the particular, and now the citing is particular, and the matter many times mistaken in general." "Few cases," he says, "were cited of old, but very pithy and pertinent; and now, in such long arguments, with such a farrago of authorities, it cannot be but there is much refuse. This were easily holpen, if the matter, which ever lieth in a narrow compass, were first discerned, and then, that every one, that argueth at the bar, would either speak to the purpose, or be short." What would he say to us, in this land of common sense, where all the books he enumerates would not be missed off the shelves of a young attorney, and where the arguments of counsel are reported by clouds of cyphers, indicating nothing but the pages of books most commonly cited as law for both sides? Would he not say, that the evil required a speedy cure?

The best reason urged for the adherence to English precedents, is the preserving of uniformity amongst the sister states. It has not, nor cannot answer this end. This evil of divergence has already begun, and can only be remedied by erecting the standard of simple wisdom, to which all may rally: for there is nothing so uniform as truth, nor so simple as wisdom. Folly cannot form a bond of union amongst enlightened men, but reason may.

Of simplicity, be it observed however, there are two periods. The first, where uncultivated human beings, with few ideas and few wants, pursue, like other gregarious animals, the instinctive habits of their species. To that state we can no more return than be again born of our mothers. The other period of simplicity is that of mature wisdom, where many ideas are referred to few and general principles. To this we must labour to attain: to this perfection we must endeavour to bring that law, which is our birthright, our blessing, and our safeguard. And let us lose no time; the moment is propitious. Whilst darkness lowers, and war threatens, and tyranny and superstition assert their ancient empire over other nations, let us improve the auspicious moments of peace and happiness to strengthen ourselves with institutions worthy of our destinies.

Whilst yet a remnant of those patriot sages to whom we

owe the blessings we enjoy, still linger on the stage where they so nobly have discharged their part, let them perceive that their generous labours are not lost, and that their children will be worthy of their bright inheritance. It is for this generation to fill up the outlines traced by the inspiration of their sires, until the glowing canvas shall present one pure harmonious image of enduring wisdom, giving to all regenerated nations a model of judicial polity equal to that already exhibited in our political institutions. When this is done, and our untrammelled jurisprudence shall expand to the measure of our growing fortunes, its history will no longer resemble that reservoir or fountain so often troubled, and so rarely limpid, but rather be imaged, if we must speak in metaphor, by a mighty river, which in some lonely barren desert, first issues from its native rock. When yet a slender stream it only serves to slake the tyger's thirst, and that of his fellow savage man. Next a foaming torrent, wild as the scenes through which it drives its headlong desultory course. By a predestined ordinance descending still, it gains the fertile plain. Uniting there with kindred waters and tributary streams it takes a milder aspect, and on its polished surface stand reflected, commerce, and arts, and all that can embellish sublunary scenes, till last of all it feels the ocean's swell, and bears upon its heaving bosom the wealth of nations and treasure of the earth.

NOTES

1 With respect to each thing as it appears.

2 Edward Livingston, Representative in Congress for Louisiana [Sampson's note].

3 Cadwallader Colden (1688–1776), *The History of the Five Indian Nations Depending on the Province of New York*, 1727.

4 By laws and not by examples.

HENRY DWIGHT SEDGWICK (1785–1831)

ON AN ANNIVERSARY DISCOURSE DE-
LIVERED BEFORE THE HISTORICAL
SOCIETY, ON SATURDAY, DECEMBER
6, 1823, SHOWING THE ORIGIN, PROG-
RESS, ANTIQUITIES, CURIOSITIES, AND
NATURE OF THE COMMON LAW. BY
WILLIAM SAMPSON (*Article VIII in* The
North American Review, *XLV, October, 1824,*
416–39)

[*The North American Review* was the literary organ of
that Boston-Unitarian culture of which Joseph Story was,
in the realm of the law, the pre-eminent ornament. Like
him, most of the foremost lawyers, foremost both for legal
acumen and classical culture, were Whigs, despised Jackson, and held the word "codification" to be obscene. Hence
it is somewhat astonishing that the editors in 1824 should
select a man to review Sampson who, though a scion of the
gentlemanly caste if any ever was, sympathized with this
movement. The *Review* did not repeat its mistake. Thereafter every article on the law is written by an anti-codifier.
This lapse is a possible indication that in 1824 the lines of
combat had not yet been rigorously drawn; the editors—
who were not lawyers—had not yet been taught that codification was a subject with which no gentleman should soil
his hands.

Henry Dwight Sedgwick, however, was indisputably a

gentleman, the second son of the mighty Judge Theodore
Sedgwick (1746–1813) of Stockbridge, Massachusetts. It
may be that his birth in that rural outpost, and his education at Williams College rather than at Harvard, gave him
a breadth of view not welcomed in the neighborhood of
Boston. It is significant, too, that he went to New York City
to study law, that he practised there, and was an ardent
champion of free trade. Sedgwick is generally given the
credit for persuading his friend William Cullen Bryant to
move from the Berkshires to New York in 1825. In 1822
Sedgwick himself had published an able book, *English
Practice of the Common Law*, which advocated a code of
procedure, expressed, however, in a New England style
quite unlike the picturesque Irish eloquence of Sampson.
Shortly thereafter Sedgwick's health failed him, and he retired to Stockbridge. His death at the age of forty-six is still
to be lamented as a loss to the profession.

Sedgwick is not, as he makes clear, a confirmed enemy
of the Common Law, as was Sampson, but he tried to
frame a reasonable argument for reform with regard to the
different social order in America and in view of the technological and economic advances already evident by that
time in the nineteenth century. He obviously underesti-
mated the force and passion of the opponents of codification. For the next three or four decades the discussion
would seldom return to the plane of Sedgwick's rational
calmness.]

ON AN ANNIVERSARY DISCOURSE, 1824

Some of the circumstances, which have retarded the improvement of the law among us, seem to be of a more accidental nature than others; and to encourage us with the
hope, that they will in some considerable degree be removed by the progress of time and increase of wisdom.
One of these circumstances is, that in this country, and in
that from which we derive our legal institutions, the law is
artificial and technical to an extent very much beyond what

is required by the reason or nature of the case. This remark, so far as it includes the principles of the Common Law, is applicable to England and to all the states of this Union, which have adopted the Common Law, but so far as it relates to the *practice* of the law so called, or to its modes and forms of proceeding, it is applicable only to England, and to such of the United States, probably a small proportion of the whole, as have adopted in mass the English practice of the Common Law.

This extreme artificialness, and technicality of the English Common Law, both as to its principles and its practice, distinguishes that system very broadly from every other. This distinction is remotely analogous to that which exists between the syllogistic mode of reasoning, and the ordinary style of argument in which a plain man would press his conclusions. It would be an interesting and instructive inquiry, to trace this peculiarity through some of the leading features of the system, such as the distinction between sealed instruments and those not under seal, the refined doctrines relating to real estates, the forms of actions, the niceties of special pleading, and the rules of practice as they exist in England. A strict research and close analysis directed to this subject would render it very evident, that these peculiarities are not usually, nor perhaps ever, the result of prospective wisdom. Their origin will be found in the history of the times, and in the particular states of society in which our English ancestors were placed. Since those periods the condition of the people has undergone a change almost radical, but the laws have not experienced a correspondent revolution. Lands in this country and in England are nearly as much the subject of traffic, as the public stocks, and yet the *theory* of the law of real estate is almost as feudal as it was in those times, when resort was had for national defence, not to the monied sources of the country, but to the lands which were held on the condition of performing military service. Society has grown and spread in every direction; wealth has increased to an immense degree, and its nature changed by the disproportionate increase of personal property; occupations and interests are in a thousand ways extended and diversified; but all this has been done silently and gradually; there has been no revolutionary period, no crisis, no epoch when the community, finding itself thrown into new circumstances, was obliged to cast about for new rules or principles to guide it in the emergency.

The lawyers and judges of the Common Law were not in advance of the age; they did not perceive the alteration, that had begun and was going on in the structure of society; on the contrary, they strove to apply old rules, with which only they were acquainted, to new relations and new things. In addition to this, and cooperating with it, was that love of quaintness, refined reasoning, and fanciful analogy, which characterises the early stages of civilisation. It was necessarily the combined effects of these circumstances, and of others not here enumerated, to give to the law in the progress of time an air of mystery, inasmuch as its reasons and principles were not to be found in the existing state of things, and its practice was unintelligible, having reference to institutions which had passed away. It has been asserted, that all knowledge is so intimately connected, that from any one truth almost every other might be deduced. This is probably extravagant, but it certainly is true, that the law, which regulates the whole mass of the people, bears a very strong affinity to most other species of knowledge, and especially to general intelligence; and yet the Common Law has been nearly excluded from the beneficial influence of those causes, which have elevated and improved the intellectual condition of the community.[1]

We now approach with due caution the separate consideration of an important part of this subject, and that is the *veneration and obedience paid to authority and precedent*, which prevail in our system of law in a much greater degree, than in most other departments of knowledge, or spheres of action. The principle on which this veneration is founded is universal in our nature, and of most salutary tendency. Without it all ancient wisdom would be useless, and uniformity would be lost in wild confusion. The inquiry of the enlightened jurist and legislator should be, how far any interference with it in relation to this subject is desirable or safe; and how far this principle should be permitted to restrain the operation of others, which are perhaps equally essential to the happiness and glory of the country?

The foundation of the English Common Law is *authority,* that is, the *dicta,* or *sayings,* and the decisions of the Judges, handed down from the earliest time to the present, each successive decision being, or being supposed to be, founded on some preceding adjudication, or at least but a new application of a principle already established. This is the theory of the Common Law, and the practical deviations from it have been rare and slight. The maxim is *stare decisis;*[2] and no argument *ab inconvenienti,*[3] that is, showing the mischievous nature of a principle, is permitted to be urged against a positive decision. Whatever has once been clearly settled, by a competent tribunal, is not again to be drawn into question before a judicial forum, and, if wrong, it can only be corrected by the omnipotence of legislative authority. . . .

When the law shall have become thoroughly conformed to the spirit of the age, authority will become of double value and efficacy. Decisions, which approve themselves to the reason and the conscience, have much greater weight, than those which oppose them. If the direct road be also the most beaten, there will be little temptation, and no apology, for turning into devious paths; but if the prescribed way be circuitous and illconstructed, there will always be apparent cause for striking into some other route.

All the states of this Union, which were British colonies, that is, all the original states, adopted the English Common Law, and the greater part of them, the English statute law in mass. This was natural and proper; indeed, under the circumstances of the case, it was inevitable. They know no other system of law, and they could practice no other. It was intimately connected with all their habits and institutions, and it is not too much to say, that the moral impossibility of changing by an act of national volition, or legislation, the established jurisprudence of a people, is as certain as the physical impossibility of changing the great geographical features of the country they inhabit. All revolutions in matters, which affect the great mass of society, to be salutary, must be gradual. The reason is obvious; the question is not what is speculatively best, but what is known and approved, what is generally understood and can be put in practice. The habits and manners, the existing opinions, and the laws which are founded on these, cannot be changed by any power short of despotism, and despotism itself has often failed in the attempt. Time is the only reformer. The expansion of a country, the increase of its wealth, its foreign and domestic intercourse, its new acquisitions moral and physical, the new relations into which it is thrown, and the changes consequent on these, all tend to produce a revolution in its jurisprudence, and nothing else can or ought to produce it.

Because changes should be gradual, it does not follow, that there should not be some periods in our progress, or *epochs,* when we should pause and look about us to ascertain what changes have been effected by the operation of time and new circumstances, and what further changes are clearly indicated as expedient by the course of things, and the new lights which have fallen upon us. In this way only can experience and 'the wisdom of our ancestors' be turned to good account. It is a truth that many will never learn, that mere *duration* is not experience, and that experience, to be of any value, must include observation and comparison at least, if not experiment.

We trust that nothing which has been said will be construed into an attack upon the Common Law. If we were compelled to make a selection among all existing, or known systems of jurisprudence, we should certainly decide in favor of the Common Law. Our chief reason for this preference would be, that it is the law of freedom. But being sovereign States we are not bound, nor is it wise to adopt, in mass, and without distinction, the jurisprudence of any country. The question rather is, whether these United States, or some of them, have not so increased in magnitude, whether their institutions, mode of society, tenure of property, and, in short, all their relations and their whole character, have not become so materially different from those existing in England, or rather from those which did exist there, when the foundations of the Common Law were laid, that the change and alienation, which have thus resulted, ought not to be formally recognised; whether we have not derived all the aid we ought to expect from the land of our ancestors; whether any farther servile dependence on a foreign country does not rather tend to retard than promote our advancement; and lastly, while we pay to England all due courtesy and respect, not only as the land of our fathers and the abode of our brethren, but also as the freest, the wisest, and most illustrious European nation, whether we should not, nevertheless, declare a final separation, not a nonintercourse, but an independence in jurisprudence, as really and nominally absolute, as it has long been in point of political sovereignty? . . .

Farther than this we are not bound to go, and here we might close this article; but as in truth our inquiries have not stopped here, we have no reluctance to state the result to which our minds have arrived; and in so doing, no merit is claimed for originality; the proposed remedy is not a novelty in speculation or practice; it is obvious, and has been frequently recommended, and, as we believe, is the only remedy which can be applied with success. We would then suggest the propriety, that at least some of the larger and more wealthy states of the Union should cause their laws to pass under a general revision, and to be formed into *written codes.*

We shall briefly state in what manner we think a code ought to be formed, and shall then leave the suggestion to make its own impressions on our readers, adding only a few remarks to prove its utility, and to remove objections.

In the first place, nothing should be done in times of political excitement. There should be no mixture of party spirit in this great work. Some of the states have incurred disgrace by the laws, which they have passed under the

influence of faction, and still more deeply by the men that
have, from a like cause, been appointed to judicial stations.
But there is no reason why, in a propitious calm like the
present, when there is nothing within or without to distract
our attention, or to give an undue bias to our efforts, there
is no reason why, at such a period, we should not subject
our jurisprudence to a revision more extensive and elementary than it has hitherto undergone, and bring about a revision of the laws, which should include the unwritten or
Common Law, as well as the statute law, which is now in
many states frequently, and in some of them periodically
revised.

The first apprehension which will strike some minds at
such a proposition is, that everything will be thrown into
confusion; that all the elements of jurisprudence would be
confounded and remodeled; and whatever might be the
theoretical beauty of the new structure to be created from
the ruins, it would be wholly untried and experimental,
"unsafe to touch and insecure to stand on." We have no
such apprehensions, nor need any entertain them if they
will but reflect who are to be the principal actors in this
revolution. They would be chiefly lawyers, and Common
Law lawyers, for we have scarcely any other—men whose
minds had been cast in the moulds of Littleton, Coke, and
Blackstone. They would also be grave and experienced
men, for none but those who had attained a high station
in the profession would be entrusted with such a task. The
danger would, in truth, be the reverse of what is appre-
hended; the reformers being acquainted with the English
Common Law, and none other, and all their habits, ideas,
and associations being connected with it, the probability is,
that their views would not be sufficiently large and liberal,
and that they would be governed too much by the bias and
prejudice of their education. Has not the fact been found to
correspond with these suppositions? Have not our lawyers,
and judges, and legislators ever shown a disposition to retain many parts of the English system, which are alike incompatible with the present state of knowledge, and with
our institutions? Our poor laws have been enacted in con-

formity to English notions. We have reënacted their usury laws. Their laws against the combinations of mechanics to obtain advanced wages from their employers are adopted in these democratic states. We have no time to pursue this branch of the subject farther. The preceding part of this essay has been written in vain, if it has not shown the prevalence of fixed ideas and principles in regard to all matters of jurisprudence, and then there is little danger of rash and unnecessary innovation in our laws. Indeed, a thorough bred lawyer *cannot* be a great innovator; his mind is saturated with the system, and he cannot wash out the tinct; his thoughts have all travelled in a certain round, and they cannot break out into space.

It is often urged, and with great sincerity, that the proposed remedy for the multiplicity and uncertainty of the law would be unavailing. It is said, and no doubt truly, that if a written code of the laws were prepared with the greatest care and ability, there would still be many lurking ambiguities; that new cases and new difficulties would arise; that comments would shortly be appended to the code; that these comments would themselves form the basis of fresh annotations; that different opinions would be entertained of the meaning of the code itself, and conflicting decisions made thereon, and thus in a short time there would grow up a mass of authority and adjudication, as ponderous and oppressive as that from which we now seek to be relieved; and, finally, that all expectations of reducing the law to a state of simplicity and certainty would prove fallacious. We admit that there is much truth in this. We have no expectation that the law ever can be reduced to a state of simplicity and certainty. On the contrary, it is in its own nature, and must ever remain, to a very great and inconvenient extent, complicated and uncertain. It is for that very reason, that it is all important to reduce the subject within as manageable a compass, and to as great a degree of certainty as possible. That there are trackless forests, and undiscovered regions, is no reason why the known and cultivated parts of the country should not be surveyed and reduced to orderly arrangement. . . .

We are not wholly without the benefit of experience in
this country in relation to this subject. We have already
hinted at the division of the law into two heads, namely,
that which binds by force of a statute or the will of the
legislature, and that which is derived from all other
sources. This distinction is not very precise, because much
of the law consists in authoritative decisions on statutes,
which are often very distinguishable from the statutes
themselves, but it is sufficiently accurate for our present
purpose. Now we believe that the experience of most of
the states has shown the expediency, not to say the necessity, of an occasional revision of the statutes to a greater or
less extent. Statutes, *in pari materia,* as they are called,
that is, upon the same subject, have been revised, collated,
amended, and reduced into one. Saving the offensiveness
of the term, this is nothing else than legislative *codification.*
It has been found not dangerous but beneficial, and we
cannot but think, that if an English jurist would take a hint
from a young country, he would not be long in discovering
that it would be no small service to his own kingdom, if the
numerous volumes of her statutes had been reduced into
order and compass; if the game laws, the laws relating to
apprentices and the poor, the bankrupt laws, and, above
all, the criminal laws, had been revised and brought
within the limits of memory and investigation.

The statute law is quite inconsiderable in comparison
with the enormous mass of the Common or unwritten Law,
that law of which the evidence is to be found in books of
reports of the English and American courts, and the books
made from them, with an occasional though rare reference
to the opinions and decisions of the jurists of other countries. If then the benefit of digesting the statute laws into
something resembling a code has been so great and so apparent, what reason is there why a similar advantage may
not be expected, by subjecting the larger and more discordant mass of the Common Law to a similar operation?

But there are still higher and more illustrious precedents
to be adduced in support of our argument. We allude to
the constitutions of the several states of this Union, and to

the federal constitution which holds them all together. What are these but a digest or *code* of fundamental principles on constitutional law? They have not excluded doubt or discussion; no human instrument could do that; language is not competent to such an effect. But they have done much; and infinitely more than those will readily believe, whose thoughts and studies have not led them to be conversant with subjects of this nature. We have had many constitutional discussions; in the infancy of this system, before its organisation had become perfect, and its parts were adapted to each other, this was unavoidable; but our written constitutions have furnished a comparatively easy and definitive test, for the resolution of doubts and decision of controversies. In England also there have been constitutional disputes, and the disputants have appealed to theoretic reasoning, vague maxims, obsolete charters, ancient usages, half forgotten statutes, concerning which it has been matter of doubtful discussion, whether they were or were not in force, and finally, there being no other absolute test, to the sword of the strongest.

The administration of justice is beyond all comparison the most important part of the government and polity of a country. An enlightened jurisprudence supposes a great advance in national character, and, more than anything else, tends to aid its further progress. That the judiciary is honest and learned denotes only a low degree of improvement in this most important of all arts. The laws should be as simple as is consistent with the multiplied relations of society, they should be homogeneous, and adapted to the existing state of things, they should be intelligible, that they may be understood, and just, that they may be approved, and they should be carried into execution in a direct, economical, expeditious, and effectual method. How far the English system of the law remains distant, not only from theoretical, but easily attainable perfection, any one may perceive, who has studied this subject with any degree of philosophical attention. Americans will not long believe, and the inhabitants of many of these states do not now believe, that there is any necessity that the forms of conducting a legal controversy should be so multiplied and expensive, that the mere costs of suit, without taking into consideration the rewards of professional eminence, should be so great, that none but the rich can indulge in the luxury of the law. This is now the case in England. Enlightened men will not long believe, that it is necessary to have such a system of law, that a vast proportion of the reports relate to distinctions having no connexion with the justice of the case in controversy, and but a doubtful existence in the nature of things, such for instance as the evanescent and scarcely discernible boundaries of the actions of trespass, and trespass on the case. These things will not always remain as they now are, but the day of change is perhaps far distant.

NOTES

[1] In the time of Cicero a few months' study was thought sufficient to render a young man, otherwise well instructed, a sufficiently accomplished lawyer. That the magnitude of this task is so much greater among us, is no doubt in the main to be ascribed to the different state of society, and the more perfect protection of rights; but one cause of the difference is certainly to be found in the extreme technicality of the law, to which we have above alluded. [Sedgwick's note].

Sedgwick's somewhat plaintive footnote is a mild expression of what in other circles was uttered more pugnaciously, a protest against the burden of scholarship which Story and his sort endeavored to impose upon the rising generations in order to stifle any dreams of simplicity. Needless to say, what Sedgwick thinks of as "technicality" has only a faint resemblance to modern connotations of the word in legal discourse; he means primarily the immense weight of the "law books" with which champions of orthodoxy sought to forestall their critics.

[2] The decision stands.

[3] From what has not been agreed upon.

THOMAS SMITH GRIMKÉ (1786–1834)

AN ORATION OF THE PRACTIBILITY AND EXPEDIENCE OF REDUCING THE WHOLE BODY OF THE LAW TO THE SIMPLICITY OF A CODE. DELIVERED TO THE SOUTH CAROLINA BAR ASSOCIATION, MARCH 17, 1827

[It is incongruous that Thomas Grimké should emerge out of "conservative" Charleston, South Carolina. Had he been a New Englander, we would have considered his devotion to a variety of "causes" as simply another manifestation of Yankee reforming zeal, but as a southerner he stands almost alone—except for the support of his two sisters, who became so outspoken against slavery that they had to migrate to the North. Thomas Grimké was a bold opponent of nullification, a classicist who yet advocated a reform of elementary education in the name of utility and science, preached the education of women and simplified spelling. He graduated from Yale in 1807 and aspired to be a minister in the Episcopal Church; under pressure from his father—a man of wealth and of solidly conservative opinions—he studied law. Despite his espousal of so many unpopular causes, he was successful at the bar.

Grimké's argument, like Sedgwick's review, is temperate. He too is not an enemy of the Common Law. Yet he is also poignantly ignorant of the passions which oppose even the most rational argument for codification. He was prodding

a hornet's nest when he mildly suggested that the example
of the civil law, and its healthy influences upon recent
English decisions, pointed toward the superiority of a code
which should replace the Common Law rather than toward such an ingenious tandem harness as Kent and Story
were assiduously constructing.]

AN ORATION, 1827

Law, in the appropriate and comprehensive meaning of
the term, includes, as essential ingredients, the ideas of
simplicity and order. For, whether we contemplate the
self-obedient agency of intelligent beings, or the involun-
tary action of material existence, order and simplicity are
still involved in our conceptions of Law. If we lift our eyes
to the heavens above, or look abroad over the surface of
our globe; if we penetrate the hidden recesses of our earth,
or the still more curious and wonderful depths of the ocean;
simplicity and order appear in all, that we behold, whatever may be its magnitude, or minuteness. Although, to the
gaze of ignorance, Creation is naught, but complexity and
chaos; yet, to the eye of Science, the works of God are
equally admirable for the simplicity of their elements, and
the completeness of their system. The Barbarian, who beholds the wilderness of greater and lesser lights which
crowd the firmament, never suspects that they are obedient
to a government, perfect in wisdom and benevolence. The
Savage, who traverses the forest, or stands in amazement
on the shore of the mysterious ocean; or launches his frail
bark on the river, or the lake, imagines not, that all are per-
vaded by the silent, secret influence of Laws, at once surprising for their simplicity and order. But Science has discovered, by the profound and unwearied studies of genius,
that all the endless variety and seeming perplexity of Nature, are reducible to systems, equally simple and harmonious in their principles.

To the eye of the Poet and the Painter, the natural world
appears invested with a sublimity, characterized by the

awful and majestic; with a beauty, distinguished for delicacy or richness. But the harmonizing magic of Philosophy gives a new elevation to the sublime, and a fresh interest to the loveliness of Nature. All, that man can know of physical existence, above, around, beneath him, has been systematized. The birds of the air, and the tribes of insects; the beasts of the forest and the fishes of the sea, have been subjected to the luminous arrangements of Science. The flowers, which adorn our gardens; the herb and the grass of the plain, the valley and the hill; the fruit-tree, yielding fruit after its kind; and the forest-tree of every clime, have been classed by the master hand of Philosophy. The fountains of living waters, the brook and the river, the tides of the deep, the mineral kingdom, clouds and lightening, wind and rain; and all the phenomena of the earth, the ocean, and the air, have become obedient to the wand of the enchanter—Science. Nor have the heavenly bodies escaped the observation of man; for the labours of Copernicus and Kepler, of Newton, Herschel, and La Place, have demonstrated, that the Laws of their being are pre-eminent in simplicity and order. . . .

All are deeply sensible of the exceedingly confused and imperfect state of our laws: and none can be more thoroughly convinced of these truths, than the Judges and the members of our profession. Hence has arisen the question, so much and so anxiously considered of late, "Is it practicable and expedient to reduce the whole body of our Law, to the simplicity and order of a code?" That it is expedient, will be denied by none. That it is practicable, has been doubted by many, perhaps by most, at the Bar and in the Legislature. If practicable, it is not only expedient, but a duty of the highest order—It is a duty which the rulers owe to the people, the people to themselves, and both to their posterity. It is an example, which is due to the sister States of our own Union: to our sister Republics of South-America: to our English ancestors: and to other civilized nations of Europe. It is a practical commentary on the great principle of the political creed of our day,

that the welfare of the people is the chief end of government. The laws are made by the Delegates of the People:
and can have no legitimate object, but to protect, improve,
and bless that people. So far as they attain not this end,
the Legislature and the Courts of Justice do not answer
the purposes of their institution. . . .

It is not uncommon for the champions of reform, in re-
plying to the arguments drawn from the character and
state of the Common Law, to pronounce that Law a chaos
of absurdity and injustice; of antiquated rules, inapplicable to modern society, and even hostile to its progressive
improvement. In a word, with them, the Common Law is,
"*Monstrum horrendum, informe, ingens, cui lumen ademp-
tum.*"[1]

But for myself, as one of the advocates of reformation,
I do protest emphatically and anxiously against such views.
So far from regarding the Common Law as a monster,
whose extermination would be a glorious achievement of
patriot chivalry, it is my admiration of the Common Law,
and the singular excellence of its standard rules and
maxims, which creates the strong desire, to see it redeemed
from the bondage of a barbarous state of society, and accommodated to the enlightened, benevolent, practical
spirit of our own times. That it ought to be done, I dare
not question. That it can be done, I doubt not. That it
will be done, I believe. . . .

Let us now examine some of those considerations of expediency, which recommend a code to our adoption, and
which are sufficient, in my judgment, to justify the attempt. And here again, I must record my dissent from such
arguments of my fellow-labourers in the cause of reformation, as presuppose two results—first, that the people at
large will become better acquainted with the laws: and
secondly, that litigation will disappear, to a very great extent. These are desirable effects but no code will ever accomplish them.

As to the first, if a code were printed and placed in the
house of every man, how few would have either time or in-

clination to peruse the book! how few could understand
or remember it! how few would know, where to find what
they wanted, or how to apply it! Such a book would be too
uninteresting to invite, much less engage the serious study
of all, even of educated persons. The pious, among the
poor and ignorant, would be contented with their Bible:
and all others accustomed to read, would prefer the Novel
and the Poem, Travels, Biography, and History, or even
Political Economy, and the abstract Sciences. A few, and a
very few men of peculiar habits, tastes, and views would
be exceptions to these remarks, and would doubtless be
devoted students of the new code. But the people at large
would have neither time nor leisure, inclination nor improvement, sufficient for the task of perusing, understanding, and applying the code to the business of life. A scheme
of laws for the regulation of the various and complex affairs of a changeable state of society, can never be reduced
within the compass of the decalogue, neither is it susceptible of the plain, matter of fact, compendious simplicity of
Christian morals.

Nor can I assent to the second supposed operation of a
code, *viz:* to diminish in a great ratio, the number of law
suits. Such, certainly, must be the effect, in some degree;
for every Lawyer of talent and experience knows, that if
the composition of any statute had been entrusted to him,
he could have prevented, by a due consideration of the
subject some at least of the questions, which have sprung
from their language. No human foresight could have anticipated all: and doubtless no mortal skill can so construct
every single clause of a general law, as to obviate all the
doubts and difficulties, which may afterwards arise. Such
is the testimony of experience; although reasoning, *a priori*
simply, may have led to a different conclusion. Let our
laws be as particular, or as general; as concise, or as voluminous, as we please. Let them shrink into one little volume, like those of San Marino; or swell to twenty ample
quartos, like the British statutes, and still cases and distinctions, without number, must crowd on each other, like
wave on wave, in endless succession. Until it shall be possi-

ble for all men to think and speak, and write alike; to adopt
the same unvarying forms of contracts; and to stand in the
same relation to kindred, neighbours, and strangers; to
debtors and creditors; to the great community of the public, and to the countless private associations of individuals:
until society shall become as uniform and unchangeable,
as the castes of Hindoostan; as servile in the transmission
of arts and trades, as the East-Indian; and as imitative, to
the very letter, as the Chinese, we cannot expect to see the
end of litigation. A multitude and a variety of suits, must
ever spring up spontaneously and prodigally, in the soil of
free institutions, free thoughts, and free actions: where
rights are valued on principle, as the noblest property, and
this is counted as worthless, except as the fruits of those.

Discarding then, such considerations as these, I proceed
to state the reasons of expediency, which are to me, decisive recommendations of a code.

1. The first, which I shall mention, will assuredly meet
the cordial approbation of all improved understandings. In
every department of human affairs, and in every branch
of human knowledge, it is considered, that a most important object has been accomplished, when method is substituted for confusion. A state of order, as contrasted with
a state of chaos, is justly esteemed, whether we regard
theory or practice, as a prize of inestimable value. In matters of little moment, regularity is held to be a merit; but in
those of a great magnitude, all acknowledge it, as a duty
and a virtue. In all the concerns of man, whether they affect an individual or a family; the social circle or a society; the community of a village or city, of a district or
State; it is a truth, equally attested by Philosophy and
common sense, that the introduction of order improves, far
beyond any previous estimate, the condition of mankind, in
happiness, usefulness, and virtue. Relying on such evidences, we might securely challenge even a disciple of
Pyrrho, to deny that a code must be eminently a public
blessing.

2. My second argument is drawn from a consideration,
somewhat similar. The value of principles, as compared

with a heterogeneous mass of facts and details, of unconnected rules and observations, will be questioned by no one. In this state of things, principles are shorn of their light, and stripped of a large portion of their power. But when they assume the organized forms of a system, they exercise a legitimate influence, at once salutary, commanding, and permanent. Our laws, in their present condition, may be called the grave, rather than the cradle of principles.

3. My third reflection, is, that a code will have the happiest effect in several important particulars on legislation itself.

(1) And first—the existence of a code will be the most efficient barrier against careless and hasty, superfluous or merely convenient legislation. At present, if we judge from matter of fact, it is considered of very little consequence, how much and how often the Law is altered. Little or no respect is felt for the Law, in its actual condition; and the opinion seems practically to be, that, as it is a chaos, the accumulations of every session will make no difference, in its justice or expediency of a new Law, additional to, or amendatory of, that code, must be clear beyond question, before the Legislature will agree to its adoption. Let that code be the result of time and mature deliberation; the harvest gathered by talents and learning, in the fields of wisdom and experience. Let it have been for some time, before the People and the Legislature, the Bench and the Bar, ere it shall have been consecrated by popular affection, and ordained by public authority, as the standard of civil jurisprudence. In such case, we may predict, that legislation will no longer be precipitate and thoughtless, superfluous or merely convenient. Something of sanctity, which has invested the Constitution, and has protected it, I may almost say, from annual innovation, will then become the property of the code.

(2) The second advantage is, that, after the establishment of a system, Legislation will be conducted on principles, and with a direct reference to an existing body of laws, in their state of clear and simple arrangement. At

present, Legislation is and can be nothing but patchwork: and the Law, while the existing order of things endures, must continue to be a fit parallel for the cabinet of Chatham, delineated by Burke, with so much felicity and pleasantry. There is no division or even subdivision of our Law, which does not admit of many, and does not require, at least some considerable improvements. Is there an act of any importance, whether ancient or modern, which may not be amended? Unless the whole body of our Law shall assume the form of a code, it is obvious, that Legislation will consist, for an indefinite period, of additions and amendments. Is it not a reflection upon our sense of justice and duty—and upon our estimate of the value of wise and stable laws, that we should submit to such a necessity for perpetual alterations? Hitherto, our acts having been suggested by particular circumstances or cases, are generally limited to them. But, under the influence of a code, cases and circumstances would be regarded only as guides to principles; and Legislation would consist, almost if not altogether, in expanding or recasting the principles of a known, fixed system.

(3) The third effect on the Legislative department relates to the forms of laws; the space, which they would occupy; the facility of reference; and the complete separation of public and private acts. The clearness and simplicity of a code require the divisions and subdivisions of books, titles, chapters, sections, and numbers. Our acts would thereafter assume an analogous character, and nothing would be easier than to connect them with the code itself, by the proper use of similar designations. It is well known, that the titles and preambles of our acts, the awkward and circuitous mode of referring to former statutes, the mass of superfluous words, the endless repetition of the same things (witness the appropriation, tax and incorporation bills) require at least twice as many pages, every year, as are necessary. Add to these considerations, that subjects totally different, are frequently mixed together; while public and private acts are confounded, instead of being kept as much apart, as the acts and resolutions. It will be like-

wise a great improvement, that, instead of a table of contents, classed only by pages, we should have a proper index, referring to each separate topic, under the numerical arrangement of the code system, and fashioned after the plan of the index to the code. It would be an obvious advantage of the new system, in connexion with the same department, that our Legislature could then act understandingly, as to the existing Law. But now, it is often next to impossible, on account of the actual condition of our laws, to ascertain what the Law is; what statutes are of force; how far they are contradicted, modified, or explained by subsequent acts; and what will be the effect of amendatory or additional clauses.

4. A fourth recommendation of a code is, that it must exercise a happy influence on the character and usefulness of the Law. The former will be elevated and dignified; because the Law will then exhibit the elements, forms, and arrangements of science. The latter will be extended and strengthened; for the law will then be more easy of comprehension, more consistent in itself, and more in accordance with common sense and natural justice. We all know, how much the respectability of the Law has been impaired by the received opinions, as to its confused and uncertain state, as to the difficulty of determining exactly what the Law is, and as to its vain repetitions, awkward circumlocutions, uncouth phraseology, and obsolete provisions. No one will deny, that the law has been exposed to much odium, contempt, and ridicule, from the causes just enumerated: nor do I believe that any intelligent man, who comprehends the causes, will question but that a code must exercise a salutary influence in moderating their effects, though it may not altogether remove them. Assuredly, I need not say, that such results will be accounted eminent blessings.

5. I cannot but mention, as a fifth argument, in favour of a code, a consequence flowing from the preceding remarks. If the Law itself shall become more respectable, in the opinion of the community at large, it seems a very fair conclusion, that the Legislator and the Judge, as well as the Professors of the Law, will rise, in a correspondent

ratio, in public estimation. Let Philosophy be again degraded by the Logic and Metaphysics of the schools, and it must again be contemptible and ridiculous. Whatever, then, can have a decisive and permanent effect on the standing of the Legislature, the Bench, and the Bar, must be regarded as invaluable, especially in a free country, where a constant action and reaction exist between those institutions and the people. It is impossible to deny, if we judge correctly of human nature, that the estimation, in which an employment is held, has, generally speaking, a decisive influence over the standing of those, who occupy that station. We may admire the sentiment of Epaminondas; but must we not acknowledge, that few have the strength of mind and the good fortune, to win the prize of true honour? We behold the same principles remarkably illustrated in the judgment of Pepin, who felt the absolute necessity of redeeming himself, by some gallant deed, from that secret contempt, which he knew would otherwise be his destiny, on account of his diminutive stature.—Human nature, in this view of it, has been ever the same.—Let us, therefore, dignify the Law, and we shall dignify the Legislature, the Bench, and the Bar.

6. Connected with the preceding, so far as the Judge, and the Profession are concerned, I may here advert to a sixth reason, in favour of a code: *viz.* the control, which Science invariably exercises over those, who are engaged in a pursuit, to which it applies. Is there any man, who beholds with more delight and approbation, than the members of the Bench and Bar, the admirable results, which are flowing from the application of the principles of science, to the various arts and trades, under the influence of mechanic institutions, in Europe and America? And shall not the very men, who rejoice so much, at the accelerated march of mind, in other departments of business, challenge also for themselves, similar improvements, from the correspondent operation of similar causes? Shall we rest satisfied, in a state of comparative chaos, when we behold the creative power of order and principles, scattering abroad

light and beauty and harmony over the works of man, in the moral and physical world?

7. A seventh argument in favour of a code, may, with propriety, have preceded the sixth, when we reflect, that the succession on the Bench and at the Bar, can only be preserved by those, who shall, at a future day, share the dignity of the one, and the reputation of the other. They are now the boys in our schools, the youths in our colleges, and the young men in our offices. We may expect at no distant period, the establishment of a Professorship of Law, in the South Carolina College, and the institution of Lectures, in emulation of those so honourable to Reeve and Gould,[2] to Kent and Dorsey. Assuredly, I need not pause a moment to point out to my superiors of the Bench, and to my brethren of the Bar, the eminent advantages of a code, not only to the professor and lecturer, but to the private instructor. Who is insensible to the superior advantages enjoyed by the students of the Civil Law, over those of the Common Law! Who will deny, that system and principles, no less than the ornaments of style, have distinguished pre-eminently the professors of the Civil, from those of the Common Law? The illustrious exceptions of Mansfield[3] and Hardwicke, of Blackstone and Jones, are to be ascribed, rather to Justinian, and his master commentators, than to Bracton, Lyttleton, and Coke.

8. The last reason, to be now assigned in favour of a code, is found in a fact, which is becoming every day more obvious and more important. Let us look abroad through our land, and see how vast an influence, educated men are every where exercising, under every possible variety of form and circumstance, over life, liberty, and property: over character and education, over public and private improvement and happiness. This is pre-eminently true, as to education and politics. And must not the same influence exist in relation to Law, so far as it gives form and being to the social business of life? Let us consider the various capacities, in which intelligent men are continually serving, and it must be cheerfully conceded, that they would find in a code, the best preparative for their duties. I speak not

now of Judges and Lawyers, but of other educated men in our community. Such persons are constantly acting as jurymen, arbitrators, and commissioners; as legislators and public officers; as guardians, executors, administrators and agents. They are continually appealed to, by friends and neighbours, and even by strangers: and, in numerous instances, advise and prepare their contracts and their wills. Law, indeed, it is obvious, pervades in its operations, all society. There is no circle, however small, which is exempt from its influence: none however extended, which does not acknowledge its power.—Hence it is the only science and the only art, of which it is the interest and duty of every man, as far as his education and opportunities permit, to know, at least, the elements. To know them, is to enable him, with comparative ease and success, to discharge the various duties, above mentioned. I have already said, that the people at large will not have time, patience, or opportunity, for the study of the code: and beyond question, the era never can arrive, when every man will be his own Lawyer; until society can subsist with a mere decalogue of civil jurisprudence. But very many of the educated men of our State (and the number must increase and never can diminish) will find it their duty, their interest, and their pleasure, to bestow much time on the study of the code. Its influence on their capacity, and fitness for public and private usefulness, needs neither comment nor illustration.

NOTES

[1] "A fearful monster, shapeless and immense, deprived of light."

[2] Tapping Reeve (1744–1823) founded in 1784 the Litchfield [Connecticut] Law School, the first professional institution of the sort in the United States. James Gould (1770–1838) was associated with Reeve in the conduct of the school and after 1820 was in sole charge of it until ill health compelled him to close it in 1833. John C. Calhoun is one among several legal minds who received in this forum the best systematic instruction available before the Harvard Law School was established (1817) or the labors of Hoffman and Du Ponceau became effective.

3 William Murray, Earl of Mansfield (1705–93), Chief Justice of the King's Bench, was universally held to be the most brilliant and far-ranging intellect in the golden age of English jurisprudence. He was the founder of English mercantile law, organizing, upon his mounting the Bench, what had been a chaotic jumble into something virtually a system. He did this work by drawing upon a thorough knowledge of Roman and continental law. Hence to American advocates of codification he appeared to bend the Common Law toward a rational order, and to use the civil law for this purpose, rather than to aim at the "blending" advocated by our Common Law lawyers.

JAMES MADISON PORTER (1793–1862)

REVIEW OF "REPORTS OF CASES AR-
GUED AND DETERMINED IN THE CIR-
CUIT COURT OF THE UNITED STATES,
FOR THE SECOND CIRCUIT." BY ELIJAH
PAINE, JR. (Article IX in The North Ameri-
can Review, *LX, July 1828, 167–91*)

[*The North American Review*, representing the mentality of New-England Whiggery (which had a strong dash
of the old Federalism) was very quick to appreciate the
error it had made in allowing Henry Dwight Sedgwick to
use its pages for even a mild plea in favor of codification.
Four years later, the magazine welcomed a reinforcement
from Pennsylvania, where the solid bar had never permitted any such argument to appear under respectable
auspices.

Porter interestingly enough was named after James
Madison, and all his life was a Democrat, though one of
the variety which historians have named "conservative."
He served briefly as Secretary of War under President Ty-
ler. He is memorable chiefly as a prime mover in the foundation of Lafayette College, where he was later professor
of jurisprudence. He was an advocate of internal improvements, of canals and railroads, and eventually president of
the Lehigh Valley Railroad. Thus, though officially a Democrat, he was in policy next door to the Whigs. Speaking
as the foremost lawyer in Northampton County, he could

magisterially refute Sampson, Sedgwick and Grimké. In his *Review* all the arguments of the anti-codifiers are marshaled fully into ranks, arrayed for battle and resolved to win or perish.

Lawyer Porter's presentation is so beautifully clear that it scarcely needs glossing. Still, I think it worth stressing how his argument for the Common Law as against codes becomes a condemnation of any "legislation" under the guise of interpretation by the courts. Here we have an early, and a delightfully explicit, formulation of the doctrine of "abstention," which has played and still plays a powerful rôle in American juridical thinking. Yet, having declared himself against "legal legislation," he makes clear almost at once that codification would be a threat to property. Students must tread their way cautiously through the logic of the complex case which may be said to have commenced its presentation with Porter's essay. The basic motivations are not difficult to decipher, however, thanks to his bland enunciation of them.

Also of more than passing interest is Porter's argument that the Common Law, by eschewing vague generalities, compels the student to hold concrete cases in the forefront of his mind, and so constantly to work from the particular to the general. We may well say that Porter has here prefigured the "case method" of study. But most striking is his concluding contention that the Common Law—and *only* such a supposedly irrational conjuration of precedents— justifies the unique constitutionalism of the United States, and so becomes the most powerful instrument for the Union, even while seeming to encourage a mad diversity.]

REVIEW OF CASES, 1827

In all ages and nations there must be common law, or *leges non scriptae*.[1] And in exact proportion, too, as those are advanced in civilization and refinement, do these become numerous, extensive, and intricate. It was so among the Greeks. It was so also among the Romans. We know

how it is in England. It is more or less so in fact, all over
the civilized world. It is the case even in France, and is
rapidly becoming more so, as we understand, and as every
rational man might have fairly expected, under the ad-
mirably digested code of Napoleon. It is so, in short, from
the uncompromising nature of things. It lies not in human
foresight to anticipate even the various classes of cases that
may arise. What legislature, for example, could have previously provided for the great questions that have presented themselves under policies of insurance, or bills of
exchange, or promissory notes, or the admissibility of evidence, or the taking of testimony, or in short under any
branch or department of law? for to attempt to enumerate
them is to limit ourselves, and to confess that they may be
enumerated, when they are in fact innumerable. New and
unimagined cases will for ever come up, for which no
legislative provision could have been made. What then is to
be done? There cannot be a great and grievous wrong,
without a violation of law. The questions therefore cannot
be laid aside; and by what laws must they be settled? By
the *leges non scriptae,* by analogies drawn from previously
adjudicated cases, by well established usages and customs,
existing among intelligent and experienced people, and
arising from, and therefore adapted to their wants, and to
circumstances in which they have been placed, and finally
ratified by the sanction of the courts of judicature. It is
this in fact which forms the first and perhaps the only
true foundation of the Common Law. And without the
liberty of judicially resorting to it, we should be in a state
infinitely worse than despotism; a state where there are
innumerable and continually multiplying violations of
right, for which, however, there can be neither redress nor
remedy. . . .

There seems to be something contradictory in the arguments, as they are usually urged, against the character of
the Common Law. By one, the judge is called a legislator,
moulding his decisions to suit his own notions of equity
and right. By another, he is thought to be so absolutely

bound down to precedent and authority, that he dares not depart from them, however unreasonable they may appear to him to be. To our apprehension neither of these statements is in any degree correct. In fact, they neutralize each other.

The legislator is free. No decree from a higher authority, except it be the letter and the spirit of the Constitution, has any restrictive force over his measures. Far different from this, however, with the judge upon the bench. In the capacity of legislator, he has authority to act only so far as is necessary in order to carry some law into execution, and then he is within the narrowest limits, and strictly and ably watched. In clearly settled cases, he is indeed bound to acquiesce; not because they were arbitrarily or peremptorily decreed, but because, as has been often observed, the points of the question in controversy were thoroughly examined by the keenest minds in competition with each other; and then deliberately pronounced to be law by cool and impartial judges; and because the principles of justice, which regulate the rights of one man, ought not to be refused to another. When the original cases were evidently not well examined in the outset, they may be reexamined, and overruled, and set aside; and this is the condition, which is always annexed to them in practice. But when they were so examined, there is every reason for giving them the obligatory force of law. We should feel the greatest insecurity of property and of rights, were it otherwise; to say nothing of the time and labor uselessly spent in searching for what had already been well ascertained.

It would be with us no ground of fear, were our judiciaries actually invested with legislative powers, far more extensive than any that they have been accused of arrogating to themselves. Judges, sharply and unremittingly watched from every side of the question in controversy, by the shrewdest and most intelligent men in the community, whom education and the warmest feelings of pride, ambition, self-interest, and rivalry of excelling in the discharge of their professional duties, combine to make acute in the detection of errors, and bold and active in publicly exposing them, will not venture, intentionally, to go very far astray from the plain principles of rectitude. They are as strongly protected, too, from unintentional wrongs. It is from the same well guarded and unexceptionable sources, that they are compelled to receive all possible light and instruction. In such a body of men, and thus situated, we should not be afraid to repose absolute legislative power, so far, at least, as is necessary to regulate the common transactions between man and man. And when we see the time and money which are now miserably wasted by many of our legislatures in making bad laws, to say nothing of the faction and the views of self-interest which reign in them, and the poor principles of qualification on which some of their members are elected, we almost wish that it were so. It is perhaps the *ultima Thule* in the career of political improvement.

In general, however, we believe that the writers against the Common Law have now given up what was formerly the most important point in the controversy. They concede that it contains some of the most admirable principles in any system or code; and the object seems to be merely to select these, and purify them from the dross, with which they say they are mingled, and then give them the sanction of some direct act from the legislature. These arguments appear to be directed against a few of its slight errors, and, in the formal part of it, against some prevailing absurdities, which its warmest admirers are now willing to allow to be such. They are errors; they are absurdities. They have brought the whole system into disrepute among the truest, and in some instances the most enlightened friends of equity and right; and although not materially, in the end, affecting the prompt and efficient administration of justice, they may be, and no doubt in some cases ought to be corrected. It is not the business of the judiciary, however, to undertake this. With all their legislative powers, which are so much complained of, and how much soever themselves may desire the reformation, they will not, they dare not attempt it. The legislatures of every state in the union come together once or twice in a year, with this as one of the principal objects of their convening; and when the evil is so great as to cry aloud for a remedy, there is no doubt that an adequate one may be applied. Let us have a care, however, lest we undermine and make the whole venerable fabric tremble, merely for the purpose of removing some of the unimportant outworks, which time and a change of circumstances may have rendered awkward and uncouth.

The only question, indeed, now actually at issue between the writers upon this subject, we believe to be this. Is it expedient for us to undertake to analyze the whole of the Common Law, select the most valuable of its principles, digest them, arrange them, embody them into a code, give them the sanction of some direct legislative act, and by the same act declare all the residue to be void or of no legal validity? We say we understand this to embrace the only important points of inquiry still unsettled among the parties in this controversy; and for ourselves, we confess we have no confidence in the practicability of the proposed measure, even were it ever so desirable. The business of fully codifying all the existing laws, we believe, never could be accomplished by one of our free legislatures. We feel almost assured of this, in fact, by actual observation. How slowly and how unwillingly do they alter any of the material principles of judicial proceeding, even when this is strongly recommended to them, and by the most enlightened men. At every period of their coming together, propositions for this end are continually brought before them, which they as continually reject. The old Norman barons used to say, when in parliament assembled, *Nolumus leges Angliae mutare.*[2] And it is still the practical maxim of our free legislative bodies. Suppose, then, they were called upon to go over the whole ground, investigate the complicated details of this most intricate and extensive and rapidly growing of all the sciences, take up title after title, rule after rule, principle after principle, examine them and the reasons on which they are founded, and the various modes by which they are to be carried into execution, and their influence on the

general administration of justice in the community,—we
know not when they would find the end of it. And all this
they must sooner or later perform; for although the business of analyzing and codifying may at first be entrusted
to a few enlightened men, the task of revising and correcting, as well as enacting into law, must be done by the
legislatures themselves; or they delegate the highest trust
committed to them to subordinate agents, without themselves seeing to its faithful execution. At least, under this
impression they uniformly act. They think it their duty to
place implicit confidence in no one. We can imagine the
innumerable alterations, amendments, and substitutions,
which almost every member thinks himself capable of introducing, and bound, perhaps, to insist upon; and it needs
but little experience to convince us of the wearing delays
and disaffections that must arise from this mode of proceeding. We venture to say, in short, that the undertaking
never could be satisfactorily accomplished by our free
legislative assemblies. We know that it was never so attempted.

It is not in lands of liberty and equal rights that the
business of codifying flourishes. It is commonly the work of
despots. A single imperial voice, commanding unqualified
instant submission throughout the community, has hitherto
ordered, directed, and enforced it in practice. In this manner only can it be promptly, harmoniously, and efficiently
done; and although the laws which were thus framed are
of a very admirable character, and still call forth the highest commendations of the wise, it is not because the people
were free for whom they were designed, but because they
were not free, and had neither the power nor the presumption to attempt to alter those, that were imposed upon them
by the sovereign authority; which, however, fortunately
for them, had the wisdom to select and employ the most
enlightened counsel in the work. If our political institutions had prevailed among them, they would not have had,
they would not have needed, the statutory codes. The evils
which called forth these important remedies, are of a
kind of which we, in this country, can form no adequate

conception; and yet they ought to be taken into the estimate, when we speak of the necessity or the utility of their so much lauded legal system. . . .

In the foregoing remarks, when we have spoken in praise of the Common Law, we have referred not to the pure, unmingled Common Law, where there is no statutory provision to guide or control it. There are comparatively few decisions of this character in our modern books of reports. The Common Law indeed naturally grows, and becomes more extensive as we advance. It accompanies us at every step of our progress in the reading of statutes, decrees, and decisions, which lie nominally beyond its reach. For the principles of interpretation and practice are borrowed from it in every branch and department of jurisprudence; and scarcely a question of litigated right can arise in any of our courts of justice, without in some way calling for its aid, or receiving from it light. So that the more other laws multiply, the more the Common Law also advances. As the sole means of improving it, we insist on able reports of well investigated cases; and we mean to make our remark particularly applicable to those of the Circuit Courts of the United States, because those are now very much neglected.

And yet there is much complaint of the great number and of the rapid multiplication of law reports. The gentleman of the bar is now under the necessity of enlarging his library and extending his researches far and wide, for the purpose of seeing all that has been decided or said by eminent jurists on the various questions submitted to him in the course of his practice. But can this be to any one a fair ground of complaint? Is it not, on the contrary, to be regarded with feelings of unmingled satisfaction? Does it not indicate clearly the increasing demand, and the more general diffusion of intelligence, on a subject, of all others the most important to the peace and good order of society? The publication of such reports is the promulgation of the laws. They are promulgated, too, with the principles on which they are founded. In no other way is it possible to

make them generally known; and as they arise out of the
actual demands for justice, they are likely to be peculiarly
well suited to the existing wants and condition of society.

We consider the prompt and full publication of law reports, to be, for a variety of other reasons than those we
have mentioned, highly beneficial. Of the importance of
it to our personal rights we cannot form too great an estimate. It secures the judiciary, by every possible motive, to
the faithful administration of justice. What wrongs from
this source may we not look for, in a community where the
decrees of the courts of judicature are suppressed and
kept from public view? Judges, who act under the impression that such is to be the fate of their decisions, although they feel the sense of duty in all its purity, yet want
the consciousness of being narrowly and extensively observed, which is a powerful incentive to great and generous
efforts, even among the most elevated minds. But when they
know, that their opinions may be severely scrutinized by
the ablest men of their own, and perhaps of coming ages;
when they reflect that those opinions will be either made
the basis of farther adjudications, or rejected as incon-
clusive and false; above all, when from fear of error they
are led, as in this country they almost universally are, to
write their opinions at length, and themselves prepare them
for the press, they have every inducement, interested and
disinterested, which can possibly be crowded upon the
mind, to be laborious, accurate, and impartial. Let then
our legal decisions be brought, as extensively as may be,
before the public; for nothing can render more unerringly
to the faithful administration of justice. If we mistake not,
this is not yet estimated as it ought to be.

True it is, the great and increasing number of the volumes of which we are speaking, makes it expensive to pur-
chase, and laborious to read them through. But this is a
difficulty attending the advancements of all the sciences.
New treatises are published. The results of new investiga-
tions must be laid before the public. New discoveries and
inventions, or new improvements or adaptations of the old
ones, are continually soliciting our examination. Yet the

man of real science does not very often complain of the multiplication of books upon 'his favorite theme; nor the man of letters, of the numerous works of literature and taste. The comparison furnishes us with a good illustration of the true character of the Common Law. It is a science, and, like all other sciences, progressive. It perpetually enlarges, and suits itself more and more closely to our wants and circumstances. And one may as well think of composing a system of natural philosophy, which shall be perfect, and without the possibility of further improvement, as a code of laws, to which advancing society is to be chained. It is not necessary to read all the law reports which are published, any more than it is to read all the essays on experimental subjects in natural philosophy, which are published. There are accurate digests of the one, as there are accurate digests of the other. Competition, too, does its mighty work of improvement here, as everywhere else. The valuable volumes of which we are speaking, soon rise to their proper elevation; the poor ones as soon sink into insignificance. The instances of this, in the history of these publications, are so many and obvious, that it is not necessary to name them particularly.

It is thus, by the publication of these volumes of reports, that the Common Law, like all the other sciences, is destined perpetually to improve. The system is becoming better, as well as more generally known. On the hearing of a question in controversy, the object is looked upon from every possible point of view. All the various and seemingly conflicting decisions upon the subject, are brought before the court and canvassed. The postulates and arguments on which they rest, are severely scrutinized; the valuable truths selected, and the material errors discarded, from each. And there is every reason for believing, that by this mode of proceeding, the really sound principles of law will inevitably be reached at last. This is precisely the way by which all the sciences improve; and it is the only way which our courts of judicature can take on the settlement of a litigated question.

We wish also to see some books of reports put earlier

into the hands of youth for their legal education, than they have been hitherto. It appears to us, that they should soon be taught to read them in the order in which they are published. If we are not greatly mistaken, they would, with proper facilities for their explanation, find them far more interesting and instructive to read, and infinitely more easy to remember, than codes, or digests, or elementary treatises. We believe these last to be commonly too abstract and general, and not best suited to the minds of those who are somewhat advanced in the science of the law. We know that the young pupil often grows tired of them, because he does not always easily or fully comprehend them, and, even if he does, cannot long retain them accurately in his memory. When afterwards, in the course of his professional practice, he is called upon to make an application of the knowledge which he has thus gone over, he finds that he has forgotten it; and when he recurs again to his books for the lost intelligence, it often appears new to him, and in nine difficult questions out of ten, he would not remember that he had ever seen it before. Not so, however, with that acquired by reading interesting law reports. The facts in these cases serve as bonds of association, by which the principles interwoven with them are held together, and kept long and strongly fastened in the mind. We appeal to the most learned of the profession, if this, even with them, is not sometimes apt to be so. The nice distinctions and the subtle refinements in their elaborate volumes of digested jurisprudence, which they have cause of recollecting only as they have read them, may pass from their thoughts; but let them be connected with some cases of actual occurrence, in which they were engaged, or which they may have been called upon carefully to examine, and they do not forget the principles then. It is also to be borne in mind, that digests and elementary treatises are only the abstracts of adjudicated cases, and not always sure therefore of stating accurately the points decided. In fact, experienced counsel will never, in a case of importance, trust to a short sentence, which, the laborious compiler says, contains in an abbreviated form the principles of a question settled, when they have the original case itself within their reach; for they have learned by observation the errors and the imperfections of digests. These are excellent as indices or tables of reference. Seldom, however, are they to be relied upon as absolute authority in themselves, when it is easy to procure the books of reports from which they were at first taken. Thus it is that the student, so far as he can read reported decisions intelligently, is sure of learning his law more accurately, as well as more pleasantly, than he can in any other way. He thus, too, will learn the questions of practice; the various forms of action; the manner in which rights are to be ascertained and settled. He sees the remedy at the same moment that he sees the wrong; and if he reads the books of reports as rapidly as they appear, and in the same order, he will be likely to know what is actually going on professionally in the world around him, from which he is almost entirely separated in the common course of early legal education. . . .

If the foregoing remarks are true of the publication of law reports generally, with what peculiar force do they apply to those of the national courts of the United States? It appears to us, that these must be interesting, not merely to the professional man and the jurist, but to every one who wishes to see clearly the true character of our political institutions. We know in fact, that there is no other way of acquiring a knowledge of them with any degree of accuracy. The constitution of the courts of which we are speaking, is entirely unexampled in the history of states. We believe indeed that it forms the only characteristic feature, which is purely and exclusively our own, in the whole frame of our national government. All our other civil institutions have been partially borrowed from abroad, and are at least faintly imitated by foreign states. But the nature of the jurisdiction, and the supreme political ascendency of our national courts of judicature, have neither precedent nor parallel in any country or age.

It had long been a favorite maxim, among enthusiastic writers on the true nature of political rights, that officers of government are but the delegated agents of the people; subservient to them; bound to give them an account of their stewardship; with clearly defined duties; with restricted powers; not authorized, under any pretence, to overstep the strict limits prescribed to them; and liable to have their doings abrogated and held for nought, when they do. The world were inclined to look upon this as rather a Utopian vision in some fancied organization of civil society, than as a practicable principle in government. In ours, however, we have actually realized it. Our high courts of judicature have carried it into execution, and we are now witnessing their powerful influence over our political character, in the protection which they give to individual rights against the encroachments of the legislative and executive powers combined. It is not merely their humble duty to administer justice between man and man. They have a far more elevated one intrusted to them. In the vast machinery of our national affairs, they are, as it were, the regulators. All our great public functionaries, even Congress itself, as well as the legislatures of the several states, they hold in salutary check. Between the people and their delegated agents they stand the supreme umpire. To these they say, "Your power of attorney is the Constitution; keep you within the limits prescribed to you by that; for when you transgress them, we are bound by our high political principles, as well as by our sacred oaths of duty, to set your doings aside, and hold them for violations of right." Is there anything comparable to this in the civil constitutions of foreign states? There the courts of judicature hold a subordinate rank in their various frames of government, and over them the legislative and the executive powers have the superintendance and control. Here they are supreme, and exhibit before us continually, in actual practice, as well as in beautiful theory, the absolute sovereignty of the law.

For the discharge of duties of such unexampled importance, the courts of which we are speaking are necessarily clothed with the most extraordinary powers. They have ultimately the power of defining their own powers; of drawing the line of demarkation between the rights of the several states and those of the Union; between the jurisdiction of the various superior courts belonging to the former, and their own; and of construing, and interpreting, and applying the provisions of the constitution, in such a manner as to their wisdom shall seem equitable and meet, for the purpose of promptly effectuating all the high purposes of national justice, for which it was originally designed. Should not the official doings of such a body of men be promptly and extensively made known? It appears to us, that the publication of the reports of adjudicated cases, from sources and on subjects like these, ought to receive, most liberally, legislative patronage and support, and be diffused as far and wide as possible, throughout our community. If there be any intelligence important to the freedom of our political institutions, it is this.

In the foregoing paragraphs we have referred only to the great questions of constitutional law which come before our national courts of judicature. The discussion of the simpler ones, occurring to them in the ordinary course of their jurisdiction, are also full of interesting matter to gentlemen of the profession. They are often called upon to decree and act on the law of nature and of nations. In many cases, they introduce us to a knowledge of the peculiar local laws of foreign states, as well as of the great international law which connects them all together. They bring also into some practice the civil law, and tend to diffuse a knowledge of it, and gradually to reconcile and incorporate it with our own, and thus give us the use of some of its admirable principles. We ask our readers to consider the cases of frequent occurrence before the courts of which we speak, for the evidence of what we have said. The examination of wrongs committed upon the high seas, or of crimes in any way affecting our sovereignty as a nation; of revenue and exchequer cases; of questions of admiralty and prize; of all those coming from the various laws of navigation and trade; of the vested or the violated rights arising under the stipulations of a treaty; of the infractions of the privileges of a patent, or of the sacred security of property con-

tained in the published works of men of literature and
science; of the great maritime contracts, growing out of
our extended commercial connexions with foreign states,
and requiring for their elucidation the great code of mercantile law, now by common consent in force, almost all
over the enlightened world;—the examination of these, we
say, has called forth in this country, to a very honourable
extent, learning, research, and ingenuity, and furnished a
rich variety of fruitful themes for valuable disquisitions, on
the most important and interesting points of law; and, for
the reason we have already given, the publication of just
reports of them must be exceedingly useful in extending
the knowledge of that law, and making it more accurate
and clear, as well as more generally known.

May we not also look to the publication of the reports
of which we are speaking, for making the Common Law of
our country more regular and uniform in its character, than
it has been hitherto? The several courts of the various
states are separate and independent of each other. The decisions in one are not considered as having any obligatory
force in those of another. Hence it is that they are often
at variance and sometimes diametrically opposite. But the
courts of the Union are joined. A most powerful bond of
association connects them together. The decrees and doings of one would be considered as having something of
more influence on those of another, than the mere opinions
of learned and intelligent men. They go moreover into
every part of the Union, and gather intelligence from the
most gifted and eminent counsel of our country, and come
together annually for the purpose of hearing, and conferring, and disposing of litigated rights, under circumstances peculiarly favorable to the clear and correct settlement of the law. No party feelings nor sectional views can
sway them. Those of one must offset and counterbalance
those of another. Their errors are reciprocally corrected. By
a judiciary thus composed of the ablest judges, and acting
under such advantages, the true principles of justice must
be reached, if they are within the reach of human genius.
Singly as well as collectively, we say, they may do much

to place our Common Law on a more steady and regular foundation, than it now has. At least, so far as their influence goes, it may be rescued from that inconsistency and variance for which it has been so long and so deservedly reproached.

NOTES

[1] Laws unwritten.
[2] We are not willing to change the laws of England.

JOSEPH STORY (1779–1845)

DISCOURSE PRONOUNCED UPON THE INAUGURATION OF THE AUTHOR, AS DANE PROFESSOR OF LAW IN HARVARD UNIVERSITY, AUGUST 25TH, 1829

[Story's inaugural oration at the Harvard Law School was for decades regarded as the supreme, the final, the victorious statement within the profession of what I have called the "orthodox" conception of its function. In thousands of similar utterances it would be repeatedly quoted or else paid the still higher compliment of sedulous imitation.

The magic of its appeal was wrought mainly by what Story's contemporaries held to be its eloquence. This eloquence may not seem so impressive to modern taste. We must forcibly remind ourselves that the literary standards of this fraternity of lawyers had been formed on neoclassical models. No doubt, injustice is done to the sublimity of the two-hour declamation by giving only a few segments of it. However, by 1829 the jurists, on such forensic occasions, had begun to vie with the clergy; soon they exceeded them in endurance. Story did not live long enough to witness the rebellion of the public patience against both abuses of the rostrum.

A further and more efficacious reason for the appeal of this inaugural—one which it takes little scholarly ingenuity to appreciate—is the fact that it was delivered six months after Andrew Jackson had been inaugurated President of the United States. Story, in brief, was here mobilizing the legal hierarchy, of which he was the high priest, against the leveling assault of Jacksonian democracy. He was marshaling every resource that the profession had so far devised for the obfuscation of the vulgar—the ritualistic character of the law, its nature as a science, the Common Law, the civil law, equity—in order to subdue the still obstinate belief of the people that jurisprudence was by its inherent nature a corrupt and corrupting business. Against this prejudice Story took advantage of the occasion to affirm, in the most compelling terms any had yet formulated, the dignity of the calling. He made it clear to younger champions that resistance to the mob can be maintained, even in the rudest of frontier regions (we inevitably think of Springfield, Illinois), by dedication to the ideal not only of reason but of classical culture.

Whereupon, by a marvelously contrived transition, Story moves from his opening portrait of the exalted moral character of jurisprudence to the assertion that the primary concern of this priesthood is with "the sacred rights of property." Thus the lawyer is stationed on the outposts of society, a "public sentinel," against an enemy who in the United States would not be an absolute monarch or a dissolute aristocracy, but a "multitude."

Even more obviously than in 1821, Story's pressing upon his students, and through publication of the address upon the public, the tremendous amount of scholarship and literary cultivation demanded of lawyers, was in reality an effort to erect a moat and a wall of unconquerable battlements around the sacred precinct.]

DISCOURSE PRONOUNCED UPON THE INAUGURATION OF THE AUTHOR, 1829

. . . But my principal object in this discourse is, to address myself to those, who intend to make the law a profession for life. To them it seems almost unnecessary to recommend the study, or press the ancient precept,

> Versate diu, quid ferre recusent,
> Quid valeant humeri.[1]

To them the law is not a mere pursuit of pleasure or curiosity, but of transcendent dignity, as it opens the brightest rewards of human ambition, opulence, fame, public influence, and political honors. I may add, too, that if the student of the law entertains but a just reverence for its precepts, it will teach him to build his reputation upon the soundest morals, the deepest principles, and the most exalted purity of life and character. One of the beautiful boasts of our municipal jurisprudence is, that Christianity is a part of the Common Law, from which it seeks the sanction of its rights, and by which it endeavours to regulate its doctrines. And notwithstanding the specious objection of one of our distinguished statesmen,[2] the boast is as true, as it is beautiful. There never has been a period, in which the Common Law did not recognise Christianity as lying at its foundations. For many ages it was almost exclusively administered by those, who held its ecclesiastical dignities. It now repudiates every act done in violation of its duties of perfect obligation. It pronounces illegal every contract offensive to its morals. It recognises with profound humility its holidays and festivals, and obeys them, as *dies non juridici*.[3] It still attaches to persons believing in its divine authority the highest degree of competency as witnesses; and, until a comparatively recent period, infidels and pagans were banished from the halls of justice, as unworthy of credit. The error of the Common Law was, in reality, of a very different character. It tolerated nothing but Christianity, as taught by its own established church, either Protestant or Catholic; and with unrelenting severity consigned the conscientious heretic to the stake, regarding his very scruples as proofs of incorrigible wickedness. Thus, justice was debased, and religion itself made the minister of crimes, by calling in the aid of the secular power to enforce that conformity of belief, whose rewards and punishments belong exclusively to God.

But, apart from this defect, the morals of the Law are of the purest and most irreproachable character. And, notwithstanding the sneers of ignorance, and the gibes of wit, no men are so constantly called upon in their practice to exemplify the duties of good faith, incorruptible virtue, and chivalric honor, as lawyers. To them is often entrusted the peace and repose, as well as the property, of whole families; and the slightest departure from professional secrecy, or professional integrity, might involve their clients in ruin. The Law itself imposes upon them the severest injunctions never to do injustice, and never to violate confidence. It not only protects them from disclosing the secrets of their clients, but it punishes the offenders, by disqualifying them from practice. The rebuke of public opinion, also, follows close upon every offence; and the frown of the profession consigns to infamy the traitor, and his moral treason. Memorable instances of this sort have occurred in other ages, as well as in our own. Even the lips of eloquence breathe nothing but an empty voice in the halls of justice, if the ear listens with distrust or suspicion. The very hypocrite is there compelled to wear the livery of virtue, and to pay her homage. If he secretly cherishes a grovelling vice, he must there speak the language, and assume the port of innocence. He must feign, if he does not feel, the spirit and inspiration of the place.

I would exhort the student, therefore, at the very outset of his career, to acquire a just conception of the dignity and importance of his vocation. Let him not debase it by a low and narrow estimate of its requisites or its duties. Let him consider it, not as a mere means of subsistence, an affair of petty traffic and barter, a little round of manoeuvres and contrivances to arrest some runaway contract, to disinter some buried relic of title, or to let loose some imprisoned wrong from the vengeance of the law. Let him not dream, that all is well, if he can weave an intricate net of special pleadings to catch the unwary in its meshes; or hang a doubt upon a subtile distinction; or quibble through the whole alphabet of sophisms. Let him not imagine, that it is sufficient, if he be the thing described by Cicero in his scorn;—"juris consultus ipse per se nihil, nisi leguleius quidam cautus et acutus, praeco actionum, cantor formularum, auceps syllabarum;" "a sharp and cunning pettifogger; a retailer of lawsuits; a canter about forms, and a caviller upon words;"[4]—or one of the tribe, defined by a master spirit of the last age, as the ministers of municipal litigation, and the fomenters of the war of village vexation.[5] God forbid, that any man, standing in the temple and in the presence of the law, should imagine that her ministers are called to such unworthy offices. No. The profession has far higher aims and nobler purposes.

In the ordinary course of business, it is true, that sound learning, industry, and fidelity are the principal requisites, and may reap a fair reward, as they may in any other employment of life. But there are some, and in the lives of most lawyers many occasions, which demand qualities of a higher, nay, of the highest order. Upon the actual administration of justice in all governments, and especially in free governments, must depend the welfare of the whole community. The sacred rights of property are to be guarded at every point. I call them sacred, because, if they are unprotected, all other rights become worthless or visionary. What is personal liberty, if it does not draw after it the right to enjoy the fruits of our own industry? What is political liberty, if it imparts only perpetual poverty to us and all our posterity? What is the privilege of a vote, if the majority of the hour may sweep away the earnings of our whole lives, to ratify the rapacity of the indolent, the cunning, or the profligate, who are borne into power upon the tide of a temporary popularity? What remains to nourish a spirit of independence, or a love of country, if the very soil, on which we tread, is ours only at the beck of the village tyrant? If the home of our parents, which nursed our infancy and protected our manhood, may be torn from us without recompense or remorse? If the very graveyards, which contain the memorials of our love and our sorrow, are not secure against the hands of violence? If the church of yesterday may be the barrack of to-day, and become the gaol of tomorrow? If the practical text of civil procedure contains no better gloss than the Border maxim, that the right to plunder is only bounded by the power?

One of the glorious, and not unfrequently perilous duties of the Bar is the protection of property; and not of property only, but of personal rights, and personal character; of domestic peace, and parental authority. The lawyer is placed, as it were, upon the outpost of defence, as a public sentinel, to watch the approach of danger, and to sound the alarm, when oppression is at hand. It is a post, not only full of observation, but of difficulty. It is his duty to resist wrong, let it come in whatever form it may. The attack is rarely commenced in open daylight; but it makes its approaches by dark and insidious degrees. Some captivating delusion, some crafty pretext, some popular scheme, generally masks the real design. Public opinion has been already won in its favor, or drugged into a stupid indifference to its results, by the arts of intrigue. Nothing, perhaps, remains between the enterprise and victory, but the solitary citadel of public justice. It is then the time for the highest efforts of the genius, and learning, and eloquence, and moral courage of the Bar. The advocate not unfrequently finds himself, at such a moment, putting at hazard the popularity of a life devoted to the public service. It is then, that the denunciations of the press may be employed to overawe or intimidate him. It is then, that the shouts of the multitude drown the still, small voice of the unsheltered sufferer. It is then, that the victim is already bound for immolation; and the advocate stands alone, to maintain the supremacy of the law against power, and numbers, and public applause, and private wealth. If he shrinks from his duty, he is branded as the betrayer of his trust. If he fails in his labor, he may be cut down by the same blow, which levels his client. If he succeeds, he may, indeed, achieve a glorious triumph for truth, and justice, and the law. But that very triumph may be fatal to his future hopes, and bar up for ever the road to political honors. Yet what can be more interesting than ambition thus nobly directed? that sinks itself, but saves the state? What sacrifice more pure, than in such a cause? What martyrdom more worthy to be canonized in our hearts? . . .

I know not, if among human sciences there is any one, which requires such various qualifications and extensive attainments, as the law. While it demands the first order of talents, genius alone never did, and never can, win its highest elevations. There is not only no royal road to smooth the way to the summit; but the passes, like those of Alpine regions, are sometimes dark and narrow; sometimes bold and precipitous; sometimes dazzling from the reflected light of their naked fronts; and sometimes bewildering from the shadows projecting from their dizzy heights. Whoever advances for safety must advance slowly. He must cautiously follow the old guides, and toil on with steady footsteps; for the old paths, though well beaten, are rugged; and the new paths, though broad, are still perplexed. To drop all metaphor, the law is a science, in which there is no substitute for diligence and labor. It is a fine remark of one, who is himself a brilliant example of all he teaches, that "It appears to be the general order of Providence, manifested in the constitution of our nature, that every thing valuable in human acquisition should be the result of toil and labor."[6] But this truth is nowhere more forcibly manifested than in the law. Here, moderate talents with unbroken industry have often attained a victory over superior genius, and cast into shade the brightest natural parts.

The student, therefore, should, at his first entrance upon the study, weigh well the difficulties of his task, not merely to guard himself against despondency on account of expectations too sanguinely indulged; but also to stimulate his zeal, by a proper estimate of the value of perseverance. He, who has learned to survey the labor without dismay, has achieved half the victory. I will not say, with Lord Hale, that "The law will admit of no rival, and nothing to go even with it;" but I will say, that it is a jealous mistress, and requires a long and constant courtship. It is not to be won by trifling favors, but by a lavish homage.

Many causes combine to make the study of the common law, at the present day, a laborious undertaking. In the first place, it necessarily embraces the reasoning and doctrines of very remote ages. It is, as has been elegantly said, "The gathered wisdom of a thousand years;"[7] or, in the language of one of the greatest of English judges, it is not "the product of the wisdom of some one man, or society of men, in any one age; but of the wisdom, counsel, experience, and observation of many ages of wise and observing men."[8] It is a system having its foundations in natural reason; but, at the same time, built up and perfected by artificial doctrines, adapted and moulded to the artificial structure of society. The law, for instance, which governs the titles to real estate, is principally derived from the feudal polity and usages, and is in a great measure unintelligible without an intimate acquaintance with the peculiarities of that system. This knowledge is not, even now, in all cases easily attainable; but must sometimes be searched out amidst the dusty ruins of antiquity, or traced back through black-lettered pages of a most forbidding aspect both in language and matter. The old law, too, is not only of an uncouth and uninviting appearance; but it abounds with nice distinctions, and subtile refinements, which enter deeply into the modern structure of titles. No man even in our own day, can venture safely upon the exposition of an intricate devise, or of the effect of a power of appointment, or of a deed to lead uses and trusts, who has not, in some good degree, mastered its learning. More than two centuries ago, Sir Henry Spelman[9] depicted his own distress on entering upon such studies, when at the very vestibule he was met by a foreign language, a barbarous dialect, an inelegant method, and a mass of learning, which could be borne only upon the shoulders of Atlas; and frankly admitted, that his heart sunk within him at the prospect. The defects of a foreign tongue, and barbarous dialect, and inelegant method, have almost entirely disappeared, and no longer vex the student in his midnight vigils. But the materials for his labor have in other respects greatly accumulated in the intermediate period. He may, perchance, escape from the dry severity of the Year-Books, and the painful digestion of the Abridgments of Statham, Fitzherbert, and Brooke. He may even venture to glide by the exhausting arguments of Plowden. But Lord Coke, with his ponderous *Commentaries,* will arrest his course; and, faint and disheartened with the view, he must plunge into the labyrinths of contingent remainders, and executory devises, and springing uses; and he may deem himself fortunate, if, after many years' devotion to Fearne,[10] he may venture upon the interpretation of that darkest of all mysteries, a last will and testament. So true it is, that no man knows his own will so ill, as the testator; and that over-solicitude to be brief and simple ends in being profoundly enigmatical. "Dum brevis esse laboro, obscurus fio."[11]

In the next place, as has been already hinted, every successive age brings its own additions to the general mass of antecedent principles. If something is gained by clearing out the old channels, much is added by new increments and deposits. If here and there a spring of litigation is dried up, many new ones break out in unsuspected places. In fact, there is scarcely a single branch of the law, which belonged to the age of Queen Elizabeth, which does not now come within the daily contemplation of a lawyer of extensive practice. And all these branches have been spreading to an incalculable extent since that period, by the changes in society, wrought by commerce, agriculture, and manufactures, and other efforts of human ingenuity and enterprise. . . .

In truth, the Common Law, as a science, must be for ever in progress; and no limits can be assigned to its principles or improvements. In this respect it resembles the natural sciences, where new discoveries continually lead the way to new, and sometimes to astonishing, results. To say, therefore, that the Common Law is never learned, is almost to utter a truism. It is no more than a declaration, that the human mind cannot compass all human transactions. It is its true glory, that it is flexible, and constantly expanding with the exigencies of society; that it daily presents new motives for new and loftier efforts; that it holds out for ever an unapproached degree of excellence; that it moves onward in the path towards perfection, but never arrives at the ultimate point.

But the student should not imagine, that enough is done, if he has so far mastered the general doctrines of the Common Law, that he may enter with some confidence into practice. There are other studies, which demand his attention. He should addict himself to the study of philosophy, of rhetoric, of history, and of human nature. It is from the want of this enlarged view of duty, that the profession has sometimes been reproached with a sordid narrowness, with a low chicane, with a cunning avarice, and with a deficiency in liberal and enlightened policy. Mr. Burke has somewhat reluctantly admitted the fact, that the practice of the law is not apt, except in persons very happily born, to open and liberalize the mind exactly in the same proportion as it invigorates the understanding; and that men too much conversant in office are rarely minds of remarkable enlargement. And Lord Bacon complains, that lawyers have never written as statesmen. The reproach is in some measure deserved. It is, however, far less true in our age than in former times; and far less true in America than in England. Many of our most illustrious statesmen have been lawyers; but they have been lawyers liberalized by philosophy, and a large intercourse with the wisdom of ancient and modern times. The perfect lawyer, like the perfect orator, must accomplish himself for his duties by familiarity with every study. It may be truly said, that to him nothing, that concerns human nature or human art, is indifferent or useless. He should search the human heart, and explore to their sources the passions, and appetites, and feelings of mankind. He should watch the motions of the dark and malignant passions, as they silently approach the chambers of the soul in its first slumbers. He should catch the first warm rays of sympathy and benevolence, as they play around the character, and are reflected back from its varying lines. He should learn to detect the cunning arts of the hypocrite, who pours into the credulous and unwary ear his leperous distilment. He should for this purpose make the master-spirits of all ages pay contribution to his labours. He should walk abroad through nature, and elevate his thoughts, and warm his virtues, by a contemplation of her beauty, and magnificence, and harmony. He should examine well the precepts of religion, as the only solid basis of civil society; and gather from them, not only his duty, but his hopes; not merely his consolations, but his discipline and his glory. He should unlock all the treasures of history for illustration, and instruction, and admonition. He will thus see man, as he has been, and thereby best know what he is. He will thus be taught to distrust theory, and cling to practical good; to rely more upon experience than reasoning; more upon institutions than laws; more upon checks to vice than upon motives to virtue. He will become more indulgent to human errors; more scrupulous in means, as well as in ends; more wise, more candid, more forgiving, more disinterested. If the melancholy infirmities of his race shall make him trust men less, he may yet learn to love man more.

Nor should he stop here. He must drink in the lessons and the spirit of philosophy. I do not mean that philosophy described by Milton, as

> A perpetual feast of nectared sweets,
> Where no crude surfeit reigns;

but that philosophy, which is conversant with men's business and interests, with the policy and the welfare of nations; that philosophy, which dwells, not in vain imaginations, and Platonic dreams; but which stoops to life, and enlarges the boundaries of human happiness; that philosophy, which sits by us in the closet, cheers us by the fireside, walks with us in the fields and highways, kneels with us at the altars, and lights up the enduring flame of patriotism.

What has been already said rather presupposes than insists upon the importance of a full possession of the general literature of ancient and modern times. It is this classical learning alone, which can impart a solid and lasting polish to the mind, and give to diction that subtile elegance and grace, which color the thoughts with almost transparent hues. It should be studied, not merely in its grave disquisitions, but in its glorious fictions, and in those graphical displays of the human heart, in the midst of which we wander, as in the presence of familiar, but disembodied spirits.

It is by such studies, and such accomplishments, that the means are to be prepared for excellence in the highest order of the profession. The student, whose ambition has measured them, if he can but add to them the power of eloquence (that gift, which owes so much to nature, and so much to art), may indeed aspire to be a perfect lawyer. It cannot be denied, indeed, that there have been great lawyers, who were not orators; as there have been great orators, who were not lawyers. But it must be admitted at the same time, that, when both characters are united in the same person, human genius has approached as near perfection, as it may. They are kindred arts, and flourish best in the neighbourhood of each other.

The eloquence of the bar is far more various and difficult than that, which is required in the pulpit, in the legislative hall, or in popular assemblies. It occasionally embraces all, that belongs to each of these places, and it has, besides, many varieties of its own. In its general character it may be said to be grave, deliberative, and earnest, allowing little indulgence to fancy, and less to rhetoric. But, as it must necessarily change its tone, according to its subject, and the tribunal, to which it is addressed, whether the court or the jury, there is ample scope for the exercise of every sort of talent, and sometimes even for dramatic effect. On some occasions it throws aside all the little plays of phrase, the vivid touches of the pencil, and the pomp and parade of diction. It is plain, direct, and authoritative. Its object is to convince the understanding, and captivate the judgment, by the strength and breadth of its reasoning. Its power is in the thought, and not in the expression; in the vigor of the blow from the hand of a giant; in the weight of the argument, which crushes, in its fall, what it has not levelled in its progress. At other times it is full of calm dignity and persuasiveness. It speaks with somewhat of the majesty of the law itself, in strains of deep, oracular import. It unfolds its results with an almost unconscious elegance, and its thoughts flash like the sparkles of the diamond. At other times it is earnest, impassioned, and electrifying; awing by its bold appeals, or blinding by its fiery zeal. At other times it is searching, and acute, and rigorous; now brilliant in point, now gay in allusion, now winning in insinuation. At other times it addresses the very souls of men in the most touching and pathetic admonitions. It then mingles with the close logic of the law those bewitching graces, which soothe prejudice, disarm resentment, or fix attention. It utters language, as the occasion demands, which melts to pity, or fires with indignation, or exhorts to clemency.

But, whatever may be the variety of effort demanded of forensic eloquence, whether to convince, or captivate, or persuade, or inflame, or melt; still its main character must for ever be like the "grave rebuke," so finely sketched by our great epic poet, "severe in youthful beauty," that it may possess an "added grace invincible." It may not stoop to ribaldry, or vulgar jests, or sickly sentimentality, or puerile conceits. It forbids declamation, and efflorescence of style. There is no room for the loquacity of ignorance, or the insolence of pride. If wit be allowable, it must be chaste and polished. The topics discussed in courts of justice are too grave for merriment, and too important for trifling. When life, or character, or fortune, hangs on the issue, they must be vindicated with dignity, as well as with force.

But I forbear. I seem, indeed, when the recollection of the wonders wrought by eloquence comes over my thoughts, to live again in scenes long since past. The dead seem again summoned to their places in the halls of justice, and to utter forth voices of an unearthly and celestial harmony. The shades of Ames,[12] and Dexter,[13] and Pinkney,[14] and Emmet[15] pass and repass, not hush as the foot of night, but in all the splendor of their fame, fresh with the flush of recent victory. I may not even allude to the living. Long, long may they enjoy the privilege of being nameless here, whose names are every where else upon the lips of praise.

Enough has been said, perhaps more than enough, to satisfy the aspirant after juridical honors, that the path is arduous, and requires the vigor of a long and active life. Let him not, however, look back in despondency upon a survey of the labor. The triumph, if achieved, is worth the sacrifice. If not achieved, still he will have risen by the attempt, and will sustain a nobler rank in the profession. If he may not rival the sagacity of Hardwicke, the rich and lucid learning of Mansfield, the marvellous judicial eloquence of Stowell, the close judgment of Parsons,[16] the comprehensive reasoning of Marshall, and the choice attainments of Kent;—yet he will, by the contemplation and study of such models, exalt his own sense of the dignity of the profession, and invigorate his own intellectual powers. He will learn, that there is a generous rivalry at the bar; and that every one there has his proper station and fame assigned to him; and that, though one star differeth from another in glory, the light of each may yet be distinctly traced, as it moves on, until it is lost in that common distance, which buries all in a common darkness.

NOTES

1 "Study for a long time what your strength will sustain, and what it will not."

2 Thomas Jefferson, "Inquiry Whether Christianity is a Part of the Common Law." Though probably written in 1764, this paper—which seems almost deliberately devised to infuriate Story—was published in this very year, 1829 (Cf. 1 *Jefferson's Reports* 137).

3 "Days exempt from legal business."

4 "A lawyer in himself is nothing, except. . . ."

5 Burke's *Reflections on the French Revolution* [Story's note].

190 JOSEPH STORY

6 Chancellor Kent's *Introductory Discourse,* p. 8. Why has this finished *Discourse* been withdrawn from his *Commentaries?* [Story's note].

7 Teignmouth's *Life of Sir W. Jones,* 100 [Story's note].

8 Lord Hale, in Preface to Rolle's *Abridgment,* 1 *Coll. Jurid.* 266 [Story's note].

9 Sir Henry Spelman (1564–1641), learned antiquarian, who wrote pioneer treatises on ecclesiastical law and on the Anglo-Saxon origins of English jurisprudence. Story loved to use this example because it so perfectly matched his own experience upon proceeding from the beauties of Blackstone to the "labyrinths" of Coke.

10 Charles Fearne (1742–94) published *An Essay on the Learning of Contingent Remainders and Executory Devises,* in 1772; it went through many subsequently enlarged editions.

11 "In laboring to be brief, I become obscure."

12 Fisher Ames (1758–1808), Federalist lawyer and publicist, ferociously anti-Jeffersonian.

13 Samuel Dexter (1761–1816), a leading Boston lawyer.

14 William Pinkney (1764–1822), foremost lawyer in Maryland, diplomat, Attorney General under Madison in 1811 and from then until his death the indisputable leader of the entire American bar; a picturesque character who affected the manners of a dandy and so might be expected to have repelled Story, his consummate mastery of the law won the profound respect of both Story and Marshall.

15 Thomas Addis Emmet (1764–1827), an Irish patriot who fled to New York where, like his fellow Irishman Sampson, he quickly became a leader of the local bar. However he was not the radical that Sampson was, and became a great constitutional lawyer.

16 Theophilus Parsons (1750–1813), a Boston lawyer, to the young Story a model of erudition, served as Chief Justice of Massachusetts.

P. W. GRAYSON

VICE UNMASKED, AN ESSAY: BEING A
CONSIDERATION OF THE INFLUENCE
OF LAW UPON THE MORAL ESSENCE
OF MAN, WITH OTHER REFLECTIONS
(New York, 1830)

[John Adams returned from the Continental Congress to
Braintree in August 1775, while the siege of Boston was
still going on. He encountered in Washington's camp a
"Horse Jockey" whom he had formerly defended. This
creature came to him full of glee because the Congress
had eliminated courts of justice in Massachusetts; he hoped
there never would be another. Adams recollects that this
event plunged him into a profound revery, if not a fit of
melancholy (he is writing in 1802):

Is this the Object for which I have been contending?
said I to myself, for I rode along without any Answer to
this Wretch. Are these the Sentiments of such People?
And how many of them are there in the Country? Half
the Nation for what I know: for half the Nation are
Debtors if not more, and these have been in all Countries, the Sentiments of Debtors. If the Power of the
Country should get into such hands, and there is great
danger that it will, to what purpose have We sacrificed
our Time, health and every Thing else? Surely We must
guard against this Spirit and these Principles or We shall

repent of all our Conduct. However The good Sense and
Integrity of the Majority of the great Body of the People, came in to my thoughts for my relief, and the last
resource was after all in a good Providence.

By 1802 he could further reflect that there had proved to
be good reason for these earlier misgivings. Such principles
as were expressed by his "Client" had triumphed even
more extensively than he had feared in 1775. "When the
Consequences will terminate No Man can say."[1]

This passage was unknown to Kent and Story, but its
sentiments were deeply cherished by them; the same anxiety, as I have had occasion to observe, informed the long
campaign of the lawyers to bring the people—the "Debtors"
—to heel. That Story, in 1829, was not fighting a phantom
of his own neurotic devising was shown the following year
when *Vice Unmasked* was published in New York. The
name on the title page, P. W. Grayson, is, as far as my researches have gone, unidentifiable. This in itself is a probable indication of the level of society on which this antagonism to the law and to lawyers stubbornly persisted. It
should be noted, also, that throughout the book Grayson
uses no Latin tags.]

VICE UNMASKED, 1830

There is a passage in Montesquieu, which says, "that it
is exceedingly difficult for the leading men of a nation to be
knaves, and the inferior sort to be honest—for the former to
be cheats, and the latter to rest satisfied with being only
dupes."

I confess, when I fell upon this passage, I was not able
to forbear making a serious application of it, to appearances in my own country.

I have already sufficiently considered the demoralizing
influence of law, as far as respects its own unaided operation, on the temper and principles of men. But I have yet
to unfold another influence, of an entirely congenial stamp

with the former, that operates, as I think, with wonderful force, to inflame its mischievous power. It is that of a certain class of men, who are professionally concerned in the administration of what is called justice. A class of men, in short, we know by the name of lawyers, whom we find swarming in every hole and corner of society. I fear I shall present in them a picture of the seeds of depravity, at which philanthropy may fold her arms, in utter despair, and weep as though the cause of mankind were indeed irredeemably lost forever!

We have seen that men in general, of their own accord, without any advice or incitement from others, feeling themselves bound up by arbitrary prescriptions, and depraved by their malign influence, would be apt enough to exert all their craft in turning the laws to their own advantage, with but little regard to the whispers of conscience, or to the dictates of justice. But who can set bounds to their iniquity, when these natural impulses come to be instructed and fomented by the learned and licensed jugglers in legal chicanery, creatures who are *ever at hand,* and ready the moment they are *roused* by a suitable *douceur* to point out the sinuous labyrinths which lead to gain, while *themselves* heroically lead the way. How can mankind resist such council and such temptations!

These men are, in truth, the lights of all the land! The very sun, moon, and stars of all intelligence. Bright bodies it must be owned they seem to the stupid gaze of innocent ignorance—the lustful admiration of congenial knavery. Yet how malignant are the beams they shoot over the whole surface of society, shedding upon it the pestilence of discord, strife, and injustice! It is, indeed, the result of inevitable necessity—the very fiat of nature, that these men should be, as we find the most of them all under the present constitution of things. That is to say, that *knaves* they must be in practice, however upright in principle. To be sure, indeed, custom and the laws, which can do anything, sanctify their conduct and loudly proclaim their indemnity. But in the meanwhile, what have become of conscience, and of right, that existed before written laws had either shape or name, and before the introduction among men of all this multitudinous machinery, in the shape of judges and justices, counsellors and attorneys, bailiffs and bumbailiffs, with the long train of congenial agents, blood suckers, and caterpillars of the state? At the very onset of this mighty corps of undertakers—these slippery factors of justice—their doom, the doom of conscience and of right, was sealed forever; that doom has been a hopeless and eternal banishment from almost every bosom into which its victims have been hurled, as dangerous pests, as *paltry things,* which enlightened experience had found too *inconvenient* to suit the newly invented, highly improved condition of society. . . .

To proceed: I have said that these men must be as we find them. Gain, I assert is their animating principle, as it is, in truth, more or less of all men. They assume their professions for a livelihood, and all their studies take that turn which seems most likely to lead them by the shortest route to the end at which they are aiming. A tremulous anxiety for the means of daily subsistence, precludes all leisure to contemplate the loveliness of justice, and properly to understand her principles.

That, indeed, would be a species of truancy—a sinful extravagance—a wild expenditure of time: common prudence would cry out against and denounce it at once as a sort of insanity.

Their business is with statutes, dictates, decisions, and authority. They go on, emptying volume after volume, of all their heterogeneous contents, till they become so laden with other men's thoughts, as scarce to have any of their own. Seldom do their sad eyes look beyond the musty walls of authority, in which their souls are all perpetually immured. And now, as soon as their minds have come to be duly instructed, first, in the antique sophistries, substantial fictions, wise absurdities, and profound dogmas of buried sages, and then fairly liberalized by all the light of modern innovation, and of precious salutary change, do we see them step forward into the world, blown with the most triumphant pretensions, to deal out blessings to mankind. Now, indeed, are they ready to execute any prescription of either justice or injustice—to lend themselves to any side—to advocate any doctrine, for they are well provided with the means in venerable print. Eager for employment, they pry into the business of men, with snakish smoothness slip into the secrets of their affairs, discern the ingredients of litigation, and blow them up into strife. *This is, indeed, but laboring in their vocation.* *

Abject slaves of authority themselves, these counterfeits of men are now to be the proud dictators of human destiny, and withal the glittering favorites of fortune! How immeasurable must be their influence, and imperial their power, holding in their hands, as they do, the *property, lives, and liberties of the citizens!* Their opinions, principles, and conduct, through all their inflexions, vindicated to the great mass of common intelligence, by their actual consequence, beside the imposing aspect of their powers, do not fail, we find, to engage the homage of general consent, and provoke, far and wide, an universal emulation. Their practices, in the general, supersede all other criterions of right, and where they fail of being imitated in a greater or less degree, the instances would be found to be rare ones, at most of uncommon integrity, or singular stupidity;

* There is in the world a very common, because it is a very convenient mode of argument, which is that of drawing large and general conclusions from a few particular facts. There is many a one, I dare say, who would be apt to be shocked here, by this severe handling of the lawyer gentry, because he might happen to know some one or two of the profession, within the circle of his own acquaintance, who were to all appearance perfect gentlemen, and very honest men. Polite and liberal at the bar, as practitioners, and in their private affairs of excellent characters and conduct, the conclusion would probably be, from these rare instances, that all the members of the profession, no matter where, with but few exceptions, were exemplary characters, too. Now this would be, I think, quite a capital mistake. For an honest lawyer, if, in strictness, there be such a phenomenon on earth, is an appearance entirely out of the common course of nature—a *violent* exception, and must therefore be esteemed a sort of prodigy.

the first of which disdains a conformity, which the latter might lack, perhaps, the faculty to achieve.

All this is, at last, nothing more than the plain and natural result of things as they are now constituted.

This order of men certainly come from the hands of nature, with as fair susceptibilities of virtue as any other creatures of mortality. But a malignant destiny overtakes them in time to turn them far off from all the benign purposes of nature, to serve the corrupt contrivances of men; and here, in this devious devotion of their powers, we see them under the tutelage of custom, and the provocations of cupidity, in proportion as they are conspicuous, depraved —and, with the power to be useful, inclined only to be vicious.

Happy were it for mankind, if instruction from these sources were to be less accessible, and more sparingly dealt out to them; but unluckily it is ever at hand, enters into every door, woos its votaries in cities and in villages, on the fields and in the highways, and, with equal insidiousness, glides into the castle and the hovel.

But is is said of these men, that they have their *good sides*, and bad, like all other men. Though their professions subject them to much imputation, and involve them, besides, in many obliquities, that still they actually render a *great deal of good* in the world, being always at hand to step in and cure the miseries of strife, that occur among men, duly compose their affairs, and restore them all back to peace and good order. This idea seems, it must be admitted, in some degree plausible; for if we will rightly examine the matter, we shall see that a very great part of all the difficulties they remove, and of the confusion they clear up, are actually engendered by themselves. So that we see them loosing knots with marvelous dexterity, which even themselves have tied, and getting well paid for it, too.

Less than this could be by no means expected; for mere policy instructs them in the necessity of rendering, at least, some *show* of good to mankind, for the high privilege of being their masters, plunderers, and sinecures.

Again we hear it urged in their favor, that from dire necessity they must be true to their clients, at whatever cost of principle to themselves—that this fidelity to their client, who consigns his dearest interests, it may be even liberty or life, to their official custody, sufficiently cancels all the claims of morality, and amply atones for every obliquity they may find it convenient to practice, in the faithful discharge of grave professional duty. By the force of this venerable custom of thought, we find it has really become a matter of conscience, of high professional honor, for these men of the law to go all lengths that are possible —snatch all advantages, too, in their crafty endeavors to gain even the most unrighteous ends of their clients. Nothing, indeed, is more common, at this time of day, than to hear them gravely extolled as patterns of excellence, for no other merit, than, merely, the cunning trick and devotion they show in the unconscientious cause of their client.

To be true and faithful to him, through all the stages and colors, lights and shades, of his knavery, and even to thunder long and loud in the arduous defence of his most wicked pretensions, is at once to lay the sure foundation of all their happiest fame, and brightest prosperity, too.

It is worth while to examine this sentiment of approbation into which most people in the world seem to have got themselves betrayed. We will see, by narrow observation, that it has proceeded from a principle of feeling in the mind, that is virtuous enough, but has certainly erred in not accurately distinguishing between the subject it praises in the instance before us, and the true one to which it justly belongs. This last, though it bear a striking resemblance to the former in its external features, will be found, when properly considered, in every essential particular, widely different. For example—a fellow being, whom I will suppose to be entirely destitute of all worth, has obtained the pledge of your support in a given emergency. It may be he has formerly rendered you some signal service, which a sense of gratitude sways you to requite, even upon one who no longer deserves the concern of any one.

You protect him with no little cost of convenience to yourself, it may be supposed, even from the pursuit of justice, having pledged your word in a moment of unreflecting sympathy, to render him so great a service.

In such a case, your fidelity, if it be not exactly worthy of commendation, surely deserves forgiveness: but it is plain that a special instance of this sort of favor to villany, into which you have been surprized by a rare and inevitable accident, from motives of gratitude and humanity, by no means constitutes you the established friend and harborer of malefactors. It is your motive of action, and the strange predicament in which you were placed, that save you from the censure of mankind, and give you, perhaps, its applause. But suppose you undertook, thenceforth, to protect and countenance knaves of every sort, and actually received from them, in the way of business, steady compensation for your care and support of their persons and their interests, how different is your character become —now, indeed, you deserve the execration of mankind! Though the instance I have first supposed, in which you have gained their applause in every outward feature, exactly resembles any single instance of the kind, which now loads you with infamy.

Will your occasional service, however cheerfully rendered to honest men, whenever it might be called for, in the slightest degree, serve to better or retrieve the last character I have given you? One would think not.

It is, perhaps, needless here to raise up a parallel in words, which must be in every one's mind, who has bestowed any attention in this place.

Can there be a more pitiable sight than that we are here constrained to behold? Quite certain it is, that the law, if it do not absorb all the talents and genius of the country, attracts, at least, the choice of it all, and leaves but little more than the refuse for other callings. What then is this sight?—*genius putting itself to sale*—the brightest intelligence of the land offering itself a loose prostitute to the capricious use of all men alike, for gold!

We shudder at the hapless female, who yields her person, indiscriminately, to the lust of libertines, for hire.

Though there is even a total wreck of virtue in these creatures, yet, in no given instance of prostitution in them, is there involved any thing like the pollution of spirit, which we must observe in your talking hireling of justice.

For he is not a passive instrument in the hands of licentious wickedness, but an active, ardent, furious, agent of injustice, that wholly supersedes, for the time, with his superior qualifications, the less gifted craft of his knavish employer.

He is set in motion, all on fire, by a purse full of vile trash, of "rascal counters," for which he freely sells all the breath of his lungs, the untiring service of his tongue, and with them, his whole heart and soul, to boot.

Surely the system, which involves such a spectacle as this, through all its parts, to its deepest depths must be *rotten!* Let us consider for a moment how genius should be employed. Certainly in the great cause of philanthropy and morals. What should be its reward? The pure *light of nature* which it would woo to its heart, the indestructible treasure of inward satisfaction with itself—an unquenchable ray of brightness, that a conscience, pure and unsullied, would shed on the soul, and the whole face of visible creation!

But this genius, we have seen, instead of flying heavenward, with the whole race of man, is *meanly sold* to knaves, for that which procures the assassin, to plunge his dagger into the bosom of innocence—its best and faithfulest service, actually bought like the meanest commodity, anywhere to be found in the filthiest market, even as it were tainted meat for the epicure, or base confectionary slimed into color and shape, for greedy brats, or silly women.

What I have written in this chapter, seems adventurous matter enough for an humble, solitary being, such as I am. If I did not feel its truth now I am at the end of it, actually sweetening the very pulsations of my heart, I would not venture it into the world; but my own conscience being entirely easy and calm on the subject, the thoughts I have

offered go from my hands as freely, and fearlessly, too, as
though they were even a grateful eulogium, framed for
the men, whose *trade* they have labored to *damn.* [*]

[*] It may serve, perhaps, somewhat to excuse the severity
with which I have treated the profession of the law, for me
to confess that I myself was one of the faculty, up to a time
that is now very recent; when, by a solemn resolution, I re-
nounced the detestable calling forever. I have learned that it is
at least some virtue for a man to condemn himself—that much,
at least, I may claim for myself, in what I have done, if *no more.*

NOTES

1 *The Adams Papers. Diary and Autobiography of John Adams*
(Cambridge, 1961) III, 326–27.

JOSIAH QUINCY (1772–1864)

AN ADDRESS DELIVERED AT THE DEDICATION OF THE DANE LAW COLLEGE IN HARVARD UNIVERSITY, OCTOBER 23, 1832

[In the colonies and in the early Republic, as in England, there was virtually no academic instruction in the law. For this reason, as President Quincy takes joy in recounting, the appointment of Blackstone at Oxford and the issuance of the famed *Commentaries* from a university were momentous events. An ordinary candidate for the American bar was trained, if at all, by the "apprenticeship" system. He "read" in the office of some senior practitioner. Though many eminent lawyers took pains with their young men, or tried to, the evils of the arrangement, as the mighty judges of England elevated the dignity and the intellectual range of legal science, became increasingly evident.

When Josiah Quincy delivered this address he was President of Harvard; he was starting the institution on the long road from a placid College toward becoming a university by giving vigorous support to the growing Law School. Quincy was a majestic figure in the Boston community. He was a son of the first Josiah Quincy, a patriot leader. Born in Braintree, he went to Phillips Academy, Andover, and to Harvard. He had "read" in an office—hence the fervor with which he pillories this method of education—and was admitted to the Boston bar in 1793.

Wealthy, handsome, elegant in manner, he was—as assuredly he could have been nothing else—an ardent Federalist. Elected to Congress in 1804, he resisted the rising West, became a friend of John Randolph, and contended against everything Jeffersonian. He fought against the Embargo and the War of 1812. Out of Congress, he was a man of affairs in Boston, for which he provided from 1823 to 1828 a vigorous administration as mayor. He was President of Harvard from 1829 to 1845, and in 1840 published his monumental *History of Harvard*. Like so many New England conservatives, he was basically antislavery—though, of course, never an Abolitionist!—and in 1860 supported Abraham Lincoln.

While on the surface a plea for the formal, systematic study of law in a classroom, Quincy's speech is another maneuver against both those *sans-culottes* like Grayson who would abolish all jurisprudence whatsoever and against those democratic legalists who would humble the Common Law into a codification. Considering that in 1832 the apprenticeship system was still the prevailing method of instruction, that the nascent law schools had barely commenced to demonstrate their superiority, Quincy ran the risk of incurring not only the scorn of these enemies but also the displeasure of the profession itself, most of whose members had come up by the traditional ladder. It took evident courage to so frankly characterize the arrangement as a debasement of the noble science. And it took cleverness to prove, as he does, that only in the universities, following the model of Blackstone, could the teaching of law become a "science," could the Common Law be transformed from an occult mystery into a "liberalized and refined" branch of learning. In short, Quincy, following such pioneers as Reeve, Gould, and Hoffman, was a stalwart protagonist of the concept of a thorough professional training, such as would eliminate the unfit and the unable, a training which the profession had gallantly maintained against the strong press of egalitarianism. Quincy's language, delivered in what we might otherwise suppose to have been, in 1832, the serenity of Cambridge's groves, shows in every phrase how deadly the struggle was.]

AN ADDRESS, 1832

The law, considered as a science, has so intimate a connexion with the sciences in general, that, at first view, we are ready to wonder, why it was not made earlier a branch of education in Universities; or how it should have ever been deemed practicable to prosecute the study of it, successfully, elsewhere. The causes of this delay to place the study of the law under the auspices of general science, will be sufficiently indicated by a brief outline of very familiar history.

"Laws," says Montesquieu, "are the necessary relations resulting from the nature of things." Now the relations of things in Great Britain, from which country our laws are chiefly derived, were, during the early periods of its historic existence, antecedent to the Norman conquest, those which naturally exist among a rude, uncultivated people, ignorant of letters. During that whole time, a knowledge of the laws was necessarily sought among its rough professors, habituated practically to pursue its loose, evanescent principles, as they were continually modified by faction, insurrection, civil wars, invasion, and conquest. Strictly speaking, there were no sciences known in the nation, with which the law could be connected as an associate of the band.

Nor was the state of things greatly different after the era of the Norman Conquest, and even down to the beginning of the last century. In the successive contests which, in the course of that long period, arose between the crown and the nobility, the people and the crown, the hierarchy and the reformers, the principles of the law followed the fates of the court, the camp, or the church. They were instruments, of which each party, in its power, availed itself to strengthen its own cause, or to depress that of its adversary, and they were shaped, or changed, according to the perpetually shifting influences of the times. "Antecedent to the revolution of 1688, the oracles of the law were dependent upon the caprice of the crown; men of pliant dispositions were raised to the bench; justice gave way to policy, and was converted into means of revenge."[1] During far the greater part of that period, as a great system of universal reason, deduced from the nature of things, and adapted to fix society on the immutable foundations of truth and justice, the English law was hardly considered by any, except perhaps by some of its most eminent professors. Strange fictions, customs of unknown origin, precedents whose reasons were hidden in an unexplored antiquity, interminable forms, mystifying verbiage, and repulsive technicalities, deprived it of all claim, in the eyes of the philosopher, as well as in those of the multitude, to the rank of a branch of knowledge resting on fixed principles. Its language was trilingual; a composite of indifferent English, bad Latin, and worse French. Its shape, "if shape it might be called, which shape had none," was "stained with the variation of each soil betwixt" the Euxine and the Baltic; Grecian, Roman, German, Saxon, Danish, Norman. In the arrangement of these contending elements, to the uninitiated eye, "Chaos seemed to sit umpire," and "high arbiter Chance to govern all." To manage these elements was an art to be learned; an affair altogether of practical skill, which the young lawyer was sent to the Inns of Court to acquire, precisely, and for the same reason, as the young soldier was sent to the camp to acquire the military art; to the end that, amid scenes of actual contest, each might learn the nature of the materials, and gain a facility in the use of the weapons for attack and defence, of their respective arts; in both of which victory was the sole object, and the means of success, equally, the subject of no scruple.

This state of things continued until after the commencement of the last century. Antecedent to that period, Sir Matthew Hale[2] had indeed composed an "Analysis of the Law," for the purpose, as he avowed, of showing that "it was not altogether impossible, by much attention and labor, to reduce the laws of England, at least into a tolera-

ble method." This analysis was nothing more than an incomplete outline, of use, comparatively, to none except
professors of the law, or professional students. So little
progress had been made, either by Sir Matthew Hale or by
any other jurist, in the work of reducing the laws of England into an orderly method, that Thomas Wood, who, in
1722, engaged in the same design, represents it as thought
to be wholly "impracticable," and states that the prejudice,
even among men of parts and learning prevailed, that a
knowledge of the English laws was only to be obtained by
"the greatest application and a long attendance on the
highest courts of justice, *and by a tedious wandering
about.*" He refers to the law, as "an art which one is to
teach," and so far from speaking of it as a science, to be
sought in its great and general principles, he calls it *"a
heap of good learning, which he hoped it would not be
impossible to sort and put into some order."* He laments
the arts of "pettyfogging, sophistry, and cavil," as too
prevalent. He represents the ways of the law to be "dark
and rugged, and full of turnings and windings." These he
declares it to be his intent to endeavour to "smooth and
shorten," and thus enable the student "to travel in a straight
line."[3]

For more than fifty years this work of Thomas Wood
was the cynosure of the law-student in this country; to
which he was taught first to direct his eye, and by which
to guide his steps. Yet how dull, how repulsive does this
work appear to the law-student of the present day! How
would he reluct at entering upon the study of the law, and
deem himself cast into a wilderness, without map or compass, if this were the only great light by which he was first
to direct his course!

Now it is a curious fact, and illustrative of the topic of
this address, that the first successful attempt to reduce the
English law into an orderly system, and to give it effec-
tively the character of a science, was made under the
auspices of a university. To the establishment of the
Vinerian Professorship, at Oxford, the English law was indebted for the *Commentaries* of Sir William Blackstone,

pronounced by Sir William Jones to be "an incomparable
work; and the most correct and beautiful outline that was
ever exhibited of any human science."

The publication of that work formed a new era in the
study of the law, both in this country and in Great Britain.
From that time the law assumed the aspect of a well-
defined science, which had its limits, its proportions, its
divisions, its principles, its objects, all arranged in an orderly method, facilitating research, aiding the memory, and
making every step of the student's progress light and satisfactory.

How different is the lot of the student at this day, from
that of him, who entered upon the pursuit of the law before the appearance of that work. By way of illustration,
hear a very condensed abstract of Lord Chief Justice
Reeve's directions for the first stage in the study of the law:

"Read Wood's *Institutes* cursorily, and for explanation of
the same, Jacob's *Dictionary*. Next strike out what lights
you can from Bohun's *Institutio Legalis,* and Jacob's *Prac-
tising Attorney's Companion,* and the like; helping yourself by Indexes. Then read and consider Littleton's *Tenures,* without notes, and abridge it. Then venture on Coke's
Commentaries. After reading it once, read it again; for it
will require many readings. Abridge it. Common-place it.
Make it your own; applying to it all the faculties of your
mind. Then read Serjeant Hawkins to throw light on Lord
Coke. Then read Wood again to throw light on Serjeant
Hawkins. And then read the statutes at large to throw light
on Mr. Wood."

It will not be necessary to adduce farther evidence upon
this point. Enough has been said to place in a strong light
the advantages derived by the student of law from the
great work of Sir William Blackstone. For the purpose of
the present argument, let it be borne in mind, that this
work was the first fruits of the connexion between the
English law and the English Universities.

Now when we recollect that it is an admitted fact, that a
great proportion of the boasted wisdom of the English
common law, was acquired by a silent transfer into it of

the wisdom of the Roman law, through the medium of the courts of justice, and that thereby the English law was "raised from its original state of rudeness and imperfection;" and when we also recollect, that a knowledge of the Roman law itself was first introduced into England, early in the twelfth century by means of Professorships, established by the monks and clergy at Oxford, and through the influence of public lectures delivered by their Professors; and when to these facts is added the undeniable and unparalleled benefit conferred upon the study of the English law, by this work of Blackstone, itself the fruit of the connexion of the study of the science of the law with that of the other sciences in the University of Oxford, is it not indeed wonderful, that doubts concerning the utility of such professorships should be entertained, even at this day, in England, and by men, also, who are eminent for their legal rank and attainments? . . .

Nor can it be concealed, that similar doubts are sometimes expressed, even in this country; though, from the habits of the community being less fixed, and the spirit of innovation more congenial to its constitution than is the case in Great Britain, probably with less universality as it respects numbers, and less eminence as it respects talents; it being generally understood, that by far the greater number of those, who are distinguished lights of the law, in this country, hail the establishment of such Professorships, as constituting a union highly propitious to the improvement of the law, and to the elevation of the character of the profession.

It will not, however, be amiss to give to this topic a more detailed examination, to the end that the community may be made to understand the real advantages to be anticipated from this engrafting of the study of the law upon seminaries destined for public education; and that lawyers themselves may be made more truly to appreciate the privileges they and their profession must derive from this association.

Lord Bacon, a great master-mind of our race, has stated, in his conclusive way, the general doctrine, and given the sound reason for it. "To disincorporate," says he, "any particular science from general knowledge, is one great impediment to its advancement. For there is a supply of light and information, which the particulars and instances of one science do yield and present for the framing and correcting the axioms of another science, in their very truth and notion. For each particular science has a dependence upon universal knowledge, to be augmented and rectified by the superior light thereof."

In no way, perhaps, can the truth of this doctrine be better illustrated, than by the history of the progress of the English law, from its ancient, barbarous, and perplexed, to its present cultivated and lucid state. So long as it was "disincorporated from general knowledge," and pursued exclusively under the guidance of professional men, in the Inns of Courts, or in offices of practitioners, its outline was obscure, its aspect forbidding and mysterious; none dared to pretend to master it, except the regularly initiated; and to some of these, its reason was a closed book, which they had not the strength or patience to open. No sooner, however, was the Common Law introduced among the branches of University education, than it became liberalized and refined. Its particular light was "augmented and rectified by the superior light of universal knowledge." Its foreign jargon was abandoned. Its technicalities were diminished. If we were to say that all the improvements, which have been introduced into the study and science of the law since the middle of the last century, were the consequence of the publication of the single work of Blackstone, we should assert, perhaps, more than we could prove, though possibly not more than is true. That work introduced the science of the English law to the acquaintance of men of general science. It was no longer a study from which such men were repelled, by the wildness of its aspect and the impervious barbarousness of its terms. By the labors of Blackstone the rough scene was changed. After the publication of his work, men of general science began to think and to speak of the English law, as of a subject which could be understood without the exclusive devotion of a whole life to it. Professional men also, their progress being thus facilitated, found more leisure themselves to pursue general science. Thus, by the reciprocal action of influences without and within the profession, its nature has been ameliorated, and its general character elevated. It is of no importance, as to our present purpose, to say, that these improvements were the consequence of the general advance of the age, and not of the connexion of the study of the law with the Universities. This connexion was either an instrument or a cause. And whether the connexion of the science of the law with the Universities be considered as an instrument, to which, in its advancing progress, the age resorted for the improvement of that science, or whether it was itself the cause of the advance of the age in the direction which led to those improvements,—on either hypothesis, the object of the present argument is attained; either as a cause, or as a selected instrument, the connexion of the study of the law with the Universities has had an efficient agency in those great improvements in the science, which have been introduced in our day. From the hour when the great magician, Blackstone, standing in the halls of Oxford, stretched his scientific wand over the "illimitable ocean, without bound," where, to the uninstructed eye, "cold, hot, moist, and dry, in their pregnant causes mixed, seemed to strive for mastery," confusion disappeared. In its stead was seen a well-proportioned, well-cemented fabric, pleasing to the sight, satisfactory to the taste, approved by the judgment, its architectural principles just, its parts orderly and harmonious, in which justice was found consorting with reason, and controversy guided by the spirit of truth, and not by the spirit of victory.

Such being the advantages already consequent upon the establishment of Professorships of law in connexion with seminaries of learning, the question arises, whether farther advantages are to be anticipated from their continuance and increase. This leads necessarily to an inquiry into the actual state of education in the science of the law, at the present day. What it is in Great Britain, Professor Park,[4] in his "Introductory Lecture" before referred to, indicates very strongly.

"Few things," he says, "will less bear looking into (with other eyes than those of habit) than the system of legal education hitherto prevailing in this country; and if the public at large could see it in its real nakedness, common sense and safety would alike dictate that such culpable neglect should no longer be permitted to insult society, and set at nought the deep interests that are at stake, in the proficiency of those who offer themselves to the public as legal practitioners." He avers, "that a great number of young men are annually let loose upon the public, calling themselves solicitors, and barristers, and conveyancers, and having perhaps personal claims upon many to be entrusted with their business, who have given no other security to the public for their having qualified themselves for a most important and arduous profession, than that of having paid a certain sum of money for articles of clerkship, or having purchased the name of pupil in the chambers of some practitioner." "I have myself," he adds," had pupils, whom no expostulations or exhortings of mine could induce to attend an average of two hours a day, or to take any pains when they did attend. I have known others, who have not come to chambers once in a week. I have known still more, who would do nothing but talk and banter when they were there." "Upon the present system," he adds, "scarcely one in every five has a single chance of attaining that proficiency, which would enable him to keep practice, even should he be so fortunate as to obtain it."

What resemblance this state of legal education in Great Britain, bears to that in the offices of practitioners of the law in this country, at the present day, it is not for me to assert. Of the state of things, in this respect, nearly half a century ago, some experience and observation enable me to speak with sufficient accuracy.

Books were recommended as they were asked for, without any inquiry concerning the knowledge attained from the books previously recommended and read. Regular instruction there was none; examination as to progress in ac-

quaintance with the law,—none; occasional lectures,—none;
oversight as to general attention and conduct,—none. The
student was left to find his way by the light of his own
mind, and obliged to take possession of the wilderness
upon which he had entered, as one of our backwoodsmen
takes possession of an American forest;—of just as much as
he could clear and cultivate by the prowess of his single
arm, in hopeless ignorance of all he did not thus personally
vanquish.

Was it the student's fortune to be placed in an office
where there was little business, and of course the spirit of
study little vexed with official manipulations? In such case,
his reading might be more, but his chances for external aid
were not therefore with certainty increased. His instructer
could not inspire a love for the profession, which perhaps
he did not feel. Very likely, by his complaints of its labors
or of its profitlessness, juvenile ardor was cooled, if not
quenched. Possibly the student was taught by example, or
even by precept, to seek wealth in the rise of lands or of
stocks; or was led to mistake the way of party strife for the
path of true glory.

Was it the student's lot to be placed in the office of one
of the greater lights of the bar;—"Hic labor ille domus, et
inextricabilis error."⁵ What copying of contracts! What filling of writs! What preparing of pleas! How could the mind
concentrate itself on principles amid the perpetual rotation
of this machinery; while at the same time it was distracted
by the sorrows of clients and the prosing of witnesses!

All this indeed gave knowledge of business, and skill in
the handicraft labor of the profession;—in the later stages
of study useful, indeed necessary; but in the earlier, posi-
tively injurious; since the eye of the student was thus first
directed to the mechanism of the art, and not to the principles of the science. He was taught, not to seek first the
divinity of the temple, and to raise his thoughts to the
glorious attributes and noble powers which its true worship requires, but, on the contrary, he was made to meet
at the very threshold whatever in it was low, selfish, and
repulsive, and condemned first to drudge at the menial

services of the altar, to live amid the offal of the sacrifice, and to look with a single eye to that which brought profit to the shrine. How could the great principles of the law, except in very propitious natures, be made to take an early root; how could deep foundations for future greatness in it be laid, by reading necessarily desultory,—attendance upon courts unavoidably casual,—and mental exercises, which could not be otherwise than occasional and listless, when conducted, without excitement and without encouragement, with just so much vagrant attention as a young man could persuade himself to give, in the midst of all the temptations which youth, society, and a sense of complete irresponsibility as to conduct, continually placed in his way?

As it respects the education for the law in private offices, at the present day, compared with that in a former period, it is said that improvements have been made;—that a more systematic intercourse between instructers and students is growing into use;—that in some places moot courts are held, at which eminent professional men preside by turns over these exercises of their students. It is even said, that, in some offices, lectures have been read. All this is well, and highly laudable. It is, however, proper on this occasion to state, that, on inquiry, it will be found that all these improvements have kept pace with the establishment of law-schools in the vicinity where they have occurred, and have been the direct consequence of the example those schools have set, or of the spirit they have diffused.

How inferior, after all, are these advantages, to those which may be attained in a law-school, connected with this University, or with any similarly endowed seminary.

First, a great body of intelligent young men are here brought together, of about the same age and general range of attainments; all of them inspired with a love of study, and ambitious of professional eminence. At least such is the fair conclusion from the fact, that they have voluntarily exchanged the absolute independence and irresponsibility of the private office, for the examination, the instruction, and responsibility established in this institution. From such minds, thus brought into contact, result honorable collision, concurrent inquiries, public discussions, comparison of themselves with each other;—all powerful stimulants of intellectual progress.

Next, a systematic course of prescribed study, selected with great deliberation by men of the highest rank in the profession; rising in just gradation from the simple to the complex, from the familiar to the abstruse; leading the young mind, by orderly induction, and by a progress secured at every step, to all the elevated points of professional attainment, where the wide view presented naturally inspires noble thoughts and generous resolutions as to truth and duty.

Lastly, a regular succession of daily examinations in study, accompanied by commentary and illustration, by one of the Professors; and, in concurrence with these, public lectures on some one or other of the great divisions of the law. To these are added appropriate exercises, having reference to practical skill in technical learning; and moot courts, superintended by men of great experience both at the bar and on the bench. Nor, in this place, will it be deemed the language of compliment, if I enumerate among the advantages of the institution the distinguished privilege it enjoys, in being under the immediate supervision of two gentlemen,[6] possessing all the endowments which constitute high professional character, and not only capable by their talents and acquirements to excite the student to raise his thoughts to the high and true sources of legal knowledge, but also singularly qualified, by the example of their past lives, as well as by their daily precepts, to inspire him with the love of severe intellectual labor; at the same time that they exhibit for his encouragement, in their own mental powers and eminent stations, the honors and rewards, which the profession of the law can confer on those who are distinguished for talent and fidelity in its pursuit.

When to all these advantages are added free access to a law library, containing upwards of three thousand volumes, and to the general library of the University, containing above thirty-five thousand; and also the genius of the

place, naturally inviting the student occasionally to seek
refuge, not in vain and vicious dissipation, but in the pursuits of general literature, from the severe and sometimes
irksome toils of legal research; and, in connexion with
these, the vicinity of a metropolis, which now is, in all
times past has been, and, from its general relations, in all
future time must be, distinguished for the number of eminent professional men residing there, the opportunity to
witness the exercise of whose skill and talents, in courts of
justice, is easy and frequent,—there is no room for question, that here unite all happy coincidences to excite, instruct and animate the law student; to relieve him from
the apathy and weariness, which at times assail the best
disposed natures; and to bring him within the influence
of the highest motives and best models of professional
merit and distinction.

Under aspects thus encouraging and useful, the Law-
School connected with this University presents itself for
the contemplation and the patronage of the lawyer, the
statesman, the patriot, the man of wealth, and the man of
learning. What interest of society can more justly claim a
liberal and enlightened support, than that which enlarges
the means and multiplies the inducements of men, destined
for the profession of the law, to be learned, moral, and
elevated, in all their opinions and conduct? What profession more deeply influences the condition of society, either
for evil or for good? Under every form of government this
is true, but eminently so in republics. The law embraces
within the sphere of its activity a greater number of relations, than any other profession. All the principles, which
guide, support, or defend the rights of individuals and
society, are within the natural scope of its action or contemplation. It deals not with man in particular classes, or
with respect to particular modes of thought or purpose,
but extends itself to his universal being, in every possible
mode in which he can act or exist. It protects the weak.
It controls the powerful. It is the refuge of the oppressed.
It is the shelter of the poor, and the guardian of the
wealthy. The great subjects of its regard are rights, truth,

morals, power, liberty. It looks to the past; it considers the present; it has respect to the future. The influences of the men of that profession are, in a greater or less degree, felt every where; in the village, the city, the county, the state, and the nation. By a few these influences are deprecated; by the great majority they are applauded, encouraged, employed and honored. How important is it that a class of men, called to act in spheres so various, on objects so numerous, and on interests so general, should have their early education consorted with their destinies! How intensely desireable is it, that their minds should not be narrowed down to the rank of mere drudges in office, or made to descend to the level of common wranglers for hire! Of what incalculable consequence is it, that, from the earliest pursuit of this profession, the minds of its students should be liberalized and generalized, and be made to comprehend and prepare for the great sphere with which it connects them! And where can the foundations of a solid and lofty structure of intellectual and moral action be laid, with better hope of success, than under the auspices of the great seats of learning, and in union with the associations and impelled by the motives, which naturally exist within their walls, or in their vicinity? Where will man's apprehensions of duty be more likely to become enlarged; and how may firmness, alacrity, and fearlessness, in the discharge of social obligations, be more certainly attained, than by the aid of general science, and under the excitement of the example of generous competition among those engaged in its pursuit?

When therefore we consider the intimate alliance, established in the nature of things and by the condition of society, between the profession of the law and those principles, both legal and constitutional, on which depend the rights of life, liberty, and property; that from the men of this profession a great number of those, who affect the fortunes of society, always have been and always must be selected; that this class, in the character of advocates, vindicate our laws, in that of judges construe them, in that of legislators powerfully contribute either to their change or continuance; that in all critical exigencies of the state, to them more than to any other class, society is accustomed to look for counsel and direction,—the duty of increasing the means and multiplying the chances of perpetuating, in that profession, a learned, talented, and conscientious body of men, can scarcely be overrated, or by any strength of language exaggerated.

To those, therefore, whom Providence has been pleased greatly to favor in the gifts of fortune, or to those whom it has still more highly favored, by granting to them the power to influence others to do good, and who may be led to inquire, how the resources of this school are proportioned to the exigencies of the study of the law, it may be proper to say, that the duties of the Royall Professor embrace instruction in every branch both of law and equity, oversight of the students, and direction and examination of them in their studies; "that those of the Dane Professor include the preparing, delivering, and publishing of lectures in law and equity, the law of nations, commercial and maritime law, federal law, and federal equity;"— spheres of duties with respect to both Professorships, sufficient exclusively to occupy the time of any two individuals, however learned and laborious. The state of the school already indicates the importance, and must soon indicate the necessity, of the foundation of another Professorship. Under these circumstances the intelligent and liberal class of men, who constitute our mercantile and manufacturing interests are respectfully invited to take into consideration the extreme desirableness and importance of a separate Professorship of Commercial and Maritime Law. In a country placed in the local condition of New England, which has, for a long time, been a competitor with the great nations of the old world in commerce, and of late rapidly vying with them in manufactures,—inseparably identified with the ocean by its habits and its harbours, and with mercantile interchange by its capital, its enterprise, its industry, and its talent,—no branch of the law more imperiously calls for attention and patronage. Commerce, as well internal as external, is ever, from its very nature, expansive and varying; in accordance with which, the principles of this branch of law necessarily vary and expand. That they may be well understood, and be diffused through the nation with a rightly grounded uniformity, nothing seems more important, than that the education of legal students should, in this respect, have the supervision and aid of some one of the greater lights of the law, whose exclusive duty it should be to lead their minds to take comprehensive and practical views of this complex subject, and to teach them, among its fluctuating interests, how to fix upon its sound and immutable principles.

In closing this address, I cannot refrain from congratulating the other constituent branches of this University on the benefit resulting from the extension of its law branch; nor from expressing to the members of the Law-School my grateful sense of the many advantages already derived from their influence and example. In every aspect their connexion has been useful and auspicious. By associating themselves with this school, they have made a wise selection among the paths which may be pursued for the attainment of legal knowledge. It is no obscure or uncertain advantage, in the pursuit of any science, to proceed from the elementary to the complex, and to ascend, by regular, well-established steps, to its difficult and commanding heights. It is no questionable or dubious good, to escape, in the early stages of the study of the law, from the annoyance and interruption of the labors of clerkship. On the contrary, it is a high and unequivocal privilege to be first introduced to the knowledge of what is formal, fictitious, and technical, not by the desultory, haphazard way of official business, but by an orderly succession of general principles, accompanied by irradiations from the combined lights of analysis and analogy. Nor is the advantage of that mutual intercourse and exercise, which, in such institutions as this, are enjoyed in so eminent a degree, to be placed at a low estimate. "Young men," says a distinguished living jurist, "as far as their mutual information extends, are the best professors for each other." By the concurrence of many minds the splendor and illumination of all are concentered upon each, and reflected by each, stimulating the spirit of research, and enkindling and keeping alive the spirit of discussion.

Above all, the opportunity of being examined upon his studies proffers to the faithful and ingenuous student the most precious of all information,—a knowledge of his own intellectual powers and defects; teaching him what to correct and how to improve; and thus leading him into the path of true glory, which is ever coincident with the paths of self-knowledge and truth.

Thus, under the joint influences of a thorough legal education and of general science, it may confidently be anticipated, that the destinies of the profession of the law will daily become more and more elevated and refined; that those generous spirits, who now have engaged, or who, from time to time hereafter, in this or in any other seat of science combining similar advantages, may engage in its pursuits, will be gradually led to embrace, within the scope of their intellectual vision, an horizon limited by no other boundary, than the utmost perfection of which their natures are capable; exalting their thoughts to the desire and design of cooperating with the goodness of the Creator, by endeavours to promote the moral and intellectual improvement of their species; and thus, in the degree which man's rank in the scale of being permits, imitating his bounty and promoting his glory.

NOTES

[1] Runnington's *Life of Sir Matthew Hale* [Quincy's note].

[2] Sir Matthew Hale (1609–76), Justice of the Common Pleas under Cromwell, Chief Justice of the King's Bench under Charles II. His *History of the Common Law of England, with an Analysis of the Law* was published in 1713.

[3] Thomas Wood (1661–1722) published *Institutes of the Laws of England; or the Laws of England in their Natural Order, according to Common Law*, in two volumes, London, 1720.

[4] Sir James Alan Park (1763–1838), Judge of the Common Pleas.

[5] "Here is that laborious and inextricable maze of the house."

[6] The "two gentlemen" President Quincy refers to are quite obviously Mr. Justice Story and John Hooker Ashmun, appointed Royall Professor in 1829. At the time President Quincy spoke, Story and Ashmun were the entire faculty; but Ashmun was already subsiding into what New England then called a "decline," and would be dead by the spring of 1833.

ROBERT RANTOUL, JR. (1805–52)

ORATION AT SCITUATE. DELIVERED ON THE FOURTH OF JULY, 1836

[P. W. Grayson, whoever he was, could be dismissed by Kent, Story, and Josiah Quincy as an ignorant demagogue of the Jacksonian mobocracy. William Sampson, we have seen, was not so summarily to be dismissed, although the tag "wild Irishman" could be affixed to him. Henry Dwight Sedgwick was a bit more alarming, yet he was a New England rationalist. The true vitality of the force against which Kent, Story, Quincy et al. contended was made supremely vocal, in the 1830s and 1840s, by the foremost Democratic member of the Massachusetts bar.

Robert Rantoul is one of the most appealing, most poignant figures in the period, and especially within a predominantly Whig area. I say this not because he was, in every contemporaneous implication of the word, a "liberal," but because he was as noble a champion of that persuasion as was Story on the opposite side. I submit that the modern student, distanced by the changes of language and of procedures, can find himself in the happy position of admiring both Story and Rantoul. Yet this may be asking too much. Possibly the issue between them is still too divisive to be treated with tolerance. If so, then Rantoul, if not admired must be remembered—unfortunately he is little remembered—as the archopponent of everything Joseph Story represented.

Rantoul was born in Beverly, Massachusetts. Like Josiah Quincy—and this is important to note—he went to Phillips Academy, Andover, and then to Harvard, where he graduated in 1826. He also "read" law, was admitted to the bar of Salem in 1829, to that of Boston in 1838. From his youth he was a Jeffersonian Democrat, and so thereafter a Jacksonian. His was no uninformed passion; he was an intellectual aware of the intoxicating ideas then blowing through the windy corridors of New England. Wherefore he became in the 1830s the most sophisticated, and the most formidable, opponent of the Common Law. All the fortifications erected by Kent and Story trembled at the blast of his horn. In this short extract from another of those two-hour orations—which our age cannot be asked to read in their entirety, but which can never be appreciated unless wholly and patiently imbibed—we find the supreme enunciation of the American democratic resistance to the pretensions of the Common Law.

Rantoul was a rigorously consistent humanitarian. Not a "cause" in the era of "reform" escaped his sponsorship. He agitated against capital punishment; he was a pioneer advocate (along with Sampson) of labor unions. He gave his services as attorney to the "Dorr rebels" in Rhode Island. He worked manfully for lyceums and tax-supported public schools, for state boards of education, for temperance. He attacked corporations. Needless to say, he was an Abolitionist. Yet, all the while, he was not a Transcendentalist: in the law he was as thoroughly a neoclassical rationalist as Joseph Story himself.

Rantoul was elected to Congress in 1851, but, exhausted by his headlong participation in a hundred crusades, he was not able to carry the burden further. His death in 1852 was an irreplaceable loss to the anti-slavery Democrats. What he might have effected in the next ten years, had he lived and retained his vigor, is one of the many sad speculations in American history.

This excerpt from the oration—which dealt with numerous other grievances, and to which, we are told, his audience listened with rapture—summarizes the solid intellectual argument, mostly homegrown though possibly encouraged by Bentham and the English reformers, against the Common Law. Rantoul eloquently affirms that, by the very nature of the society, America must rapidly enact its legal forms exclusively through statute. Nothing in this new land can grow by prescription, and precedent is useless. The democracy speaks only through enactments. To achieve rationality in American law the only possible solution is a codification of these statutes. Wherefore America can readily dispense with such medieval sophistries as equity and special pleading, along with all those other perversions of simple common sense which devious pundits, such as Kent and Story, have endeavored to inflict upon us in the name of a specious "reason." Most importantly Rantoul raises, in an alarming declaration, the issue of whether judges, unless they be confined to a strict administration of the statute, instead of being permitted the mysterious whimsey of the Common Law, will not become the judicial legislators of the country. In these paragraphs Rantoul enunciated, as none had before, the problem which in the Jacksonian era became the central one of American jurisprudence—a problem which has remained an annoying one to the federal system ever since, and which at this writing seems not yet finally adjudicated.]

ORATION AT SCITUATE, 1836

The Common Law sprung from the dark ages; the fountain of justice is the throne of the Deity. The Common Law is but the glimmering taper by which men groped their way through the palpable midnight in which learning, wit, and reason were almost extinguished; justice shines with the splendor of that fulness of light which beams from the Ineffable Presence. The Common Law had its beginning in time, and in the time of ignorance; justice is eternal, even with the eternity of the allwise and just Lawgiver and Judge. The Common Law had its origin in folly, barbarism, and feudality; justice is the irradiance of divine wisdom, divine truth, and the government of infinite benevolence. While the Common Law sheds no light, but rather darkness visible, that serves but to discover sights of woe,—justice rises, like the Sun of Righteousness, with healing on his wings, scatters the doubts that torture without end, dispels the mists of scholastic subtilty, and illuminates with the light that lighteth every man that cometh into the world. Older, nobler, clearer, and more glorious, then, is everlasting justice, than ambiguous, base-born, purblind, perishable Common Law. That which is older than the creation may indeed be extolled for its venerable age; but among created things, the argument from antiquity is a false criterion of worth. Sin and death are older than the Common Law; are they, therefore, to be preferred to it? The mortal transgression of Cain was anterior to the Common Law: does it therefore furnish a better precedent?

Judge-made law is *ex post facto* law, and therefore unjust. An act is not forbidden by the statute law, but it becomes void by judicial construction. The legislature could not effect this, for the Constitution forbids it. The judiciary shall not usurp legislative power, says the Bill of Rights: yet it not only usurps, but runs riot beyond the confines of legislative power.

Judge-made law is special legislation. The judge is human, and feels the bias which the coloring of the particular case gives. If he wishes to decide the next case differently, he has only to *distinguish*, and thereby make a new law. The legislature must act on general views, and prescribe at once for a whole class of cases.

No man can tell what the Common Law is; therefore it is not law: for a law is a rule of action; but a rule which is unknown can govern no man's conduct. Notwithstanding this, it has been called the perfection of human reason.

The Common Law is the perfection of human reason,— just as alcohol is the perfection of sugar. The subtle spirit of the Common Law is reason double distilled, till what was wholesome and nutritive becomes rank poison. Reason is sweet and pleasant to the unsophisticated intellect; but this sublimated perversion of reason bewilders, and perplexes, and plunges its victims into mazes of error.

The judge makes law, by extorting from precedents something which they do not contain. He extends his precedents, which were themselves the extension of others, till, by this accomodating principle, a whole system of law is built up without the authority or interference of the legislator.

The judge labors to reconcile conflicting analogies, and to derive from them a rule to decide future cases. No one knows what the law is, *before* he lays it down; for it does not exist even in the breast of the judge. All the cases carried up to the tribunal of the last resort, are capable of being argued, or they would not be carried there. Those which are not carried up are not law, for the Supreme Court might decide them differently. Those which are carried up, argued, and decided, might have been decided differently, as will appear from the arguments. It is, therefore, often optional with the judge to incline the balance as he pleases. In forty *per cent* of the cases carried up to a higher court, for a considerable term of years, terminating not long ago, the judgment was reversed. Almost any case, where there is any difference of opinion, may be decided either way, and plausible analogies found in the great storehouse of precedent to justify the decision. The law, then, is the final will or whim of the judge, after counsel for both parties have done their utmost to sway it to the one side or the other.

No man knows what the law is *after* the judge has decided it. Because, as the judge is careful not to decide any point which is not brought before him, he restricts his decision within the narrowest possible limits; and though the very next case that may arise may seem, to a superficial observer, and even upon a close inspection by an ordinary mind, to be precisely similar to the last, yet the ingenuity of a thorough-bred lawyer may detect some unsuspected shade of difference upon which an opposite decision may be founded. Great part of the skill of a judge consists in avoiding the direct consequences of a rule, by ingenious expedients and distinctions, whenever the rule would operate absurdly: and as an ancient maxim may be evaded, but must not be annulled, the whole system has been gradually rendered a labyrinth of apparent contradictions, reconciled by legal adroitness.

Statutes, enacted by the legislature, speak the public voice. Legislators, with us, are not only chosen because they possess the public confidence, but after their election, they are strongly influenced by public feeling. They must sympathize with the public, and express its will: should they fail to do so, the next year witnesses their removal from office, and others are selected to be the organs of the popular sentiment. The older portions of the Common Law are the work of judges, who held their places during the good pleasure of the king, and of course decided the law so as to suit the pleasure of the king. In feudal times it was made up of feudal principles, warped, to be sure, according to the king's necessities. Judges now are appointed by the executive, and hold their offices during good behavior,—that is, for life, and are consequently out of the reach of popular influence. They are sworn to administer Common Law as it came down from the dark ages, excepting what has been repealed by the Constitution and the statutes, which exception they are always careful to reduce to the narrowest possible limits. With them, wrong is right, if wrong has existed from time immemorial: precedents are every thing: the spirit of the age is nothing. And suppose the judge prefers the Common Law to the Constitutions of the State and of the Union; or decides in defiance of the statute; what is the remedy? An astute argument is always at hand to reconcile the open violation of that instrument with the express letter of the Constitution, as in the case of the United States Bank, —or to prove an obnoxious statute unconstitutional, as would have happened in the case of the Warren Bridge, but for the firmness of Judge Morton.[1] Impeachment is a bugbear, which has lost its terrors. We must have democratic governors, who will appoint democratic judges, and the whole body of the law must be codified.

It is said, that where a chain of precedents is found running back to a remote antiquity, it may be presumed that they originated in a statute which, through lapse of time, has perished. Unparalleled presumption this! To suppose the legislation of a barbarous age richer and more comprehensive than our own. It was without doubt a thousand times more barren. But what if there were such statutes? The specimens which have survived do not impress us with a favorable opinion of those that may have been lost. Crudely conceived, savage in their spirit, vague, indeterminate, and unlimited in their terms, and incoherent when regarded as parts of a system, the remains of ancient legislation are of little use at present, and what is lost was probably still more worthless. If such laws were now to be found in our statute book, they would be repealed at once; the innumerable judicial constructions which they might have received would not save them. Why then should supposed statutes, which probably never had any but an imaginary existence, which if they ever existed were the rude work of barbarians, which cannot now be ascertained, and if they could be, would be despised and rejected as bad in themselves, and worse for our situation and circumstances,—why should such supposed statutes govern, in the nineteenth century, the civilized and intelligent freemen of Massachusetts?

These objections to the Common Law have a peculiar force in America, because the rapidly advancing state of our country is continually presenting new cases for the decision of the judges; and by determining these as they arise, the bench takes for its share more than half of our legislation, notwithstanding the express provisions of the Constitution that the judiciary shall not usurp the functions of the legislature. If a Common Law system could be tolerable anywhere, it is only where every thing is stationary. With us, it is subversive of the fundamental principles of a free government, because it deposits in the same hands the power of first making the general laws, and then applying them to individual cases; powers distinct in their nature, and which ought to be jealously separated.

But even in England, Common Law is only a part of a system, which, as a whole, would be incomplete without *equity*. We strive to make the part supply the place of the whole. Equity is the correction of that wherein the law by reason of its generality is deficient; yet we have taken the law, deficient as it confessedly is, without the correction, except in certain cases, where by degrees, and almost without the knowledge of the people, equity powers have been given to the courts. A court of chancery would not be tolerated here, for reasons which I have not time to enter upon; and without that adjunct, the Common Law system would not be tolerated in England. The remedy is to fuse both into one mass, adopting such principles of equity as are really necessary, from time to time, supplying defects and omissions, as they are discovered. It is hardly necessary to observe, that in doing this, opportunity should be taken to reform and remodel the great body of the law, which stands in need of such a revision more than any other science. Some immense advances, it is true, have been made within the last two years, of which the total abolition of special pleading is not the least remarkable. But instead of being satisfied with what has been gained, it should only encourage us to step forward more boldly in what remains to do. All American law must be statute law.

NOTES

[1] Marcus Morton (1784–1864), associate justice of the Supreme Court of Massachusetts, 1825–40. The famous case of *Charles River Bridge* v. *Warren Bridge* arose out of an effort to break the "monopoly" held by Harvard College in receiving tolls for the only connection between Boston and Cambridge. The Warren Bridge was intended to be a free bridge. Daniel Webster was counsel for the monopoly. Judge Morton and one other colleague supported the Warren Bridge argument in the hearing of 1828. Morton was a Democrat, antislavery, champion of the laboring classes and of trade unions; hence he was much admired by Rantoul.

The case of the bridges was eventually carried to the Supreme Court, where the Warren Bridge won in 1837. This hearing is remarkable because, while Joseph Story dissented with the minority against Warren Bridge, the argument for it was delivered by Simon Greenleaf, Story's colleague in the Harvard Law School, who had become Royal Professor in 1833 upon the death of Ashmun. (The faculty still consisted of only two instructors in 1837.) What was at stake in the case appears in a letter Kent addressed to Story, congratulating him on his stand and deploring the majority decision: "It abandons, or overthrows, a great principle of constitutional morality, and I think goes to destroy the security and value of legislative franchises. It injures the moral sense of the community, and destroys the sanctity of contracts."

JAMES RICHARDSON (1771–1858)

AN ADDRESS DELIVERED BEFORE THE
MEMBERS OF THE NORFOLK BAR, AT
THEIR REQUEST, FEBRUARY 25, 1837

[While not known to be specifically a reply to Rantoul, Richardson's address is typical of the sort of treatment the "conservatives" meted out to him. The description of the lawyer who betrays the high moral standard of the profession and who then, instead of remaining the pure and moral dispenser of justice, becomes "the agitator of the passions of the vile" makes very clear that the deep division on codification had steadily widened. With the reign of "King Andrew,"—that is, President Andrew Jackson—the gulf became unbridgeable. Hence it is important to note Richardson's intensification of Story's theme that the ideal lawyer is a man of rigorous moral integrity and that he avoids the evils of small-minded partisanship by keeping up his literary (i.e., mainly classical) culture.

Richardson was born in Medfield, Massachusetts, and worked on a farm until he was twenty-one. He was largely self-educated, a "man of the people," not of the upper classes. Yet he managed to enter Harvard in 1793, graduating in 1797 and taking an M.A. in 1800. He read his law with Fisher Ames, which possibly explains why he became an almost fanatical, stoutly anti-democratic Federalist and Whig. He soon became, and to the end remained, the leading figure in the Norfolk County bar, serving as its president from 1822 to 1858. He also ventured into insurance, and made money. He was widely read in the classics and in eighteenth-century authors, but surprisingly enough, he enjoyed Byron.]

AN ADDRESS, 1837

Among nations where the mandate of the despot is the only rule of action, and every thing is disposed of according to his will, the investigation of questions of right and justice is superfluous, because unavailing; but where life, liberty and property are protected by standing laws, the construction and application of those laws, and the investigation of the numerous causes and questions arising under them, are closely connected with the security, tranquility and prosperity of the body politic; and under all such governments, the legal profession has had extensive influence;—the honest and able advocate has been respected, honored and rewarded, his opinions confided in, and his influence extended; and thus his duties have become more important, and more solemnly obligatory. He becomes responsible, not only for his legal opinions and professional conduct, but for the correctness of his moral and political course, and in some degree for the peace and tranquility of his neighborhood, and for the sentiments, principles and conduct of those of the circle in which he moves. From the nature of his pursuits, he has an opportunity, and indeed it is a part of his duty, to study the tempers, feelings, passions and prejudices of men in all ranks of society, and in all the various walks of life, and under all the influences of hope, fear, anger and interest; he may become instrumental in calling forth the noble and generous sentiments of our nature, as well as the sense of justice, love of truth, and desire to promote peace and tranquility in society; or instead of allaying and soothing, of exciting, the angry passions of litigants, of making himself the instrument of those passions, of operating upon their hopes and fears, upon their cupidity or spirit of revenge, and thus, instead of being the pure, elevated, moral, intellectual and social man, the dispenser of justice, the promoter of peace, the advocate of truth and protector of innocence, he may become the agitator of the passions of the vile, an instrument in the hands of the dishonest, and a "sower of discord among brethren."

In this view, of what immense importance it is, both to the professional individual and to society, that a foundation should be laid, early and deep, of all the virtues that dignify and adorn our nature, and restraint be put on all the passions and propensities that deform and degrade it. Let not then the young aspirant content himself with merely acquiring a knowledge of the forms of business in the courts, and a readiness and tact in the management of causes; but let him look, above and beyond this, to the deep foundation of the principles of the law, as bottomed on justice;—let him imbibe a reverence for truth, from which no influences can make him swerve; let him consider himself not merely the pupil of, but the fellow laborer in the cause of justice, with the great givers and expounders of the law, protectors of innocence and defenders of right, who have appeared in all ages and nations to adorn society and bless mankind. Animated with these views, and looking for encouragement, not to the applauses of the multitude, but to the confidence of the wise, the veneration of the good, and the approval of his own heart, he may pursue his course unfaltering. With this standard of action, this encouragement, and these hopes, he will acquaint himself with all the various arts, sciences and pursuits, which occupy civilized and social man,—trace the principles of the law to their sources,— pursue its history through all the changes in the state of society, ancient and modern; converse with the illustrious orators, statesmen and poets of all nations and ages; incorporate into his mind, heart and soul, their beauties, their graces, and their etherial spirit; adopt all the elegant proprieties of language, that give impulse and direction to the mind,—for language is the voice, and the wing and the rudder of thought,—and thus become, what every lawyer ought to be, the recipient and actual possessor of every excellence and grace, which perfect the orator, adorn the man and citizen, and render society secure, tranquil and happy. . . .

Among the lesser evils to which we, as a profession, are exposed, are the prejudices of the low, the vulgar and narrow minded, sometimes excited and inflamed by the wit of those better informed in mind, but not more elevated in spirit. That there are those occasionally creeping into the profession, who lie open to the censure of the high and the low, to the shaft of the witty, and to the contempt or commiseration of all; who are the "scourges of grammar," the "blunderbusses of law," and the panders of petty controversies, is not denied; but where is the justice of pointing the finger of scorn, or aiming the shaft of ridicule, at a whole profession, many of whom have been, and are the glory of their country,—the safe expounders of her laws, the guides of her councils, and the champions of her rights and liberties, because all its members are not learned, eloquent, sagacious, and honorable?

There are, however, other and superior classes of men, who hold, or pretend to hold, the legal profession in too low an estimation. These are theorists without practical knowledge, and practical men without theory;—those possessing general without particular knowledge, and those possessing particular without general knowledge. These contend that the study and practice of the law contract the mind, narrow the range of thought, induce a habit of attention to little things, incapacitate the intellect for large and liberal views, and for such an expansion as to take in all that appertains to great and important questions. This may be the case with those who practise the law as a trade, not study it as a science; who press into the practice without preparation—who have never explored the recesses of ancient mind, nor traced legal principles to their sources, to whom the past has afforded but little instruction, and the future can afford but little hope; but can the mind that has been conversant with the whole history of the law, including the history of men and nations,—enriched by the contemplation of all the beauties of thought and diction, that imagination and taste have originated and displayed in all ages, and disciplined by the conflicts of the forum, and the collision of mind with mind, where all its powers of imagination, memory and sagacity, have been employed to collect,—of discrimination to marshal, arrange and apply, every fact, reason and argument, that may avail to sustain his position—be contracted by attention to nice distinctions, and by weighing the reasons on both sides of the question? On the contrary, it is this very practice which tends to enlarge the mind, as well as to render it more acute and discriminating, and more capable of arriving at correct results.

The beautiful reveries of Plato, in his perfect Commonwealth, the fanciful and fascinating picture of Harrington, in his *Oceana*,[1] and of Bolingbroke in his *Patriot King*,[2] still serve to delight the imagination; and even the *Political Justice*[3] of Godwin is read with interest, as the production of a vigorous mind; but these are the productions of isolated intellect, of genius in the closet, of men perhaps equal in natural endowments to the great founders of our republican institutions, and the framers and expounders of our laws; and had their minds been disciplined in the same school, by conflicts with other powerful minds, instead of producing systems fitted only to entertain and amuse, they might have been among the distinguished instructors and benefactors of mankind.

There is also an evil incident to the members of our profession individually, and to which the gifted and eminent are most exposed; a malady, which no medicine can reach, and whose ravages the healing art hath been hitherto unable to arrest. It has its origin in the mysterious connection between the mind and the body, the physical and intellectual man—a connection, perceived and acknowledged by all, but beyond the power of mind fully to investigate. The faithful advocate soon becomes absorbed in the cause of his client,—the principles, the facts, and the legal deductions take entire possession of his mind; he

pours out his whole intellectual soul in the cause. The
client can find repose when the investigation is finished;
not so, in many instances, the advocate. Another cause
commands his attention before the traces of the former
have been obliterated. Sleep, that soothing power,

> That on the giddy mast, seals up the ship-boy's eyes,
> And steeps his senses in forgetfulness,

though wooed, can not be won. The intellectual triumphs
over the physical man,—the fine fibres of the brain, amid
which the wonder working power of thought resides, become attenuated by severe exertion; the whole frame feels
the shock; by extreme tension, "the silver cord is loosed,
the golden bowl is broken," and the too etherial spirit quits
its earthly abode forever! Witness the fate of Emmet, of
Pinkney, of the elder Webster, of Henry—and we may add
to the melancholy catalogue, when in the discharge of
their highest duties, our own revered Sewall[4] and Parker.[5]
Can this fatal termination of life be avoided? Can we
mitigate this immedicable malady? The discoveries of
modern times have not reached it; and we may look in
vain for a remedy in the libraries of the learned in the
healing art. Where then shall we go? Could the soul but
escape from its enthralment, and leaving the real world,
with all its exciting, and all its depressing and disturbing
cares, and enter the ideal, the world of imagination, with
all its glories and beauties, it might there find solace,
tranquility and repose. The remedy then, if remedy there
be, must be sought, not among the nostrums of the drug-
gists, nor the prescriptions of the skilful, but in the friendship of kindred spirits, and by the early cultivation of the
taste and imagination; by forming and perfecting a relish
for whatever is grand, beautiful and touching, in the natural and moral world, and a habit of flying from scenes
that exist, to scenes that may be shadowed forth; of holding communion with the muses, the fair daughters of memory and mind, whose high and holy office is to purify and
elevate the soul,—who scattered the blossoms of heaven,
wet with Castalian dew, over the spirits of a Mansfield, a

Blackstone, and a Jones, giving additional dignity and
purity to their manners, their thoughts, and their language,
and adding to their intellectual immortality a wreath of
celestial beauty, whose freshness and fragrance will endure
and charm forever.

To a soul thus disciplined, elevated and inspired, all creation and all time become tributary. He may inhale the first
breath of spring in the bowers of paradise,—sing with the
morning stars, call up and hold communion with the venerable shades of the instructors and benefactors of mankind, taste all the joys of friendship, and the communion of
kindred minds. Thus may we make all that the poet loves
subsidiary to the health of the mind; thus would the shades
of Parnassus refresh the spirit, and the fountains of Helicon
flow with the waters of life. . . .

The lawyer, like the poet, is not destined to opulence;
the streams of Pactolus lave not his dwelling,—and should
Jupiter again descend in a shower of gold, he would again
fall into the lap of some fortunate Danae, rather than into
the coffers of any modern Demosthenes. Like the bee, he
gathers honey, but not for himself:

Sic vos non vobis mellificatis apes[6]

is his motto. Yet aside from the rewards and honors of
exalted station, which but few can hope to attain, and
which are due only to great, and pure, and gifted minds,
disciplined by unremitting study and reflection; but which
are frequently usurped, and soiled, and degraded by the
artful intriguer, and selfish, hungry, hollow-hearted politician; he hath rewards and consolations proportioned to,
and coextensive with, his successful exertions to limit his
desires, purify his affections, discipline his mind, enlarge
his views, exalt his faculties, and employ them in the cause
of truth, justice and humanity. Though the world's honors
are not his portion, though he have sustained none of the
high and guiding offices of the State,—though he have
never ministered at the altar of justice, nor, like Moses, attended at the giving of the law,—though his exertions have

been confined to professional duties, though compelled by
the *"res angusta domi"*[7] to labor in the most burdensome
parts of the profession,—so that he might well exclaim,

> Hence it is that my life receives a brand,
> And hence almost my nature is subdued
> To what it works in, like a dyer's hand;

yet if he have holden fast his integrity—if he have sustained
his spirit, if he have exalted his feelings, and kept his soul
pure and free from the canker of avarice, the poison of un-
hallowed ambition, the leprosy of a love of popular applause, and the lubricity of political intrigue,—if he have
recognized and practised the obligation of every moral and
social duty,—if he have gathered and deposited in his mind
the rich gems of the gifted minds of all nations and ages,
interwoven them with, and made them his own treasures,
increased their richness and radiance by arranging and pol-
ishing them, and formed a taste for every thing beautiful
and grand in sentiment and in action, in nature and in art;
when the frosts of life's winter gather around him, when
the excitements of the forum and the collision of mind with
mind cease to animate, he will have rewards and consolations, that will render his days of retirement cheerful and
serene. Retrospection will present him with cases of fraudu-
lent arts detected, and innocence rescued from the snare;—
looking around him he may recognize some made more
prosperous by his advice, or more happy by his exertions,
and perhaps some made better by his example. In society,
and mingling with the friends of his earlier and brighter
years, he may dispense of his intellectual treasures, or by
interchange increase them—in solitude, regale himself with
the beauties of nature and art, for which he has formed a
relish—exercise his intellect in the contemplation of things
as yet unseen, or listen to the whisperings of faith and
hope;—nor need he

> Murmur though his fate shut out
> The gorgeous world's tumultuous din;
> He recks not of the world without,
> Who feels he bears his world within.

NOTES

[1] James Harrington (1611–77) published *Oceana* in 1656.

[2] Viscount Henry St. John Bolingbroke (1678–1751) composed *The Patriot King* in 1738; it was published in 1749.

[3] William Godwin (1756–1836) published *The Inquiry Concerning Political Justice, and its Influence on General Virtue and Happiness* in 1793.

[4] Jonathan Mitchell Sewall (1748–1808) eminent lawyer of Portsmouth, New Hampshire, whose career was sadly hampered by periods of ill-health brought on by overwork.

[5] Isaac Parker (1768–1830), Chief Justice of Massachusetts from 1814 to 1830, the moving spirit in the founding of Harvard Law School.

[6] Thus like the bees, you make honey not for yourselves.

[7] "Confined circumstances of the house."

TIMOTHY WALKER (1802–56)

INTRODUCTORY LECTURE ON THE DIGNITY OF THE LAW AS A PROFESSION, DELIVERED AT THE CINCINNATI COLLEGE, NOVEMBER 4, 1837

[Timothy Walker's address to the society of that Cincinnati which had been devastatingly ridiculed only five years before in Mrs. Trollope's *Domestic Manners of the Americans* (1832) is a splendid example of how lawyers trained in the East to worship the ideals of scholarship set forth by Mr. Justice Story carried with them into the crudity of the West a sense of mission. In Cincinnati, Walker dared to advocate codification. It may be, of course, that Walker was simply responding to the Western dislike of tradition. We should note that, on this topic, Story was never quite so hysterical as Kent. Story could see a value for codes in certain areas, such as maritime law. Walker, as he here reveals himself, is certainly no such radical as was Rantoul; on this occasion, at least, he derives consolation from the reflection that our lack of codes only makes the intellectual challenge to the lawyer that much more exhilarating.

Walker appears to be distinguishing and describing the various areas of the law—those to each of which Story would devote a massive *Commentary*—on the premise that this now established wisdom would come as fresh news to the rustics of Cincinnati. A great part of this tone must be discounted as merely another recitation of those obvious beauties of the law (when aesthetically considered), to which assemblies of jurists could in this period listen with unwearied delight. At the same time, more pointedly than in the usual encomiums uttered in the East, Walker takes care to explain how the law, though based upon man's social "nature," is perforce an "artificial" organism. (At this point, one is reminded for a moment of the Vermonter Chipman.) This point of view had to be propounded over and over in what were but recently frontier communities. Thus one may observe in this apparently artless address the art by which legalists subdued the "uprooted" peoples to at least a modicum of respect for order. Invoking the mighty names of the civil law, Walker demands that young Ohioans bow to the "moral sublimity" of the "law of nations," which probably seemed to his auditors to have nothing whatsoever to do with commerce on their spacious inland river.

Walker's parade of subdivisions within the empire of the law leads most understandably, therefore, to another denunciation of "pettifoggers," and finally to an adroit refutation of the obstinate popular prejudice against lawyers as such. Walker, like Story, constantly reinforces his argument with the admonition that the great lawyer, the moral being entrusted with an earthly (not heavenly) duty, must prove his virtue in this society of the West by immense labors, and by a profundity of study which in itself will silence the snarls of his opponents.

Timothy Walker was born in Wilmington, Massachusetts, of poor farm folk, like James Richardson. Like Richardson, too, he was mainly self-educated, gained admission to Harvard by a narrow margin, and became a leading scholar of that institution. He graduated in 1826, and for a few years taught with George Bancroft at the revolutionary school the latter endeavored to set up at Round Hill near Northampton. After this "transcendental" experiment he went to the Harvard Law School, there studied under Joseph Story and so may be said to be almost the first who carried the message directly from the lips of the master. He

migrated to Cincinnati in 1830 and was there admitted to
the bar. A private law school, which he organized in 1835,
became two years later a part of Cincinnati College. For
his first series of formal lectures he gave the one here ex-
cerpted as an inaugural. The complete sequence, entitled
Introduction to American Law, went through thirteen editions between 1837 and 1905; thousands of American lawyers were trained by it. Walker also edited with immense
distinction, and against formidable difficulties, *The Western Law Journal,* in which several articles seminal to the
jurisprudence of the nation were published.]

INTRODUCTORY LECTURE, 1837

I have said that the necessity for law grows out of man's
social nature. It contemplates him, not as a single, solitary
being, moving on alone to his final destination, but as making part of a vast multitude of similar beings, performing
their earthly career in company; and therefore requiring
numerous regulations to prevent convulsion. These regulations constitute the science of law, which it is my province
to expound. If men were angels, no such regulations would
be necessary. The eternal principles of right and wrong,
emblazoned by a revelation from on High, and applied by
a sleepless and unerring monitor within, would be all-suffi-
cient for their government; and they might be safely left
in that state of nature where their Creator left them. But
being men, and not angels, they require, in addition to the
restraints of religion and morality, the positive regulations
of municipal law. Society dares not leave the human will
in the same absolute freedom, in which God has left it;
but to the indirect sanctions of duty, has added the direct
sanctions of law.

And this consideration serves to designate the proper
scope of the science of which I speak. It is not a part of
religion or ethics, but is so much superadded to them both.
They commit an egregious error, who consider jurisprudence as looking forward into eternity. It begins and ends

with this world. It regards men only as members of civil society. It assists to conduct them from the cradle to the grave, as social beings; and there it leaves them to their final Judge. I would that this attribute of law were more generally appreciated. I say, then, that its proper voice from Heaven, or from the depths of the human soul, proclaimed another world beyond the present. Religion and morality embrace both time and eternity in their mighty grasp; but human laws reach not beyond the boundaries of time. As immortal beings, they leave men to their conscience and their God. And though this consideration may seem, at first view, to detract from their dignity, I rejoice at it as a consequence of our absolute moral freedom. I rejoice, that in this country, at least, government dares not interfere between man and his Creator; and that the blasphemous union between church and state, and the impious usurpation of Almighty jurisdiction, of which that union has so often been made the pretext, can never pollute our legal annals. I know no higher subject of congratulation, than the fact, that we have confined our legislators to their proper sphere; which is, to provide for our social welfare here on earth, and leave each to select his own pathway to immortality. But let me not be misunderstood. I do not say that human law has no concern with our moral condition; for it should do much to improve it. But why? Not because we are the subjects of future retribution; but because our social welfare, here on earth, is intimately connected with our moral condition. So far, then, as the dignity of the law depends upon the relation in which it contemplates man, I claim for it no more, than it would have had, if death, instead of being the introduction to another life, had been an eternal sleep. Even then, human laws would aim to make this brief existence as happy as possible; and this is all they now aim to do. Doubtless they succeed infinitely better now, from having the powerful aid of religion, which would then be wanting; but still their proper function remains the same. Having, then, ascertained the general relation, in which our profession contemplates man, let us consider some of the subjects which it presents for our study. If these be of an elevated character, the profession will be one of corresponding elevation, so far, at least, as its theory is concerned. The actual behavior of lawyers is indeed another and distinct matter. It is very possible that an eminent lawyer may be a debased man; for groveling conduct may co-exist with the most exalted studies. Even the religious profession has not always kept its votaries pure and spotless. Still I hope to show, in their proper order, that both the theory and practice of law are calculated to dignify and elevate the character; and that it is only in their perversion, that they fall short of this effect. I proceed, then, in the first place, to call your attention to some of the prominent subjects embraced in a course of legal study. To you, as to a jury, I will submit the facts, and then ask for your candid verdict. I would that I could so treat the subject as to excite your interest; but, for fear I shall fail in this, I will, at the outset, invoke your patience. The subject is grave, and I shall treat it with seriousness.

Beginning, then, with the aggregate of human beings, spread over the whole surface of the earth, the law first contemplates them as divided into distinct *nations;* each supreme within its own limits, and independent of every other, so long as there is ability to maintain this supremacy and independence. Yet these nations are not isolated and disconnected, like the inhabitants of different planets. They exist together on the same planet; and, therefore, like individuals, require rules to regulate their intercourse. These rules constitute the *law of nations,* which may be set down as the first and highest branch of jurisprudence. Passing over individuals, it deals only with sovereignties. It is, in fact, the gravitation of the social system, causing nations, like planets, to revolve in their proper orbits. What are the rights and duties of nations, in peace and in war, on the land and on the ocean?—These are the grave and solemn questions, which it is the province of the law of nations to answer. But it may be asked, what power there is to ordain laws for nations, which acknowledge no common government? There is no great international legislature—no general congress of nations. Whence, then, comes this

branch of law? I answer that nations, like individuals, are
bound to observe the immutable principles of natural justice; and these, accordingly, profess to form the basis of
the international code. But as nations might not, in all
cases, concur in the deductions to be drawn from these abstract principles, recourse is had to past usage; and the
doctrine is, that nations are bound by what custom has
settled. The law of nations, then, is a collection of usages
and precedents, dating back from the earliest historical
traditions, and gradually accumulating with the progress
of ages, until the aggregate has become a comprehensive
code of established law; the study of which, is of the highest interest, as well with reference to the nature of its inquiries, as to the dignity of the parties concerned. The con-
querors, and statesmen, and diplomatists, of all past time,
come up in review before the student; and he scrutinizes
their conduct amidst the lights which have been shed
around it, first, by philosophical historians, and, afterwards,
by the luminous minds of Grotius, Puffendorf, Vattel,
Burlamaqui, Mackintosh, our own Wheaton,[1] and other
distinguished commentators on this branch of jurisprudence. Moreover, there is high moral sublimity in the very
idea of associated millions, constituting the highest supremacy this side of Heaven, yet bound by laws, the observance of which is invited by the public opinion of the
whole civilized world, and the violation of which is sure
to be punished by the countless horrors of war; for such
are the awful sanctions which secure obedience to the law
of nations. The assembled world is the court in which this
law is adjudicated; and destroying armies are commis-
sioned to carry its sentence into execution. Who, then, will
question the dignity of this branch of legal study? Next to
religion, I know not that the human mind can employ itself in contemplations more interesting or sublime; and if
the law of nations be not as practical, as the branches
which follow, it certainly makes up in grandeur, what it
lacks in every day utility. When I have followed the great
masters in this science, through their profound disquisitions
upon national rights and obligations, I have felt reluctant to

descend from the heights to which they have conducted
me, and take up those questions which only involve the
concerns of individuals, however weighty these concerns
may be.

The next division of legal study, nearly allied to the preceding, grows out of the *conflict of laws* between different
nations; a subject upon which our distinguished jurist,
Judge Story, has recently given us a most learned commentary. No two nations have precisely the same internal laws.
On the contrary, the diversity is so great, as almost to occasion a doubt whether there be any thing like immutable
principles in jurisprudence. Now it results from the very
nature of sovereignty, that each nation, without reference
to extent, numbers, or situation, has unqualified supremacy
within its own limits. Hence no law, made in one nation,
can have force in another, without the consent of that
other. Yet, in the close and constant intercourse of nations,
it must often happen, that in deciding in one nation, upon
rights which originated under the law of another, complete
justice cannot be done, without recognizing the law of
that other. Here, then, is opened to the student a field of
research, at once extensive and interesting. When the *lex
loci*[2] and *lex fori*[3] come into conflict, in what cases shall
the right of sovereignty yield to *comity*, and one nation
recognize and enforce the law of another? If this be done
in all cases, sovereignty is shorn of half its beams; if not
done at all, the harmony of nations and the rights of individuals may be alike jeoparded. There must be, then, a
system of general rules, to determine when the law of the
place of adjudication shall prevail, and when not. Such
rules there are; and they are to be found in the treatises on
the conflict of laws. What was originally an open question,
addressed to the *comity* or good feeling of nations, is now
settled by precedent; and when the citizens of one nation,
remove to or travel in another, and make contracts, acquire
property, marry, or die there, it is no longer a matter of
doubt, by what law their rights will be determined. Thus,
the conflict of laws forms the second important and interesting branch of legal study. The mind becomes ele-

vated and expanded by the contemplation of great principles broadly applied. Human nature, too, presents itself under its most inviting aspect. The very idea that a branch of law has sprung up, from sacrificing the strict and imperative right of sovereignty to the accommodating principle of national comity, is in itself a subject of the most gratifying reflection. The ancient and barbarous notion that nations are natural enemies, and disposed, not merely to exact the last tittle of their rights, but also to do each other as much harm as possible, is shown to be a foul libel on the human race. The student finds, on the contrary, that the feelings of courtesy and benevolence are cherished with even greater constancy between neighboring nations, than between neighboring individuals; and he leaves the study with a higher opinion of his species, than he commenced with.

And now, having explored these two divisions of international law, the course of study brings the student home to his own hearth and fireside. For the rest, he is to investigate that internal or domestic law, by which the rights of his own fellow-citizens are regulated within the jurisdiction of his own country. He has descended from the height which overlooks the nations, to the vale which contains his most cherished hopes and interests. But here again, there are gradations in the dignity and importance of the different branches of legal study, which require to be noticed.

First of all is *constitutional law*, which, in this country, lies at the foundation of the social fabric. I say in this country, because it has been our glory to give the first example of a political organization based upon written constitutions. We hear much said, it is true, of the British constitution; but what is it? A mere collection of usages and precedents, gathered up in the progress of some twenty centuries, and subject to be modified or abrogated by the omnipotent will of a British Parliament. Not so with the American idea of a constitution. We understand by a constitution, a solemn written declaration of the sovereign will of the people, in their original capacity, as the highest earthly power, prescribing the form and limiting the powers

of the government, which they have thus voluntarily created. And this idea is as simple, as it is new and grand.
A sufficient number of people to form a nation, enter into a
compact for that purpose, and reduce the terms to writing.
That instrument is their constitution; in conformity with
which, as their organic and fundamental law, all other
laws are to be made, and all delegated powers executed.
But this primary idea of a constitution acquires some complexity from the peculiar organization of our political system. The people of the United States might have agreed to
form themselves into one consolidated government; and, in
that case, we should have had but a single constitution.
But, for a variety of reasons, they preferred state governments, united under a federal government. This renders
the department of constitutional law less simple, than it
would otherwise have been. For, in the first place, we
have the federal constitution, which speaks the sovereign
voice of all the people of the United States, and is supreme
over the subjects to which it extends; and next we have a
constitution for each State, which is subordinate to the
federal constitution, but supreme in all other respects. Notwithstanding, however, this double aspect of constitutional
law, it is still very far from being a difficult study; illustrated as it has been by the most able commentators. And
as to its dignity and importance, I presume there cannot
be two opinions on the subject. Whatever may be said
about subordinate branches, no American citizen can hesi-
tate about this. He can but poorly appreciate the freedom
he enjoys, who does not understand the great charter which
secures it. I was about to go further, and say, that he
does not deserve to be free, who will not inform himself in
what his freedom consists. But when I consider how many
of our citizens have no opportunity of studying our constitutions, for want of suitable provision in our seminaries
of learning, I forbear. At the same time, I rejoice that arrangements have been made for instruction in this branch,
in the academical department of this college. It speaks well
for the wisdom of those to whom its organization has been
committed. And I trust that no youth will be sent forth as a

graduate, who has not informed himself of his rights and duties, as a citizen of a free and constitutional government. I can assure him that he will find no knowledge more entirely gratifying, as well in the acquisition as in the future use. In Rome, had Rome been blessed with a constitution, instead of the law of the twelve tables, every citizen would have been required to know it by heart. And shall the many here, whose high prerogative it is to rule the few, leave the study of the constitution only to the few? Lawyers must study it, as the foundation of all other law; and shall not others study it, as the foundation of their liberty? I trust this disgrace is not always to attach to our systems of education. And, again, I congratulate this institution, that it has made provision for teaching constitutional law, as a branch of general education.

In the next place, having mastered the provisions of constitutional law, and thus laid firm and strong the foundations of the legal edifice, the student is prepared to commence the superstructure. He now understands the limits of delegated power. He has seen what laws may, and what laws may not be made; and how the permitted laws are made and administered. It remains, then, to inquire, what the existing laws do in fact provide? And in following out this inquiry, consists the chief labor of the student. Nor is it an easy task, which he proposes to himself. A stranger might think that this knowledge could be easily procured from a diligent perusal of our statutes. Adverting to the beautiful theory of our system, according to which a legislature is provided to make the laws necessary for our government, he might naturally conclude, that the acts of this legislature would comprise the entire body of our law, with the exception of what is embraced in our constitutions and treaties. Finding in these constitutions no other law-making power than the legislative department, the inference would be obvious, that we have no other internal laws, than our legislative acts. Were this, indeed, the fact, the law would be a simple and easy study. Could our whole law be found in our statute books, we might dispense with law schools, and almost with lawyers. In ordinary cases, every man might find for himself the law he wished to know, by a good index to the statute book. But what would that stranger say, if I should tell him, that although in our theory, the legislature makes our laws, yet, in fact, our legislative acts do not contain, perhaps, a fiftieth part of the law which governs us? I doubt not that he would be amazed at this discrepancy between our theory and practice. Yet, nevertheless, it exists. No where, in this country, is there to be found any thing approaching to a complete code of statute law. But, on the contrary, until very recently, those who have proposed measures for enlarging our codes, and thus gradually approximating them toward completion, have been sneered at, by the profession, as visionary schemers. Because the age so abounds in humbug, codification has been condemned as but another humbug; and the consequence is, that, up to this moment, the people of the United States are contented to live under a system of law, only a small fraction of which has ever received an express legislative sanction. But why should I complain? As it is, we have a profession embracing such a vast compass of study; so much of doubt and uncertainty; such a singular mixture of formality and technicality; so many curious and convenient fictions; and, at the same time, so many astonishing specimens of acute discrimination and profound logic, that when, by the persevering toil of years, we have at length climbed up into "the gladsome light of jurisprudence," we need feel no apprehension, lest every man should undertake to become his own lawyer, by doing what we have done. On the contrary, so long as our statute law shall be permitted to remain thus meager and imperfect, we may rest assured that the mass of our citizens, while they may find now and then a little law in the acts of our legislature, will be compelled to seek for a great deal in the heads of our lawyers. Whatever, therefore, may be my feelings, as a man and a citizen, as a lawyer, I am bound to rejoice in those difficulties of acquisition, which render our profession so arduous, so exclusive, so indispensable, and, therefore, so respectable. I would not be understood as saying that the most perfect

code of statute law would render this profession entirely
unnecessary; but it is quite evident, that, by rendering the
acquisition of the law more simple and expeditious, it
would tend to diminish the importance which at present
attaches to this profession.

And now, since the main body of our law is not to be
found in our legislative acts, the uninitiated may be disposed to ask whence it comes, and where it is to be found?
I will endeavor, briefly, to answer these questions. First,
then, there is what we call the *Common Law*. This is a
vast collection of judicial precedents, commencing with the
earliest glimmerings of English history, accumulating there
up to the present moment. These precedents are contained
in some hundreds of volumes of reports, embracing the decisions of all the English and American courts, which have
been reported; which decisions have been condensed, digested, abridged, and commented upon, in some hundreds
of volumes more, for the convenience of the profession.
And, next, there is the system of *equity* or *chancery law*,
which had its origin in the early deficiencies of the English
statutory and common law. This, like the other, consists of
judicial precedents, running through nearly the same lapse
of time, and contained in similar, though not quite so many
repositories. In round numbers, the books containing the
common and chancery law, including reports, digests,
abridgments, and commentaries, may be set down at one
thousand volumes. Now, even if all these precedents were
of the same binding force as legislative acts, so that when
you had once found a principle decided, you might rest
upon it as unquestionable law, it would still be a Herculean
labor to master the contents of so many volumes. But this
is not the fact. When you have found a precedent to suit
your case, you must look downward through all subsequent
reports to ascertain whether it has not been *overruled*. For
to avoid the evil of being bound absolutely by precedents
settled some hundreds of years ago, under an entirely different state of society, judges have been under the necessity of treating prior decisions, rather as lights to inform
their judgment, than as imperative rules to govern their

decisions. And hence the proverbial uncertainty of the law. In the first place, you may not find the precedent you want. If you do find one, it may turn out to have been overruled. And if not yet overruled, you have no assurance that it will not be overruled, in the very case before you. To say nothing, then of the imperfection of human language, which occasions ambiguity in written, as well as unwritten law; contact with each other, making it difficult to determine to which jurisdiction a given case belongs, there is enough in the very nature of Common and chancery Law, as above explained, to try the strength and tax the patience of the strongest and most resolute mind. To most of the sciences you may discern some limits—some stage, at which the mind may repose upon its acquisitions. But to jurisprudence, as at present constituted, I know not where the limits are. If the aged veteran, at the close of a long life of persevering labor, has been able to say to himself,—"I am perfect in the law,"—he has attained a condition, of which I cannot now even form a conjecture. I say not these things to discourage the student; for he can still do what others have done before him; and eminence in the profession does not mean perfection. But I speak thus, because the difficulties to be overcome, are what pre-eminently give dignity and importance to this profession. If reward is to be commensurate with toil, we deserve, at least, as much as any other profession. . . .

My object thus far has been, to demonstrate the dignity and importance of the legal profession, by hasty references to the various branches of law, to the sources of information, and to the subjects with which the law is conversant. If I have at all succeeded in this object, I have verified the declaration of Blackstone, that "the law employs in its theory the noblest faculties of the soul." He further declares, that "it exerts in its practice the cardinal virtues of the heart;" and this is what I shall now endeavor to demonstrate.

I begin then with the remark, that the employment of the lawyer is pre-eminently one of *trust* and *confidence*.

The *law* itself so regards it; for it exempts the lawyer from revealing what his client has confided to him, while it compels a disclosure even from a religious confessor. But what is still more to the purpose, *men* so regard it. The province of a lawyer is to vindicate rights and redress wrongs; and it is a high and holy function. Men come to him in their hours of trouble. Not such trouble as religion can solace, or medicine cure; but the trouble arising from innocence accused, confidence betrayed, reputation slandered, liberty assailed, property invaded, promises broken, the domestic relations violated, or life endangered. The guilty and the innocent, the upright and the dishonest, the wronging and the wronged, the knave and the dupe, alike consult him, and with the same unreserved confidence.

In the next place, the practice of law affords the best possible opportunity for the study of human nature. Indeed it has often occurred to me, that no diary could be more interesting and instructing, than that of an eminent lawyer's experience. Of what fearful secrets has he been the depository, when the murderer, the robber, or the incendiary, have been his clients. What a deep insight has he gained into the dark caverns of the human heart, from the plots, conspiracies, and stratagems, which have been laid open to his view. How have the fountains of sympathy swelled within him, at the discovery of wrongs for which he could find no adequate remedy. And what triumphant satisfaction has been his, when he has broken the proud oppressor's rod, or rescued innocence, wrongfully accused, from the grasp of avenging justice. It is not given to man to see the human heart completely unveiled before him. But the lawyer perhaps comes more nearly to this, than any other; for there is no aspect in which the character does not present itself, in his secret consultations. All the passions, all the vices, and all the virtues, are by turns subjected to his scrutiny. He thus studies human nature, in its least disguised appearances; and his diary therefore would furnish its most authentic history. He has watched it under all trials; in the light and in the shade, in ecstasy and in despair, in glory and in shame. But his diary may not be pub-

lished. His secrets must be buried with him. His honor is
pledged never to violate professional confidence. Otherwise
he could a tale unfold, compared with which all fictions
would be stale and vapid.

But let us leave his *office,* and pursue him to the *forum.*
Here is his field of triumph and renown, or of defeat and
shame. Here he meets his antagonist, in the sharp en-
counter of wit, reasoning, and persuasion. He has pledged
his best exertions to his client; he has a liberal compensation in prospect or possession; and his reputation is at stake
in the result of the cause. Here then is every incentive to
eloquence, and every opportunity to display it. He is in
the field where the great advocates who have gone before
him, have won their laurels. He speaks indeed to *convince*
the court, and *persuade* the jury. But a listening crowd
are hanging upon his accents, and making up a verdict for
or against himself. And above all, his client is there, intently
watching every word and gesture, because on them are sus-
pended all he holds dear. But the argument is finished, the
charge is given, and the jury have retired: all is deep silence, and trembling expectation. The jury return; their
verdict is pronounced—the client is acquitted. And the advocate—but who shall describe his feelings? There are no
words to depict moments like this. The approbation of the
bench, the applause of the crowd, the gratitude of the
client, the admiration of all, even of the antagonist himself,
conspire to make such moments the most intensely gratifying, which mortals can know.

At length we follow the successful lawyer, from the bar,
to the bench. The counsellor has at last become the judge.
The topmost round of the ladder is now reached. And here
all the high qualities of his nature are called into exercise.
The sagacity which cannot be misled by sophistry; the integrity which nothing can shake or bribe; the stern im-
partiality, which forgets the parties and looks only at the
cause; the dignified courtesy, which rebukes levity, while
it wins respect: these are the qualities, without which all
the learning of a Coke would not make a worthy judge;
and which no where shine so conspicuously as from the

bench. Of the power which belongs to the judicial office, of the all-pervading influence exerted by a Mansfield or a Marshall, for example, I need not here speak. Such men live in their decisions, through all coming time. These decisions go to swell the great aggregate of common law, and thus determine the rights of generations yet unborn.

Nor is it to the judicial office alone that the lawyer may aspire. His studies pre-eminently fit him for every civil office. In the halls of legislation, he must ever occupy a conspicuous place, because no man is so well prepared to suggest and frame new laws, as he who knows what the existing laws contain. It is a well known fact, that from the days of the revolution down to the present time, no single class of the community has performed so much of the public service of the country, as the members of this profession. I do not mention this as a motive to study law, but as a proof of the estimation in which the profession has been held. As a motive I should rather hold it in contempt. I know not a greater vice of the times, than the all prevalent hankering after office. It is degrading alike to electors and elected. The old idea was, that office should seek the man; now the man seeks the office; and he descends to the most humiliating compliances in order to obtain it. I of course have no reference to any party or set of men, for the evil prevails universally. Men seem to forget their self respect, when they seek honor from office; as if that which is factitious, could alter that which is inherent in the man. But this is a digression. I would hold up the legal profession, as an end in itself, not as a stepping stone to something higher. In fact there is nothing higher. He who stands at the head of this profession, is on a level with the most elevated in the land; and instead of owing his eminence to the solicited suffrages of others, he has the proud satisfaction of having achieved it for himself.

Nor is this all. If such be the influence of the profession, in calm and peaceful times, what must it not be, when the elements of society are thrown into unwonted commotion? Hitherto, indeed, since the formation of our government, the political horizon has been comparatively calm. There have been some threatening clouds now and then, but no destroying tempests. In the main, the fundamental rights of men have been scrupulously respected, and the laws duly observed and administered. A learned bench, and an upright bar, have quietly preserved the order of the system, while the busy and protected public have hardly felt their influence. But imagine a reverse; for it is at least possible, and the enemies of free government are loudly predicting it. We are trying the greatest political experiment the world ever witnessed; and the experience of all history warns us not to feel too secure. A voice from the tombs of all the departed republics tells us, that if our liberty is to be ultimately preserved, it is at the price of sleepless vigilance. I refer not to foreign aggression, for of this we have nothing to fear; our only foes are those of our own household. Domestic aggression may come from two quarters; from those who govern, or from those who are governed. On the one hand, power is always tending to augmentation. Those who have some, employ it to gain more; and if not seasonably withstood, become too strong to be resisted. And on the other hand, liberty is always tending towards licentiousness. The more men have, the more they are likely to want. Being free from many restraints, they would do away with all. We have had recent symptoms of this alarming tendency. The sacred landmarks of law have been torn down by mobs, and temporary anarchy has gained the ascendant. Now when dangers threaten, from either of these quarters,—when rulers would trample the law under their feet, or mobs would rise to overthrow it,—who are the sentinels to give the alarm? Do I assume too much, in saying, society looks with confidence to that class of men, whose profession it is to watch over the law? No: their station is on the watch towers of society, and they will be the first to sound the tocsin. Nor will they stop there. They will argue for the law, while argument will avail; they will fight for it, when reasoning is silenced; and when its supremacy can no longer be maintained, they will not survive its downfall.

We have now followed the lawyer through his whole career of study, practice, and distinction. Rising with the dawn, and trimming assiduously the midnight lamp, we have seen him exploring the law of nations, the conflict of laws, constitutional law, the law of persons, the law of property, the law of crimes, and the law of procedure; and for this purpose, ransacking the precedents of all ages, to supply the immense chasms in actual legislation. Having thus stored his mind with the vast and various lore of jurisprudence, we have seen him in secret consultation with his clients, contending at the bar, deciding from the bench, and filling the high places in his country's service. And now what say you? Is the legal profession dignified, or not?

But methinks I hear some one whisper, that one side only has been heard. I am well aware that there are prejudices against the profession. It is said to abound with pettifoggers, who pervert the law to the purposes of knavery; with quacks, who sacrifice their clients through their ignorance; and with needy hangers-on, who will foment lawsuits, rather than not have them. Lawyers are said to delight in tricks, stratagems, and chicanery; to argue as strenuously for the wrong as for the right, for the guilty as for the innocent; and to hire out their conscience, as well as their skill, to any client who will pay the fee. What shall be said to these charges? I, for one, am willing to admit their truth, to some extent. Our profession abounds with opportunities and temptations to abuse its high functions; and it would be strange indeed, if it had not some unworthy members. We lay no claim to superhuman virtue. We see unworthy members in every other profession, and therefore take no shame to ourselves that they are sometimes to be found in ours. Besides, we take refuge behind the principle, that supply corresponds to demand. If there were no dishonest or knavish clients, there would be no dishonest or knavish lawyers. Our profession, therefore, does but adapt itself to circumstances; and it depends upon the community, whether it shall be elevated or degraded; or rather, in what degree it shall incline one way or the other: for there is no bar, any where, which has not its ornaments, as well as blemishes; and these must be well known to the community. We stand conspicuously before the public eye. At first our reputation may be limited to the town in which we live; anon it extends through the county; at length, if we continue to rise, we become known throughout the state; and finally, to a select few it occurs, to be celebrated throughout the country, and perhaps throughout the world. But the leading idea I would convey is, that there need be no deception or mistake about a lawyer's standing. If therefore clients will employ those who are unworthy, they do it with their eyes open, and have no right to find fault with the profession in general.

I have thus far confined myself to facts: but perhaps you may be influenced by the *opinions* of great men. I have already quoted the declaration of Blackstone, that "the law employs in its theory the noblest faculties of the soul, and exerts in its practice the cardinal virtues of the heart." Burke, in one place, declares the law to be, "the pride of the human intellect, and the collected wisdom of ages; combining the principles of original justice, with the boundless variety of human concerns." And in another— "one of the first and noblest of human sciences; a science which does more to quicken and invigorate the under-standing, than all other kinds of learning put together." Sir William Jones says: "If law be indeed a science, and really deserve so sublime a name, it must be founded on principle, and claim an exalted rank in the empire of rea-son." But, like the great Mansfield and Blackstone, he was a poet, as well as a lawyer; and he thus poetically eulogizes his favorite theme:

> And sovereign LAW, the world's collected will,
>   O'er thrones and globes elate,
> Sits Empress—crowning good, repressing ill;
>   Smit by her sacred frown,
> The fiend DISCRETION, like a vapor, sinks;
>   And e'en the all-dazzling crown
> Hides his faint rays, and at her bidding shrinks.

And now, in professional phrase, the case is with you. Let it not suffer for want of an abler advocate. The leading impression I desire to leave upon your minds is, that lawyers, as a class, deserve all they obtain, whether of honor or emolument. Let no man, therefore, enter the profession as a sinecure. Genius, without toil, may, to some extent, distinguish a man elsewhere; but here he must labor, or he cannot succeed. No quickness of invention can supply the place of patient investigation. A clear mind might determine at once what the law ought to be, but actual inspection alone can determine what the law is. Let those, therefore, who would prepare themselves "for untying the knots and solving the enigmas of jurisprudence," first of all make up their minds to hard work. Let them weigh well the fact, that, "to scorn delights and live laborious days," is the indispensable condition of professional eminence. On somewhat easier terms they may prepare themselves "to prowl in courts of law for human prey;" but nothing short of resolute, emulous, persevering study, can raise them to that height, which alone should satisfy a generous ambition. And for their solace, let them also remember, that nothing great or good, in any calling, was ever achieved without corresponding effort.

> It was not by vile loitering in ease,
> That Greece obtained the brightest palm of art;
> That soft, yet ardent Athens learned to please,
> To keen the wit, and to sublime the heart—
> In all supreme, complete in every part!
> It was not thus majestic Rome arose,
> And o'er the nations shook her conquering dart:
> For sluggard's brow the laurel never grows;
> Renown is not the child of indolent repose.

NOTES

[1] Henry Wheaton (1785–1848), reporter for the United States Supreme Court, 1816–27, published *Elements of International Law* in 1836.

[2] Law of the place.

[3] Law of the court.

RUFUS CHOATE (1799–1859)

THE POSITION AND FUNCTIONS OF THE AMERICAN BAR, AS AN ELEMENT OF CONSERVATISM IN THE STATE: AN ADDRESS DELIVERED BEFORE THE LAW SCHOOL IN CAMBRIDGE, JULY 3, 1845

[By no possible exercise of the imagination can we conceive that Rufus Choate would ever have followed Timothy Walker into the wilderness of Ohio. He was born—in all respects even more than either Story or Webster—for conservative, Whig New England. His conception of conservative nationalism—a word he stressed in the published title of this address—was so powerful, that after three decades of intense hatred of Jackson and his successors, he went over to the Democrats in 1856 and supported Buchanan, in a last desperate effort to preserve the Union according to the only lights by which he could see any hope for its survival.

Choate's final action, followed by what apparently was a flight from the whole mess (he died in Nova Scotia while on the way to England) may, I believe, be taken as symbolic of the fate of a large portion of the "conservative" bar in the confusing decades before the outbreak of hostilities in 1861. Choate, as the disciple of Story and Kent, was a scholar in the law, and supplemented his erudition by immense readings in Greek and Latin. He was dedicated, heeding their instruction, to the terrible task of curbing the democratic anarchy by the majestic power of the law. He went to pieces when the issue which forced itself upon him, as on all the lawyers, proved to be not that of mob vs. intrenched property, but that of utterly irrational and illegal conflict within the profession itself.

Rufus Choate was born in Essex, Massachusetts, and from childhood exhibited a precocious intellect. He was sent to Dartmouth rather than Harvard, and in the year of his graduation, 1819, his ears were ringing with the peroration of Daniel Webster's argument in the Dartmouth College Case. He resolved on the spot that he would learn to orate in Webster's vein; this ambition he more than accomplished.

Choate attended the Harvard Law School, but also read with William Wirt in Washington. He was admitted to the bar at Ipswich in 1822, and at Boston in 1834. He was the most successful pleader of his day. A large man, of immense energy, omnivorous reading, terrific presence, he was a master of cross-examination, and a stupendous forensic orator. He could have had a judgeship for the asking, and was several times offered a professorship; he preferred the arena. He did serve in Congress, 1830–32, and part of a term in the Senate, 1841–45; but these he regarded as distractions from his true calling, which was trying and winning cases in court. All through this period, he hated Jackson and excoriated Abolitionists.

This address, pronounced to the Harvard Law School in 1845, is as much as any in the volume self-explanatory. Yet I must again point out, as evidenced therein, that the victory of the learned profession over the recalcitrant populace was but barely being won when the political issue cast its dire shadow over the happy assumptions of the Kent and Story school of thought. They may have felt, with justified complacency, that by 1845 (the year of Story's death) the voice of Grayson was silenced in the land; but they had still not disposed of the challenge of codification when they were called upon to invoke the law, which they had so eloquently celebrated as the sole instrument of social cohesion, to prevent a conflict with which the law by itself proved incompetent to deal.

Possibly the most remarkable element in this forthright utterance is Choate's appreciation that in America the "conservative" position has nothing in common with that of English or European conservatives, that from their point of view it is indeed still radical. Otherwise, one can but admire the progression by which he works out of this form of Americanism an impassioned plea for the preservation of everything which has already been decided, constructing finally what seems to him a conclusive argument against any and every fantasy of a code.]

THE POSITION AND FUNCTIONS OF THE AMERICAN BAR, 1845

Let me premise, too, that instead of diffusing myself in a display of all the modes by which the profession of the law may claim to serve the State, I shall consider but a single one, and that is its agency as an element of conservation. The position and functions of the American Bar, then, as an element of conservation in the State,—this precisely and singly is the topic to which I invite your attention.

And is not the profession such an element of conservation? Is not this its characteristical office and its appropriate praise? Is it not so that in its nature, in its functions, in the intellectual and practical habits which it forms, in the opinions to which it conducts, in all its tendencies and influences of speculation and action, it is and ought to be professionally and peculiarly such an element and such an agent,—that it contributes, or ought to be held to contribute, more than all things else, to preserve our organic forms, our civil and social order, our public and private justice, our constitutions of government,—even the Union itself? In these crises through which our liberty is to pass, may not, must not, this function of conservatism become more and more developed, and more ar͏͏ ͏͏re operative?

May it not one day be written, for the praise of the American Bar, that it helped to keep the true idea of the State alive and germinant in the American mind; that it helped to keep alive the sacred sentiments of obedience and reverence and justice, of the supremacy of the calm and grand reason of the law over the fitful will of the individual and the crowd; that it helped to withstand the pernicious sophism that the successive generations, as they come to life, are but as so many successive flights of summer flies, without relations to the past or duties to the future, and taught instead that all—all the dead, the living, the unborn—were one moral person,—one for action, one for suffering, one for responsibility,—that the engagements of one age may bind the conscience of another; the glory or the shame of a day may brighten or stain the current of a thousand years of continuous national being? Consider the profession of the law, then, as an element of conservation in the American State. I think it is naturally such, so to speak; but I am sure it is our duty to make and to keep it such. . . .

In proceeding to this, I think I may take for granted that conservatism is, in the actual circumstances of this country, the one grand and comprehensive duty of a thoughtful patriotism. I speak in the general, of course, not pausing upon little or inevitable qualifications here and there,—not meaning anything so absurd as to say that this law, or that usage, or that judgment, or that custom or condition, might not be corrected or expunged,—not meaning still less to invade the domains of moral and philanthropic reform, true or false. I speak of our general political system; our organic forms; our written constitutions; the great body and the general administration of our jurisprudence; the general way in which liberty is blended with order, and the principle of progression with the securities of permanence; the relation of the States and the functions of the Union,—and I say of it in a mass, that conservation is the chief end, the largest duty, and the truest glory of American statesmanship.

There are nations, I make no question, whose history,
condition, and dangers call them to a different work. There
are those whom every thing in their history, condition, and
dangers admonishes to reform fundamentally, if they would
be saved. With them the whole political and social order
is to be rearranged. The stern claim of labor is to be provided for. Its long antagonism with capital is to be reconciled. Property is all to be parcelled out in some nearer
conformity to a parental law of nature. Conventional discriminations of precedence and right are to be swept away.
Old forms from which the life is gone are to drop as
leaves in autumn. Frowning towers nodding to their fall
are to be taken down. Small freeholds must dot over and
cut up imperial parks. A large infusion of liberty must be
poured along these emptied veins and throb in that great
heart. With those, the past must be resigned; the present
must be convulsed, that "an immeasurable future," as Car-
lyle has said, "may be filled with fruitfulness and a verdant shade."

But with us the age of this mode and this degree of reform is over; its work is done. The passage of the sea, the
occupation and culture of a new world, the conquest of
independence,—these were our eras, these our agency, of
reform. In our jurisprudence of liberty, which guards our
person from violence and our goods from plunder, and
which forbids the whole power of the State itself to take
the ewe lamb, or to trample on a blade of the grass of the
humblest citizen without adequate remuneration; which
makes every dwelling large enough to shelter a human life
its owner's castle which winds and rain may enter but
which the government cannot,—in our written constitutions,
whereby the people, exercising an act of sublime self-re-
straint, have intended to put it out of their own power for
ever, to be passionate, tumultuous, unwise, unjust; whereby they have intended, by means of a system of representation; by means of the distribution of government
into departments, independent, coordinate for checks and
balances; by a double chamber of legislation; by the
establishment of a fundamental and paramount organic

law; by the organization of a judiciary whose function, whose loftiest function it is to test the legislation of the day by this standard for all time,—constitutions, whereby by all these means they have intended to secure a government of laws, not of men; of reason, not of will; of justice, not of fraud,—in that grand dogma of equality, equality of right, of burthens, of duty, of privileges, and of chances, which is the very mystery of our social being,—to the Jews, a stumbling block; to the Greeks, foolishness,—our strength, our glory,—in that liberty which we value solely because it is a principle of individual energy and a guaranty of national renown; not at all because it attracts a procession and lights a bonfire, but because, when blended with order, attended by law, tempered by virtue, graced by culture, it is a great practical good; because in her right hand are riches, and honor, and peace; because she has come down from her golden and purple cloud to walk in brightness by the weary ploughman's side, and whisper in his ear as he casts the seed with tears, that the harvest which frost and mildew and canker-worm shall spare, the government shall spare also; in our distribution into separate and kindred States, not wholly independent, not quite identical, in "the wide arch of the ranged empire" above, —these are they in which the fruits of our age and our agency of reform are embodied; and these are they by which, if we are wise,—if we understand the things that belong to our peace,—they may be perpetuated. It is for this that I say the fields of reform, the aims of reform, the uses of reform here, therefore, are wholly unlike the fields, uses, and aims of reform elsewhere. Foreign examples, foreign counsel,—well or ill meant,—the advice of the first foreign understandings, the example of the wisest foreign nations, are worse than useless for us. Even the teachings of history are to be cautiously consulted, or the guide of human life will lead us astray. We need reform enough, Heaven knows; but it is the reformation of our individual selves, the bettering of our personal natures; it is a more intellectual industry; it is a more diffused, profound, and graceful, popular and higher culture; it is a wider develop-

ment of the love and discernment of the beautiful in form,
in color, in speech, and in the soul of man,—this is what we
need,—personal, moral, mental reform,—not civil—not political! No, no! Government, substantially as it is; jurisprudence, substantially as it is; the general arrangements
of liberty, substantially as they are; the Constitution and
the Union, exactly as they are,—this is to be wise, according
to the wisdom of America. . . .

It is one of the distemperatures to which an unreasoning
liberty may grow, no doubt, to regard *law* as no more nor
less than just the will—the actual and present will—of the
actual majority of the nation. The majority govern. What
the majority pleases, it may ordain. What it ordains is
law. So much for the source of law, and so much for
the nature of law. But, then, as law is nothing but the will
of a major number, as that will differs from the will of
yesterday, and will differ from that of to-morrow, and as
all law is a restraint on natural right and personal independence, how can it gain a moment's hold on the reveren-
tial sentiments of the heart, and the profounder convictions
of the judgment? How can it impress a filial awe; how can
it conciliate a filial love; how can it sustain a sentiment of
veneration; how can it command a rational and animated
defence? Such sentiments are not the stuff from which the
immortality of a nation is to be woven! Oppose now to this
the loftier philosophy which we have learned. In the language of our system, the law is not the transient and arbitrary creation of the major will, nor of any will. It is not
the offspring of will at all. It is the absolute justice of the
State, enlightened by the perfect reason of the State. That
is law. Enlightened justice assisting the social nature to
perfect itself by the social life. It is ordained, doubtless,
that is, it is chosen, and is ascertained by the wisdom of
man. But, then, it is the master-work of man. *Quae est
enim istorum oratio tam exquisita, quae sit anteponenda
bene constitutae civitati publico jure, et moribus?*[1]

By the costly and elaborate contrivances of our constitutions we have sought to attain the transcendent result of

extracting and excluding haste, injustice, revenge, and folly from the place and function of giving the law, and of introducing alone the reason and justice of the wisest and the best. By the aid of time,—time which changes and tries all things; tries them, and works them pure,—we subject the law, after it is given, to the tests of old experience, to the reason and justice of successive ages and generations, to the best thoughts of the wisest and safest of reformers. And then and thus we pronounce it good. Then and thus we cannot choose but reverence, obey, and enforce it. We would grave it deep into the heart of the undying State. We would strengthen it by opinion, by manners, by private virtue, by habit, by the awful hoar of innumerable ages. All that attracts us to life, all that is charming in the perfected and adorned social nature, we wisely think or we wisely dream, we owe to the all-encircling presence of the law. Not even extravagant do we think it to hold, that the Divine approval may sanction it as not unworthy of the reason which we derive from His own nature. Not extravagant do we hold it to say, that there is thus a voice of the people which is the voice of God.

Doubtless the known historical origin of the law contributes to this opinion of it. Consider for a moment—what that law really is, what the vast body of that law is, to the study and administration of which the lawyer gives his whole life, by which he has trained his mind, established his fortune, won his fame, the theatre of all his triumphs, the means of all his usefulness, the theme of a thousand earnest panegyrics,—what is that law? Mainly, a body of digested rules and processes and forms, bequeathed by what is for us the old and past time, not of one age, but all the ages of the past,—a vast and multifarious aggregate, some of which you trace above the pyramids, above the flood, the inspired wisdom of the primeval East; some to the scarcely yet historical era of Pythagoras, and to Solon and Socrates; more of it to the robust, practical sense and justice of Rome, the lawgiver of the nations; more still to the teeming birthtime of the modern mind and life; all of it to some epoch; some of it to every epoch of the past of which history keeps the date. In the way in which it comes down to us, it seems one mighty and continuous stream of experience and reason, accumulated, ancestral, widening and deepening and washing itself clearer as it runs on, the grand agent of civilization, the builder of a thousand cities, the guardian angel of a hundred generations, our own hereditary laws. To revere such a system, would be natural and professional, if it were no more. But it is reasonable, too. There is a deep presumption in favor of that which has endured so long. To say of any thing, that it is old, and to leave the matter there,—an opinion, a polity, a code, a possession, a book,—is to say nothing of praise or blame. But to have lived for ages; to be alive to-day,—in a real sense alive,—alive in the hearts, in the reason of to-day; to have lived through ages, not swathed in gums and spices and enshrined in chambers of pyramids, but through ages of unceasing contact and sharp trial with the passions, interests, and affairs of the great world; to have lived through the drums and tramplings of conquests, through revolution, reform, through cycles of opinion running their round; to have lived under many diverse systems of policy, and have survived the many transmigrations from one to another; to have attended the general progress of the race, and shared in its successive ameliorations,—thus to have gathered upon itself the approbation or the sentiments and reason of all civilization and all humanity,—that is, *per se*, a *prima-facie* title to intelligent regard. There is a virtue, there is truth, in that effacing touch of time. It bereaves us of our beauty; it calls our friends from our side, and we are alone; it changes us, and sends us away. But spare what it spares. Spare till you have proved it. Where that touch has passed and left no wrinkle nor spot of decay, what it has passed and left ameliorated and beautified, whatever it be, stars, sea, the fame of the great dead, the State, the law, which is the soul of the State, be sure that therein is some spark of an immortal life.

It is certain that in the American theory, the free theory of government, it is the right of the people, at any moment of its representation in the legislature, to make all the law, and, by its representatives in conventions, to make the Constitution anew. It is their right to do so peaceably and according to existing forms, and to do it by revolution against all forms. This is the theory. But I do not know that any wise man would desire to have this theory every day, or ever, acted upon up to its whole extent, or to have it eternally pressed, promulgated, panegyrized as the grand peculiarity and chief privilege of our condition. Acting upon this theory, we have made our constitutions, founded our policy, written the great body of our law, set our whole government going. It worked well. It works to a charm. I do not know that any man displays wisdom or common sense, by all the while haranguing and stimulating the people to change it. I do not appreciate the sense or humanity of all the while bawling: true, your systems are all good; life, character, property, all safe,—but you have the undoubted right to rub all out and begin again. If I see a man quietly eating his dinner, I do not know why I should tell him that there is a first-rate, extreme medicine, prussic acid, aquafortis, or what not, which he has a perfectly good right to use in any quantity he pleases! If a man is living happily with his wife, I don't know why I should go and say: yes, I see; beautiful and virtuous; I congratulate you,—but let me say, you can get a perfectly legal divorce by going to Vermont, New Jersey, or Pennsylvania. True wisdom would seem to advise the culture of dispositions of rest, contentment, conservation. True wisdom would advise to lock up the extreme medicine till the attack of the alarming malady. True wisdom would advise to place the power of revolution, overturning all to begin anew, rather in the background, to throw over it a politic, well-wrought veil, to reserve it for crises, exigencies, the rare and distant days of great historical epochs. These great, transcendental rights should be preserved, must be, will be. But perhaps you would place them away, reverentially, in the profoundest recesses of the chambers of the dead, down in deep vaults of black marble, lighted by a single silver lamp,—as in that vision of the Gothic king,—to which wise

and brave men may go down, in the hour of extremity, to
evoke the tremendous divinities of change from their sleep
of ages.

*Ni faciat, maria, ac terras, coelumque profundum
Quippe ferant rapidi secum, verrantque per auras.*[2]

To appreciate the conservative agency and functions of
the legal profession, however, it is time to pass from an
analysis of the sentiments and opinions which distinguish it,
to the occupation by which it is employed. The single labor
of our lives is the administration of the law; and the topic
on which I wish to say a word in conclusion is, the influence
of the actual administration of law in this country on the
duration of our free systems themselves. The topic is large
and high, and well deserves what I may not now attempt,
a profound and exact discussion.

I do not know that in all the elaborate policy by which
free States have sought to preserve themselves, there is
one device so sure, so simple, so indispensable, as justice,
—justice to all; justice to foreign nations of whatever class
of greatness or weakness; justice to public creditors, alien
or native; justice to every individual citizen, down to the
feeblest and the least beloved; justice in the assignment
of political and civil right, and place, and opportunity; justice between man and man, every man and every other,
—to observe and to administer this virtue steadily, uniformly, and at whatever cost,—this, the best policy and the
final course of all governments, is pre-eminently the policy
of free governments. Much the most specious objection to
free systems is, that they have been observed in the long
run to develop a tendency to some mode of injustice. Resting on a truer theory of natural right in their constitutional
construction than any other polity, founded in the absolute and universal equality of man, and permeated and
tinged and all astir with this principle through all their
frame, and, so far, more nobly just than any other, the
doubt which history is supposed to suggest is, whether
they do not reveal a tendency towards injustice in other
ways. Whether they have been as uniformly true to their

engagements. Whether property and good name and life have been quite as safe. Whether the great body of the *jus privatum*[3] has been as skilfully composed and rigorously administered as under the less reasonable and attractive systems of absolute rule. You remember that Aristotle, looking back on a historical experience of all sorts of governments extending over many years—Aristotle who went to the court of Philip, a republican, and came back a republican—records, in his Politics, *injustice* as the grand and comprehensive cause of the downfall of democracies. The historian of the Italian democracies extends the remark to them. That all States should be stable in proportion as they are just, and in proportion as they administer justly, is what might be asserted.

If this end is answered; if every man has his own exactly and uniformly, absolutism itself is found tolerable. If it is not, liberty—slavery, are but dreary and transient things. *Placida quies sub libertate*,[4] in the words of Algernon Sydney and of the seal of Massachusetts,—that is the union of felicities which should make the State immortal. Whether Republics have usually perished from injustice, need not be debated. One there was, the most renowned of all, that certainly did so. The injustice practised by the Athens of the age of Demosthenes upon its citizens, and suffered to be practised by one another, was as marvellous as the capacities of its dialect, as the eloquence by which its masses were regaled, and swayed this way and that as clouds, as waves,—marvellous as the long banquet of beauty in which they revelled,—as their love of Athens, and their passion of glory. There was not one day in the whole public life of Demosthenes when the fortune, the good name, the civil existence of any considerable man was safer there than it would have been at Constantinople or Cairo under the very worst forms of Turkish rule. There was a sycophant to accuse, a demagogue to prosecute, a fickle, selfish, necessitous court—no court at all, only a commission of some hundreds or thousands from the public assembly sitting in the sunshine, directly interested in the cause—to pronounce judgment. And he who rose rich and honored might be flying at night for his life to some Persian or Macedonian outpost, to die by poison on his way in the temple of Neptune.

Is there not somewhat in sharing in that administration, observing and enjoying it, which tends to substitute in the professional and in the popular mind, in place of the wild consciousness of possessing summary power, ultimate power, the wild desire to exert it, and to grasp and subject all things to its rule,—to substitute for this the more conservative sentiments of reverence for a law independent of, and distinct from, and antagonistical to, the humor of the hour? Is there not something in the study and administrative enjoyment of an elaborate, rational, and ancient jurisprudence, which tends to raise the law itself, in the professional and in the general idea, almost up to the nature of an independent, superior reason, in one sense out of the people, in one sense above them,—out of and above, and independent of, and collateral to, the people of any given day? In all its vast volumes of provisions, very little of it is seen to be produced by the actual will of the existing generation. The first thing we know about it is, that we are actually being governed by it. The next thing we know is, we are rightfully and beneficially governed by it. We did not help to make it. No man now living helped to make much of it. The judge does not make it. Like the structure of the State itself, we found it around us at the earliest dawn of reason, it guarded the helplessness of our infancy, it restrained the passions of our youth, it protects the acquisitions of our manhood, it shields the sanctity of the grave, it executes the will of the departed. Invisible, omnipresent, a real yet impalpable existence, it seems more a spirit, an abstraction,—the whispered yet authoritative voice of all the past and all the good,—than like the transient contrivance of altogether such as ourselves. We come to think of it, not so much as a set of provisions and rules which we can unmake, amend, and annul, as of a guide whom it is wiser to follow, an authority whom it is better to obey, a wisdom which it is not unbecoming to revere, a power,—a superior—whose service is perfect freedom. Thus at last the spirit of the law descends into the great heart of the people for healing and for conservation. Hear the striking platonisms of Coleridge: "Strength may be met with strength: the power of inflicting pain may be baffled by the pride of endurance: the eye of rage may be answered by the stare of defiance, or the downcast look of dark and revengeful resolve: and with all this there is an outward and determined object to which the mind can attach its passions and purposes, and bury its own disquietudes in the full occupation of the senses. But who dare struggle with the *invisible* combatant, with an enemy which exists and makes us know its existence, but *where* it is we ask in vain? No space contains it, time promises no control over it, it has no ear for my threats, it has no substance that my hands can grasp or my weapons find vulnerable; it commands and cannot be commanded, it acts and is insusceptible of my reaction, the more I strive to subdue it, the more am I compelled to think of it, and, the more I think of it, the more do I find it to possess a reality out of myself, and not to be a phantom of my own imagination; —that all but the most abandoned men acknowledge its authority, and that the whole strength and majesty of my country are pledged to support it; and yet that *for me* its power is the same with that of my own permanent self, and that all the choice which is permitted to me consists in having it for my guardian angel or my avenging fiend. This is the spirit of LAW,—the lute of Amphion,—the harp of Orpheus. This is the true necessity which compels man into the social state, now and always, by a still beginning, never ceasing force of moral cohesion."[5]

In supposing that conservation is the grand and prominent public function of the American Bar in the State, I have not felt that I assigned to a profession, to which I count it so high a privilege to belong, a part and a duty at all beneath its loftiest claims. I shall not deny that to found a State which grows to be a nation, on the ruins of an older, or on a waste of earth where was none before, is, intrinsically and in the judgment of the world, of the largest order of human achievements. Of the chief of men are the *conditores imperiorum*.[6] But to keep the city is only not less difficult and glorious than to build it. Both rise, in the estimate of the most eloquent and most wise of Romans, to the rank of divine achievement. I appreciate the uses and the glory of a great and timely reform. Thrice happy and honored who leaves the Constitution better than he found it. But to find it good, and keep it so, this, too, is virtue and praise.

It was the boast of Augustus,—as Lord Brougham[7] remembers in the close of his speech on the improvement of the law,—that he found Rome of brick and left it of marble. Ay. But he found Rome free, and left her a slave. He found her a republic, and left her an empire! He found the large soul of Cicero unfolding the nature, speaking the high praise, and recording the maxims of regulated liberty, with that eloquence which so many millions of hearts have owned,—and he left poets and artists! We find our city of marble, and we will leave it marble. Yes, all, all, up to the grand, central, and eternal dome; we will leave it marble, as we find it. To that office, to that praise, let even the claims of your profession be subordinated. *Pro clientibus saepe; pro lege, pro republica semper*.[8]

[1] What speech of those men is indeed so perfect that it is to be preferred to a state well established by law and customs? [Cicero, *De Republica*, 1.2.]

[2] "Unless he acted thus, [the winds] would surely bear off swiftly with themselves the seas, the land, and the vault of heaven, and sweep them through space." [Virgil, *Aeneid*, 1, 58–59.]

[3] Private law.

[4] A serene peace beneath liberty.

[5] *The Friend* [Choate's note]. Comparison of this passage with Coleridge's original (*Works*, New York, 1868, Vol. 11, p. 159) reveals that Choate tampered with the punctuation and made slight verbal changes in his version. The calculated irony of this citation may easily be missed by modern readers: Coleridge had early become a sort of patron saint among Transcendentalists and other converts to the categorical imperative—

persons whom Choate despised. These quoted Coleridge in defense of their radical ideas, philosophical and political, in total disregard of his revulsion against the French Revolution and his adherence to a Tory, Anglican position. Choate was endeavoring, by this use of Coleridge, to hoist not only such jurists as Rantoul but such liberalizing philosophers as Emerson with one of their own petards.

[6] Founders of states.

[7] Henry Peter Brougham, Baron Brougham and Vaux (1778–1868), Lord Chancellor 1830–34. Choate here refers to Brougham's great speech in Parliament on the need for legal reform, February 7, 1828. Because of the general antipathy among American jurists to the philosophy of Utilitarianism, the arguments of Jeremy Bentham for codification were little regarded, but Brougham was respected, and was a name to conjure with. Hence, by striking at Brougham in his conclusion, Choate is striking indirectly at American codifiers.

[8] On behalf of clients, often; on behalf of the law, always.

JAMES JACKSON (1819–87)

LAW AND LAWYERS. IS THE PROFESSION OF THE ADVOCATE CONSISTENT WITH PERFECT INTEGRITY? (The Knickerbocker Magazine, XXVIII, November 1846, 378–83)

[*The Knickerbocker Magazine*, edited in the 1840s by Lewis Gaylord Clark, a man whom genteel New York considered the beau ideal of sartorial and intellectual elegance, made a great point of maintaining communications with its correspondents in diverse regions of the hinterland. Thus it nobly kept up an exchange with southern and western contributors (most of whom were professional lawyers), with the New York and even the Boston branches. The magazine was consistently Whig, nationalist, and would-be-cosmopolitan.

In its pages the popular conviction that lawyers were, by the nature of their profession, dishonest, had to be constantly refuted. *The Knickerbocker Magazine* was the principal—indeed, the only—non-technical journal in which, along with the relaxed and genial literary forms of a Washington Irving, could also be presented the gentlemanly aspect of the law. Among its correspondents was James Jackson of Athens, Georgia, who was decidedly not of New England origin—which editor Clark hated—but who could echo in Southern terms the arguments of Story and

Walker, and for basically the same reasons. The profession needed as much defense in Georgia as in Ohio.

James Jackson was born in Jefferson County, Georgia, son of a man who had been governor. Graduated from the University of Georgia in 1837, he practiced law in Athens and was active in various state functions. He served with Stonewall Jackson in the Civil War; afterwards he was a Justice of the Supreme Court of Georgia and in 1880 Chief Justice. He was a cultivated classical scholar—in the standard pattern—yet also a pious Methodist.]

LAW AND LAWYERS, 1846

It is one of the dicta of the infallible mob, that the legal profession necessarily involves many practices inconsistent with elevated integrity, or even common honesty. A successful lawyer is a sort of licensed knave, refined perhaps in his mode of cheating, but really little better than a prime minister of Satan, or at least a member of His Majesty's cabinet. To conceal truth, to pervert evidence, to mislead juries and brow-beat judges, are supposed to be the great attainments of legal ambition.

It needs but little philosophy to account for this prejudice against the votaries of the law. The reasons for the obloquy cast upon the legal profession are numerous. At present we shall notice only two; the expense attending to a suit of law, and the delay. The complaints made against the law on account of its expense arise from the fact that men are prone by nature to consider the possession of their property as an indisputable right, and to regard whatever is spent in defending it as lost. The "law's delay" is undoubtedly a serious evil, which we hope will soon be amended; but the party who suffers from it can rarely blame his lawyer. The fault lies rather at the door of the legislature, or whoever constitute the courts of a state, for not establishing a reasonable number of judicial tribunals; or it is more frequently attributable to the trickery of the other party litigant, who contrives by dishonesty to obtain

continuances and raise obstacles to a speedy settlement of
a dispute. The advocate is the last person to be held responsible for this great stain upon our legal system. Excellence of any kind has a tendency to produce envy in the
minds of some men; and intellectual superiority and eminence in a learned profession are sufficient causes to arouse
the bitter feelings of an ignorant rabble, and to incur their
upbraidings. The effects of the vulgar and mistaken notion
of which we have spoken are as pernicious as its origin is
apparent; for men are apt to be virtuous or vicious according as they are considered to possess the one or the other
of these qualities. Once let a man know that he is looked
upon with suspicion and scorned, and the golden chain
which bound him to virtue is severed, and the way paved
to all sorts of meanness.

For ourselves, we have no more respect or faith in the
cynicism of the modern rabble than we have in that of the
ancient philosopher who lived in a wash-tub. We do not
believe that a candle in broad daylight is necessary to find
a man among the human race, or that any extraordinary
means need be resorted to to find honest men in the legal
profession. We do not pretend however to deny that the
advocate is perhaps exposed to greater temptations to
wicked practices than any other person in society. The
profession of the advocate is eminently one of confidence,
and there is no method of gaining an ascendancy over the
minds of others so direct and complete as that of becoming
master of their secrets. Many chances also occur in a science
so intricate and mysterious as that of the law, to pervert
its true object, and in the name of Justice itself to thwart
justice. Moreover, by becoming intimately acquainted with
the circumstances of his client, the lawyer has better opportunities to defraud him without detection, or even suspicion; but it is certain that to do this the lawyer must
boldly commit a sacrilege at the altar of which he is ordained high priest; he must contradict in practice the system to which he is professedly attached; in short, he must
"steal the livery of Heaven to serve the devil in." But the
same can be said of the other liberal professions. Such re-

flections are by no means peculiar to the legal profession. The physician can be in a family like the serpent in the garden of Eden. Many a pure woman, or hapless husband, has been perfectly convinced, and is daily convinced, of the truth of this remark. These evils all flow from the fact that the medical profession, like the legal, is one of confidence. Noxious doctrines can be promulgated from the pulpit; and in the secret bethel of the homestead the confiding heart may find that the black cloth and the white cravat are but disguises assumed by the traitor to his GOD and to his fellow-man. The politician or the statesman, by wily arts seducing the mass, can introduce false principles into the government of a nation, and thus corrupt the fountains of the happiness of a whole people. Why not argue from this that these professions too are more refined inventions for the practice of villany? Why not change the plan of attack upon the medical profession, and brand physicians as scientific murderers and pompous quacks? Why not call the ministers of the gospel a troop of hypocrites? Why not stigmatize the statesman as a destroyer of human happiness and as an evil genius to the confiding and the trustful? In short, in every profession where mental discipline and superior abilities raise a man above the level of the surrounding crowd, and equip him with extraordinary influence, the avenues of dishonesty and treachery are a thousand-fold increased. "Let him who standeth take heed lest he fall!" But that there is any thing in the science or the practice of law which necessarily involves a stifling of conscience, the sacrifice of one iota of principle, a support of injustice or inevitable dishonesty, we do most firmly and solemnly deny.

In maintaining our position we shall examine and try to show the groundlessness of some of the chief objections which have been brought against the legal profession. Among other calumnies thrown out against the advocate, it is triumphantly asserted by some wiseacres of the present day that he often enlists in a cause without knowing or even caring which side is in the wrong; that it is impossible when the interests of two parties conflict, as in a case at law, that both can have the right, and therefore the advocate of one at least is of necessity guilty of dishonesty. But on this point the voice of reason and common sense is far different from that of the rabble. To see the fallacy of the charge, it is only necessary to bear in mind that all matters of opinion are not capable of perfect mathematical demonstration; that they are not so obvious as to make it necessary that either party should prosecute his claim at the expense of integrity; that the affairs of mankind are not so nicely adjusted as that one party in a law-suit should be entirely right and the other entirely wrong; and that truth cannot be elicited and justice awarded unless both sides of a case are fairly represented. Consider the intricacies of contracts and commercial relations; the difficulty in many cases of ascertaining the true meaning of the will of testators; and above all, the nice distinctions to be made in determining the degree of criminality. It were palpably absurd for the advocate to prejudge the questions to which these and a thousand other subjects, equally complicated, give rise. Beside, it is not for the advocate to say whether a cause is just or unjust; for him to decide upon the justice or injustice of a case would be to usurp the province of the judge. Many cases which at first seemed to be bad have on examination proved to be good. Nay, it often happens that the advocate is unable to see the justice of his client's cause until it is brought before the court. In short, the advocate is bound to represent his side of the case, *right or wrong*, in the best possible light, and to enforce the strongest arguments he can devise in favor of his client, leaving the validity of those arguments and the true merits of the case to the decision of the judge, whose business alone it is to decide. Let the advocate prejudge a case, and you bar the citizen from seeking redress in a court of justice; you defeat the very object of trials at law; in a word, you introduce mob-law, and make every man his own judge and his own avenger.

It is also charged against the profession that the advocate appears in defence or prosecution of a claim which he believes to be unjust; that he defends the wrong side, knowing it to be wrong. For example, he defends a person whom he knows to be *morally* guilty. Is this consistent with perfect integrity, or is it not? Now there is such a thing as justice to a depraved criminal, and the interests of society demand that justice should be done to him as well as to the offended law and the outraged community; and it is a maxim established since the "time whereof the memory of man runneth not to the contrary," that every man shall be presumed innocent until proved guilty. It is also an important rule of justice that punishment shall be apportioned to crime; and in order that these fundamental principles of justice may be maintained and their strict applications secured, the services of an advocate must, from the very nature of the circumstances, be obtained, that he may expound the law; suggest every reasonable doubt; insist upon palliating circumstances; and in short, put the most favorable construction upon the conduct of the accused which the principles of justice will allow. If this be not done, the very objects for which courts exist will be utterly defeated, and trials at law become a mere farce. It is asserted that the advocate, by appearing in defence of a person whom he knows to be guilty, tacitly acknowledges his belief in his innocence, becomes an abettor in crime, and thus swerves from the path of integrity. Now actions are moral or immoral according as the motives by which the agent is actuated are good or bad. And is it not strange that sensible men should say that an advocate defends a criminal from any love of crime? Beside, the law under which punishment is inflicted has not the same facilities of information as private individuals; the only way in which it can ascertain crime and award justice is by a fair hearing of both parties. No matter how certain the community may be of the criminal's guilt, it would be a palpable subversion of law to allow this fact to detract one iota from his privilege of defence. Without this faithful scrupulousness of the law it would lose its authority and we its protection. And this same glorious caution must also be exercised in determining the degrees of guilt; for the *degree* of guilt is as necessary to be ascertained as the fact of the *existence* of the guilt. It would be palpably absurd to convict a man of murder who had merely committed the crime of manslaughter, or to convict a person of manslaughter who had merely committed a justifiable homicide. In the majority of instances the shade of difference between the first two crimes is so slight, depends so much upon the color given to the transaction by the witnesses, and a reasonable explanation of the various circumstances of the case, that the learning and ingenuity of counsel are absolutely necessary to make as clear and favorable a definition of legal terms as possible; to explain the relation of circumstances to each other; to apply the strict test of cross-examination; to ascertain the credibility of the witnesses, and sift from the evidence the prejudices of those who detail the facts. Here then, on the immutable principles of justice, do we take our stand, and maintain that *every case, however bad, every criminal, however depraved, has a claim upon the services of the advocate, and that the advocate may honestly defend a person whom he knows to be guilty of some crime;* and we hold that in attempting to avert from his client a penalty disproportioned to his offence, he is discharging a duty as truly just and noble as if he were holding the shield of his eloquence over the most pure and innocent. It is upon this principle that the humanity of modern law provides, in contradistinction to the barbarism of former ages, that the most abandoned criminal may confront the majesty of the law and the sternness of his accusers through the mediation of an advocate. Those certain wise nobodies who charge the members of the legal profession with dishonesty, seem to forget that there is in the human mind a tendency to imbibe prejudice in favor of the side of a question which it hears first, or for which it has sympathy on account of the relation which it sustains to the person who is intrusted in it, as the relation of client and lawyer. Probably in the majority of cases which turn out unfavorably to the advocate, he really believes himself to be in the right.

Another charge brought against the profession is, that

the advocate, knowing his client to be guilty, endeavors to prove him innocent. Is this right? To answer this question correctly, it will be necessary to glance at the objects of trials at law. Laws are presumed to be so framed as to promote the good of the greatest number by saving the innocent from condemnation and convicting the guilty. For this purpose TECHNICAL RULES have of necessity been adopted. The intricacy of the law, arising from its technicalities, has been and still is the cause of much censure upon the profession of the advocate. Some men seem to regard the law as a mere piece of mechanism; a form without spirit; words destitute alike of philosophy and meaning. But every science has its forms. Grammar and mathematics have their rules and figures of demonstration; and it is only through the technicalities of the law that its spirit can be imparted and the understanding reached. When a man commits some heinous crime, say that of murder; when he is arraigned before a court of justice; when the community think he ought to suffer the penalty of death; when the feelings of men are excited against the offender, if the advocate for the criminal appears and proceeds to show that, owing to some flaw in the indictment, the trial cannot proceed, and thus clears the criminal, it is not strange that superficial reasoners, and even men of sense, should become prejudiced against him who "made the worse appear the better cause." But then it is not the advocate who clears the criminal. He only performs his duty to his client, leaving the result of his arguments to the judge and jury. Why not throw the blame, if blame there be, upon them? Every avenue of escape for the prisoner should be kept open. The learning and ingenuity of skilful and practiced men are absolutely necessary to explain and apply the technicalities of the law in regard to evidence. For if all evidence is to be indiscriminately admitted, then the most perjured villain has the most spotless character completely under his control. On this account, proceeding upon the reasonable doctrine that it is better that many guilty should escape than that one innocent person should be punished, the law requires that a certain amount of proof shall be necessary to establish guilt. In short, the evidence must be such as to exclude every rational doubt. Whatever is less than this, if allowed to be sufficient, is an injury to society for the sake of avenging a single crime. The advocate, therefore, may honestly and conscientiously, with a view to the interests of society and the security of innocent men, labor with all his might to show that the evidence adduced in a given case does not justify a conviction. We do not say that he may have recourse to bribery or trickery, or any other sort of meanness, to gain a verdict in his favor; but we do say that it is the advocate's sacred duty to use all fair means and himself to the utmost to make it appear that the law does not declare his client guilty. "No matter," he might boldly proclaim in the eye of common judgment or common prejudice, "how great the moral iniquity of my client may be, if on this account he can be convicted upon slight evidence, a precedent is established which controverts the very object of all law, and endangers the purest virtue, the most complete innocence."

Another objection not unfrequently urged against the profession of the advocate is, that he keeps within his own bosom facts which the confidence of his client has entrusted to him, and thus *cheats* the law out of its proper victim. But it must be remembered that the advocate stands in the very place of the accused; that he becomes acquainted with what he would not know upon any other condition. And we would ask upon what principles of reason or justice can a man be made to testify against himself; or by what right can the advocate, standing in the place of the accused, be compelled to do the same? Of course a system of law so weak as to require, in order to sustain itself, the confession of the accused, would be too contemptible to be dignified with the name of law; a system founded upon such inquisitorial tyranny would be too gross to be called the child of equity and justice; it would be impracticable; it would defeat itself; in short, it would be wretched lawlessness.

Far be it from us to say that trials at law are never

scenes of dishonest wriggling and palpable falsehood. That the law itself is defied and mocked and tricked by its own ministers, we do not pretend to dispute. But if a few yield to temptation, and become, instead of lawyers, usurers and gamblers and sharks and thieves, we should ask by what rule of logic it follows that the whole class must be stigmatized as rogues unwhipped of justice, unbranded felons, uncaged wolves? Of course we do not say that a man is honest merely because he is a lawyer; but we do religiously believe that it is equally ridiculous and absurd to say that because a man is a lawyer he is therefore a knave. The true lawyer, imbued with lessons of wisdom, and accustomed to labor in all that ennobles the soul and refines the mind and chastens the feelings, is one of the ornaments of his race. The vindicator of the laws of GOD and man; a guardian of morality and conservator of right; the distributor of justice and the protector of the injured and the innocent; a public sentinel to sound the alarm on the approach of danger; he is one of the firmest safe-guards of society. His profession is one of transcendent dignity. Its object is to shield the oppressed from the oppressor; to equalize the disparity which nature has fixed between the weak and the strong; which circumstances have made between the rich and the poor, the favorite of fortune and the beggar-brat of misfortune; to defend the fatherless and the widow; to protect innocence against the wiles of its enemies, and the prejudices of a world which was more ready to crucify CHRIST than Barabbas. Whoever then perverts this object, and commits a sacrilege at the altar of justice at which he is sworn to minister, shame on him! —and equal shame on him who endeavors to convict a class for the vices of a few, and dares attempt to make the law appear, instead of the handmaid of justice, the slave of injustice; and the profession of the advocate, dignified and noble as it is in all its *true* objects, to seem a mere school of refined knavery!

Of LAW, the world's collected wisdom, the good man's defence, the bad man's dread, founded as it is on moral rectitude and the principles of eternal truth, "no less can

be said, than that its seat is the bosom of GOD, its voice
the harmony of the world; all things in heaven and earth
do it homage; the least as feeling its care, the greatest as
not exempt from its power; both angels and men and the
creatures of what condition soever, though each in different sort or manner, yet all, all with uniform assent, recognize it as the life of their being, the giver of their peace,
the safeguard of their happiness!"

DAVID DUDLEY FIELD (1805–94)

REFORM IN THE LEGAL PROFESSION AND THE LAWS. ADDRESS TO THE GRADUATING CLASS OF THE ALBANY LAW SCHOOL, MARCH 23, 1855

[With David Dudley Field we reach the culmination —or what might more aptly be called the explosion—of those forces which since the Revolution had persistently advocated reform by codification. Field was no doubt influenced by English and Continental jurists, but on the whole he was a product of native experience. He devoted his whole life and his tremendous energies to this cause. Indeed, he seems to have been born with a consuming predilection for it. His was a more coherent, more systematic, rebellion against the Common Law than that of either Sampson or Rantoul; and he had considerable effect on American jurisprudence, whereas they had little or none. Yet Field never wrought the complete revolution he intended.

He was born the son of a Congregational minister in Haddam, Connecticut, of a gifted family—one of his brothers would be a Justice of the Supreme Court, another would lay the Atlantic Cable. He attended Williams College but did not graduate, and read law in Albany. He started his practice in New York City and quickly demonstrated enormous ability. Though not a courtroom orator like Choate, he was a much more profound student. He

argued several important cases before the Supreme Court
and accumulated a fortune. An ardent Democrat, he nevertheless opposed the Mexican War. He was outspoken in
his anti-slavery feeling and in 1860 supported Lincoln.
After the war he shocked and alienated many of his followers by serving as counsel for the notorious Jay Gould
and Jim Fiske in the Erie Railroad Litigation (1869) and
for the still more notorious "Boss" Tweed (1873–78). In
his last years he campaigned with characteristic vehemence
for a code of international law.

He commenced his agitation for the codification of
American law in 1839 and kept it up with such force as to
compel, in the 1850s, the state legislature to appoint a
commission to review the situation. Several codes were
prepared but only one, the penal code, was adopted. However, Field exerted great influence in several other states,
notably California.

In the 1840s Field was intimate with the literary group
in New York City that called itself "Young America," the
most important member of which, to our eyes, is Her-
man Melville, but who in the eyes of contemporaries was
a lesser hanger-on and soon a fugitive from it to the Berkshires. (*The Knickerbocker Magazine* heaped scorn upon
the brotherhood.) This group talked boisterously about
creating a new, fresh, original literature of America, which
should be as loud as Niagara, as powerful as the Mississippi River, as sublime as the Rocky Mountains. It particularly rebelled against the domination of American taste
by things English and the slavish imitation of English
writers by the genteel and most successful of American
authors. Field was not active in the strictly literary performances of this band, though he wrote for it a few
articles which show his entire sympathy with its aims.
As this Address makes explicit, his hostility to the Common Law was a specifically American hostility to English
domination; the imposition of an "artificial" contrivance
upon the virgin wilderness of America was to him an out-
rage. In the realm of the law, therefore, he was moved by
a spirit akin to that which inspired Melville and Walt

Whitman. And just as they were derided by those who felt that rude democracy required the discipline of English culture, so Field was heartily abused by the majority of lawyers, who held that a native codification would be a descent into barbarity. But Field was a fighter and could not be intimidated. The conclusion of this address reveals the deep sources of his dedication.]

REFORM IN THE LEGAL PROFESSION, 1855

The present condition of our law is anomalous. For the main part, it is derived from the Common Law of England, but so mixed and blended with other rules and usages that it can hardly be called a system at all. The Constitution of the State declares that "such parts of the Common Law, and of the acts of the Legislature of the Colony of New York, as together did form the law of the said colony, on the 19th day of April, 1775," and the resolutions of the Congress of the said colony and of the Convention of the State of New York, in force on the 20th day of April, 1777, which have not since expired or been repealed or altered, and such acts of the Legislature of this State as are now in force, "shall be and continue the law of this State, subject to such alterations as the Legislature shall make concerning the same." The Constitution thereupon requires the Legislature, at its first session after the adoption of the Constitution, to "appoint three commissioners, whose duty it shall be to reduce into a written and systematic code the whole body of the law of this State, or so much and such parts thereof as to the said commissioners shall seem practicable and expedient." The wisdom of the latter provision will be apparent by-and-by.

What was this Common Law to which the Constitution referred, and which are those parts of it that formed the law of the colony in 1775? The Common Law, properly so called, is the customary law of England, as it existed before the coronation of Richard I, which was in 1189. But, as this would throw us back, nearly seven hundred years, upon a mass of usages which would not be thought tolerable for any existing civilization, the Courts have been obliged to hold that such acts of the English Parliament, in amendment of the Common Law, as were passed before the emigration of our ancestors, and are applicable to our situation, are to be considered as part and parcel of the Common Law. What an explanation is this to give to the citizen of the laws according to which he is to live! If he be certain that he knows what were the customs of England in the reign of Richard, how is he to know to what period of emigration the Constitution refers (for be it remembered that from the first emigration to the Revolution there passed a hundred and fifty years), and by what means can he guess which English statutes the Courts will consider applicable to our situation? . . .

To this unwritten or Common Law are to be added, according to the construction put by our Courts upon the constitutional declaration, the statutes of England applicable to our situation. Thus it is seen that the English portion of law which our English progenitors brought with them was not a homogeneous system, but an irregular mass of usage and statute, derived partly from the traditions of various and discordant tribes and races, partly from the enactments of tyrannical kings and struggling Parliaments, and partly, it may be added, from interpolations by judges and chancellors from the civil or canon law.

But, before the arrival of the English, there had settled in the land, and ruled for nearly half a century, a dissimilar people, whose laws, founded chiefly on the Roman codes, were yet modified by the local customs of the different provinces of the Netherlands. These laws, "the precious customs of Fatherland," as the Dutch settlers delighted to call them, and particularly the customs of Friesland, were the first laws of the colony, and, though long since, in most respects, supplanted by the English, traces of them still exist, and affect property in the oldest of the Dutch settlements.

Upon this English and Dutch stock was ingrafted colonial legislation, which consisted mainly of efforts to adapt the law of aristocratic and kingly England to the circumstances and wants of settlers in the forest on a different side of the ocean. No attempt was made to frame a new system, conformable to the new country, and to the new people that were to be born in it; but the old laws of old nations, strangely compounded of Saxon, Norman, and Dutch customs, of the laws of the Heptarchy, of Alfred, and the Conquest, of the statutes of Merton of Marleberge, Winchester, and Gloucester, were transferred from one continent to the other. Thus it happened that those feudal laws of real property were impressed upon the virgin wilderness, with which the Gothic invaders had afflicted the fair lands where the mild and rational system of the Roman law had prevailed before that fierce onslaught from the North:

> . . . when her barbarous sons
> Came like a deluge on the South, and spread
> Beneath Gibraltar to the Libyan sands.

And thus also it happened that a most artificial system of procedure, conceived in the midnight of the dark ages, established in those scholastic times when chancellors were ecclesiastics, and logic was taught by monks, and perfected in a later and more venal period, with a view to the multiplication of offices and the increase of fees, was imposed upon the banks of the Hudson and the quiet valley of the Mohawk. . . .

Let us return now from the consideration of these minor reforms to that greatest reform of all, *the establishment of "a written and systematic code of the whole body of the law of this State."* And first let me explain how the matter stands at present.

At the same time that the commission enjoined by the Constitution was created for the purpose of framing a gen-

eral code, or code of rights and crimes, another commission, also enjoined by the Constitution, was created for
the framing of a code of remedies. The former commission was dissolved without reporting a code. The latter
framed, and reported to the Legislature, codes of civil and
criminal procedure. . . .

The prejudices that prevail on this subject among the
members of the profession, both on the bench and at the
bar, are well known, and I would not disguise the impediment which these prejudices create. But I have seen
greater prejudices than these pass away: and, believing
in the power of reason and the spread of truth, I feel
confident that the day is near when we shall all smile at
the fallacies which are now so dominant. It may well
be true that not one lawyer in five believes in the practicability or expediency of a civil code; but not one in a
hundred, ten years ago, believed in the possibility of administering legal and equitable relief in the same action,
and by a uniform mode of proceeding; but who in this
State doubts it now, or would go back to the separate
processes if he could? And I may add that not one in
twenty, here or in England, ten years ago, believed in the
advantage or safety of making witnesses of parties, though
the most conservative bar in Christendom now, as one man,
pronounces in its favor, and the old rule of exclusion is
thrown contemptuously aside for jest and derision.

How the establishment of a code should have been so
long a problem with us is a curious subject of speculation,
for certainly all the instincts of republicanism are in its
favor. One of the distinctions of our scheme of government
is the written Constitution. A written law rests upon the
same principle. In monarchical or aristocratic governments
it would not be so much to be wondered at that a class
should arrogate to itself the knowledge and interpretation
of laws; but that this should happen in a republic, where
all the citizens both legislate and obey, is one of those
anomalies which, however susceptible of explanation, seem
at first sight incredible.

Is a civil code practicable, and, if practicable, expedient? These questions present the whole case, and should be answered in connection; for it is the habit of objectors to retreat in a circle from one to the other. If you answer the objection that the code is impracticable, you are then told that, though it might be practicable, it would not be expedient; and if you follow by proving the expediency, not unlikely you will hear again that, though expedient, it is not practicable. Show first that the work is practicable, and, that being done, let not your adversary escape from the position that the whole question has been narrowed to the one point of expediency, and that the decision of this closes the question.

How, then, stands the question of practicability? Is a civil code practicable? The best answer to this question should seem to be the fact that civil codes have been established in nearly all the countries of the world, from the time of the Lower Empire to the present day. Are we not as capable of performing a great act of legislation as Romans or Germans, as Frenchmen or Italians? The very doubt supposes either that our abilities are inferior or our law more difficult. The suggestion of inferior abilities would be resented as a national insult; and who that knows anything of it believes that Roman, French, or Italian law is easier to express or explain than our own? And he who does believe it should, in very consistency, straightway set about the amendment of our own, to render it as easy to learn and as facile to express as these foreign laws.

If it were assumed as essential to a code that it should contain a rule for every transaction that in the compass of time can possibly arise, the objection might have some force; but no sane person holds any such idea. We know that new relations will hereafter arise which no human eye has foreseen, and for which new laws must be made. The plan of a code does not include a provision for every future case, in all future times; it contemplates the collecting and digesting of existing rules and the framing of new ones, for all that man's wisdom can discern of what is to come hereafter. Every existing rule of law is written in some book; the books are infinite in number and abound in contradictions and anomalies. To have a code is to have these rules collected, arranged, and classified; the contradictions reconciled; the doubts settled; the bad laws eliminated, and the result written in one book, for the instruction and guidance of citizen and magistrate, lawyer and client.

This brings us to the remaining question of expediency. Is it better to have written or unwritten law; law collected in one book or scattered through a thousand; one system, congruous with itself, where the parts can be seen in their relation to the whole, or disjointed pieces of law, collected from different languages and nations?

There are two objections, which are the only ones that seem to me to be put forth with any appearance of confidence. The first asserts that an unwritten or customary law has this advantage over a written code, that the former is more pliable, and can be extended and molded to correspond with a changing and expanding social state. This is a favorite argument, but I conceive it to be altogether fallacious. It assumes two things, neither of which is true: first, that law is more flexible because unwritten; and, second, that flexibility in law is excellence. A law is a rule of action; to say that the rule is not fixed, that is, flexible, is to say that it is no rule at all. When a decision is made upon the Common Law, it is announced as an authoritative declaration of an existing rule; if it be not really that, then the Judges, instead of interpreting, are making law. If it be an exposition of existing law, then it is not alterable by the Judges, and, of course, is no more flexible in their hands than a statute would be. A flexible Common Law, means, therefore, judicial legislation. Is that desirable? If there be any reason for the policy of separating the different departments of government, the Judges should no more be permitted to make laws than the Legislature to administer them. All experience has shown that confusion in functions leads to confusion in government. Judges are not the wisest legislators, any more than legislators are the wisest Judges. And if it were otherwise, there is this difference between the two modes of legislation, that legislation by a Legislature is made known before it is executed, while legislation by a court occurs after the fact, and necessarily supposes a party to be the victim of a rule unknown until after the transaction which calls it forth.

The judiciary have no rightful concern with the policy of laws. If they need to be changed, the Legislature is the proper judge of the time and the manner of change. And before all other nations, ours is the one by which this rule should be inflexibly enforced; for, more than others, we hold to the entire separation and independence of the different departments of government, so that neither shall encroach upon the other, and the judiciary shall be independent of the executive, the executive of the judiciary, and the Legislature of both.

Then it is said that, if a code were once enacted, it would soon be overloaded with glosses and comments upon the texts, as numerous and contradictory as the cases upon the common law, which now fill the books. This, if it were true, would only prove that the process of codification must be repeated at certain intervals—an objection of no great force, especially as it assumes that, until the accumulation of glosses and comments, the code would prove an advantage. But the fact is overstated. There would be glosses and comments, of course; but with a common tribunal to settle questions of doubtful construction, it should seem impossible that there should arise half the questions which now occur upon the common law, since the latter regards not merely the meaning but the existence of a rule, the extent of its design, its applicability to our situation, and also its policy.

This objection, moreover, is inconsistent with the first objection which I answered; for, if there are to be so many commentaries and different interpretations, the text and the comments will soon come to have that flexible character which is thought by some to be so beneficial an element of the common law.

Considering, then, these two objections to the expediency of a code to be satisfactorily answered, and turning to the other side, how great are the advantages which we can

see in its accomplishment! The numerous collections of
law-books upon the shelves of our libraries superseded by
a single work; the whole law brought together, so that it
can be seen at one view; the text spread before the eyes
of all our citizens; old abuses removed, excrescences cut
away, new life infused—these will be the beneficent effects
of this vast work. . . .

No undertaking which you could engage in would prove
half so grand or beneficent. Your canals, your railways,
your incalculable wealth, your ships cutting the foam of
every sea, the enterprise of your merchants, the skill of
your artisans, the fame of your ancestors—all would not
exceed in glory the establishment of a code of laws, containing the wisest rules of past ages, and the most matured
reflections of our own, which, instinct with the free spirit
of our institutions, should become the guide and example
for all the nations bearing the tie of our common language.

Shall this imperial State be outstripped in the noble race
by either of her sisters, or by that queenly island, mother
of nations, which, having been our parent, is now our rival?
In material public works, in commerce with all the world,
in the accumulation of wealth, in the possession and display of power, and in all the arts, we are contending with
her for preëminence; it is now to be determined which
shall be the lawgiver of the race. Whether this crown
shall be upon the head of the mother, or the youngest of
the nations, is the problem which the men of this generation shall solve. May it be so resolved as that we shall
win the well-deserved prize; that we shall have a book of
our own laws, a CODE AMERICAN, not insular but continental, as simple as so vast a work can be made, free in
its spirit, catholic in its principles! And that work will go
with our ships, our travelers, and our armies; it will march
with the language, it will move with every emigration, and
make itself a home in the farthest portion of our own continent, in the vast Australian lands, and in the islands of the
southern and western seas.

Let us not fear that anything valuable will be lost from

the accumulations of past generations. Whatever is beneficial as well as venerable, whatever is most wise, whatever is approved by time and or consecrated by habit, will be preserved and reënacted. Only that which is hurtful, unsuitable, or obsolete, will be laid aside, as it ought, no matter how long it may have lasted, or how strong become.

To the young men of this generation, more than any other that have ever lived, to you who are now going forth from study into professional life, the great task is committed of reforming and establishing the law. You are now enrolled in that profession upon which, more than any other, rest the functions of government and the preservation of social order. You stand in that great congregation, where also stand the most illustrious men of the past and present ages. Demosthenes, Aeschines, Ulpian, Cicero, Daguessau, Bacon, Mansfield, and our own Marshall, Kent, and Story, are your professional brethren. To be worthy to stand in such presence, to be influenced by such examples, to catch a portion of their spirit, are distinctions in themselves.

You stand, moreover, in the very portals of a new time. The world is soon to take its impulses from this side of the ocean. The language we speak, the institutions in which we participate, are to spread with our dominion—

From the world's girdle to the frozen pole—

and beyond our dominion to remote islands and continents. Whence shall come the lawgiver of the new time? From our own soil, I would fain hope and believe. The materials are at hand, and the time is propitious. A new people, grown suddenly to the strength and civilization of the oldest and mightiest, with laws for the most part borrowed, finds that they need to be reëxamined, simplified, and reconstructed. The task is great, the object is greater, and the reward is ample. Let us, then, be up and doing, that we may have the merit and the satisfaction of having accomplished something toward it, before we rest from our labors.

THEODORE SEDGWICK (1811–59)

A TREATISE ON THE RULES WHICH GOVERN THE INTERPRETATION AND APPLICATION OF STATUTORY AND CONSTITUTIONAL LAW (New York, 1857

[In the very decade, 1850 to 1860, when Field was pressing his argument most vigorously and was being most violently attacked, a new frame of mind, of temper, was arising among many of the more thoughtful practitioners. It came out of a weariness over the whole debate about codification, pro or con. The American experience, these men began to realize, had demonstrated that the law did not have to be all one thing or the other, that it could get along in practice with a combination of methods which seemed in theory utterly incompatible. Joseph Story was a prophet of this pragmatic solution, but in the work of Theodore Sedgwick we find it quietly assumed that this and not doctrinaire codification is *the* American way. For that reason, Sedgwick's remarks, though not so vigorous as some we have heard, signify the close of an epoch. After the Civil War technological and financial transformations in our society would pose a whole new set of problems, of a sort that had been either nonexistent or else not of major concern in the earlier part of the century.

Theodore Sedgwick was born in Albany, a grandson of Judge Theodore Sedgwick of Stockbridge and a son of

Theodore the second, who was also an eminent lawyer. But unlike his forebears, he was a Jeffersonian and a Democrat. He graduated from Columbia in 1829, was admitted to the bar in 1833, and built up a successful practice in New York City. Ill-health compelled him (as it had forced his uncle) to give it up and to retire to Stockbridge. His *Treatise*, of which the portion here reprinted is the opening, was long used as the standard textbook on its subject in several law schools.]

A TREATISE ON THE RULES, 1857

Man, in whatever situation he may be placed, finds himself under the control of rules of action emanating from an authority to which he is compelled to bow,—in other words, of LAW. The moment that he comes into existence, he is the subject of the will of God, as declared in what we term the laws of nature. As soon as he enters into society, he finds himself controlled by the moral law (more or less perfect and active according to the condition of the community to which he belongs, and the degree in which it has accepted the divine precepts of our religion), and also by the municipal or civil law. When States come to be organized as separate and independent governments, and their relations grow frequent and complicated, there is superadded the law of nations. These codes are variously enforced, but each has its own peculiar sanction. They are curiously interwoven together, and in their combination tend to produce that progress and improvement of the race which we believe Christianity teaches, and to which we hope civilization leads.

Thus, the law of nature, the moral law, the municipal law, and the law of nations, form a system of restraints before which the most consummate genius, the most vehement will, the angriest passions, and the fiercest desires, are compelled to bend, and the pressure of which the individual is forced to acknowledge his incapacity to resist.

Of these various systems of rules for the government

and control of men, the municipal or civil law asserts its claim emphatically as a distinct branch of knowledge, and is that to which we refer when we speak of the profession of the law, the study of the law, the science of the law.

Municipal law is defined by the great English commentator, as "a rule of civil conduct prescribed by the supreme power in a state, commanding what is right and prohibiting what is wrong." Our American Kent describes it "as a rule of civil conduct prescribed by the supreme power of a state."

Both of these definitions are perhaps obnoxious to criticism. Either of them sufficiently answers our present purpose.

Before entering on the precise subject of this treatise, it is necessary to have an accurate idea of the various elements constituting that system of municipal law which controls the conduct of the active millions who compose our race.

The two great sources of municipal or civil law, in all countries of which we have the means of tracing the jurisprudence, are unwritten law or usage, and written or statute law; in other words, custom and positive enactment. . . .

To this source is also chiefly to be traced the great body of the original English law, "that ancient collection of unwritten maxims and customs called the COMMON LAW" which still exercises such extensive sway in both England and America, and on which we daily see engrafted regulations owing their origin to the same principle. *Sine scripto jus venit, quod usus approbavit, nam diuturni mores consensu utentium comprobati legem imitantur.*[1]

As, however, societies advance, and become consolidated or crystallized into regular governments, they do not wait for the slow process of custom to establish general rules. In order to create more certain and rapid uniformity they resort to positive enactments, to statute laws. And these enactments, in many cases, more or less supplant the usages which precede them. Such is the gradual tendency of civilization.

So, the first demand of that extraordinary people which has been to the world the great exemplar of organization and administration, of order and discipline,—its first serious internal struggle, was for a body of written law to replace the vague and undefined customs and usages by which they had till then been governed. This was the origin of the law of the Twelve Tables, which united the functions of a constitution and a code, and was for nearly a thousand years, until the time of Justinian, the basis of the jurisprudence of Rome.

So, we see in France, the old multifarious customs which, before the Revolution, ruled the various provinces of the kingdom, giving way to the code, the greatest and most permanent work of the central authority of the empire.

So again in England, although the Common Law, the great customary law, as fixed by the art of printing, expounded and extended by judicial interpretation, retains, even to our time, so great a sway, still, we daily see it modified by and giving way before the inroads of the lawgiver.

But wherever a great body of customary law exists, or has ever existed, a familiar knowledge of its provisions and its history is indispensable to the jurist. First, in point of time, it is often first in point of importance, as explaining and even to a certain extent controlling the statute law to which it apparently gives place.

The importance of bearing this in view in the consideration of our present subject, will be recognized when it is recollected that the great body of unwritten usages called the Common Law of England, is also the basis of the law of this country. The sources, indeed, of American and English jurisprudence, are identical. This is universally true, with the exception only of those States, like Louisiana, Florida, Texas, and California, which, before they were annexed to the United States, belonged to countries governed by the civil law. The colonists who settled this coun-

try, were Englishmen, with the feelings, the attachments,
and the prejudices of Englishmen. It became necessary
for them to establish or recognize and adhere to some system of law from the moment they landed. That system
was of necessity the English, and accordingly, we find the
doctrine to have always been that the colonists were subject to, and, as it were, brought with them, the great principles of the Common Law of the mother country, with
such modifications as the legislative enactments of Parliament had at that time introduced into it, or the particular
situation of the colonists in their new condition required.
It is to be understood, then, as a general principle,—that
the basis, the fundamental element, the starting point, of
the jurisprudence of the States of the Union, is the Common Law of England, so far as the same is not actually
repugnant to our system. The exceptions we shall hereafter consider; but so it has been repeatedly decided and
affirmed in the thirteen old States, as they are called,
which in 1776, threw off the English sovereignty. The declaration of rights made by the first Continental Congress,
in 1774, declares that "the respective colonies are entitled
to the Common Law of England, and to the benefit of such
of the English statutes as existed at the time of their colo-
nization, and which they have, by experience, found to be
applicable to their social, local, and other circumstances."

This is the uniform language of our judicial decisions,
whether of the federal or State tribunals. It has been declared by the Supreme Court of the United States, that our
ancestors brought with them the general principles of the
Common Law as in force at their emigration, and claimed
them as their birthright. Nevertheless, that the common
law of America is not to be taken in all respects, to be
that of England, but that the settlers brought with them,
and adopted, only that portion which was applicable to
their situation.

The Supreme Court has also declared that English statutes passed before the emigration of our ancestors, being
applicable to our situation, and in amendment of the law,
constitute a part of our Common Law, and the construc-

tion of such statutes which prevailed at the Revolution, is the rule for the Courts of the United States. English judicial decisions, therefore, pronounced previous to our Declaration of Independence, construing or interpreting such statute law of the mother country as we have adopted, are to be received here as a part of such statutes; but judicial decisions on such statutes, pronounced subsequently to our Revolution, though treated with great respect, are not to be admitted as authority. . . .

It is very important to bear in mind the exception already mentioned, that only so much of the English common law was adopted by the colonies as was applicable to their condition. So, the English law of fixtures permitting the tenant to remove trade fixtures, but forbidding him to disturb those made for agricultural purposes, was never the law of this country. "The country was a wilderness, and the universal policy was to procure its cultivation and improvement. The owner of the soil, as well as the public, had every motive to encourage the tenant to devote himself to agriculture, and to favor any exertion that should aid this result." Such is the intimation of the Supreme Court of the U. S.; and in the State of New York, the right of the tenant to remove any "erections that he may have had occasion to make for his own use or enjoyment, if he can do so without injury to the inheritance" and without reference to their particular character, has been specifically declared.

So, again, on the same principle, it has been held in the same State that the English law of ancient lights was never adopted in this country; and, in the absence of any special covenant, that when an owner of two adjoining lots in a city leased one of them on which was a building receiving its light and air through an open space on the adjacent lot, that the proprietor had a right to build on the lot in question, so as even to darken or stop the windows of his tenant, and that his absolute right of property could not be interfered with by injunction.

Such then, we learn from the highest authority, was the

silent and practical adoption of the Common Law, by the colonists who on the shores of the Atlantic laid the foundations of empire. But when the Revolution broke out, and the inhabitants of the new States with that provident forecast to which attention will hereafter be called, undertook by solemn instruments, to declare and fence in their rights and liberties, it became necessary to determine the fundamental law of the sovereignties just springing into life. So shall we find that at the Revolution of 1776, by the constitutions of most if not all the States, the great body of the Common Law, and such of the English statutes as were not repugnant to our system, were preserved and adopted as binding on us. But the Common Law of England is perpetually fluctuating; and it would have been altogether inconsistent with proper notions of national independence to give the law of a foreign country any permanent control over our tribunals or our people. It was, therefore, necessary to fix a time after which any changes effected in the Common Law of the mother country would have no effect here. And that period is the Revolution. That epoch is the era of our independence, legal as well as political, and we recognize no foreign law posterior to that period, binding on us as authority. . . .

At the same time it has been declared by the Supreme Court of the United States, to be clear that there can be no common law of the Union. The federal Government is composed of twenty-four sovereign and independent States, each of which may have its local usages and common law; but there is no principle which pervades the Union, and has the authority of law, that is not embodied in the Constitution or Laws of the Union. The Common Law could be made a part of the Federal system only by legislative adoption. It is settled that the federal courts have no jurisdiction of common law offences, and that there is no common law of the Union. When, therefore, a common-law right is asserted, we must look to the State where the controversy originated. What is common law in one State may not be, and frequently is not so considered, in another. The judicial decisions, the usages and customs of the respective States, must determine how far the Common Law has been introduced and sanctioned in each.

It is often said that Christianity is part and parcel of the Common Law; but this is true only in a modified sense. Blasphemy is an indictable offence at Common Law; but no person is liable to be punished by civil power who refuses to embrace the doctrines or follow the precepts of Christianity; our Constitutions extend the same protection to every form of religion, and give no preference to any. Still, though Christianity is not the religion of the State, considered as a political corporation, it is nevertheless closely interwoven into the texture of our society, and is intimately connected with all our social habits and customs, and modes of life.

The great body of the Common Law of England, and of the statutes of that country as they existed in 1776, are, then, so far as applicable to our condition, the basis of our jurisprudence. Upon this foundation we have erected a great superstructure of law, the fabric of judicial decisions and the product of the numerous legislative bodies to which the government of the States and of the Union is confided. As we shall have occasion to see in the progress of this work, the statute law of the United States, and of the different members of the confederacy, form a vast body jurisprudence, in many cases complicated, peculiar, and novel, but eminently adapted to our unprecedented situation, and of equal interest for the citizen and the lawyer.

To these two sources of municipal law, viz. Common and statute Law, must be added in America a third. We have thought it wise to set limits to the law-making authority, and by the direct action of the people themselves to establish certain rules and principles of action which can be varied by no power less than that supreme will which calls the legislator into being. In other words, we have imposed *constitutional* restraints on the legislature.

Something of this same disposition is to be found in the

annals of the mother country. The history of the race to
which the people of America belong, in all their struggles
for the attainment and preservation of freedom, shows their
marked and sedulous care in obtaining and preserving formal acknowledgments and records of their rights and liberties, muniments of title, as they might in technical language be termed. . . .

These, however, are all but parliamentary enactments,
or regal concessions, intended to operate as checks on the
kingly prerogative. They furnish no safeguard against abuse
of the legislative authority.

Our ancestors went further, and seeking to guard against
the abuses of popular, as their English progenitors did
against those of monarchical power, both in the formation
of the government of the separate States, and in laying the
foundation of the great confederacy of the Union, they
carefully asserted and defined those individual rights which
not even the law-making power, not even the people itself, shall be permitted to infringe. . . .

It is as forming a system of written limitations or restraints on legislative power that we shall have to consider
them, and in this aspect it will be interesting and instructive to study their operation, to compare their analogies,
and to observe their interpretation. For the present, it is
sufficient to remark, . . . that the parliamentary or legislative history of this country is remarkable for nothing more
than for the care with which we have endeavored to define
the boundaries of the various powers which in the aggregate form the complex machine of government, and the
rigor with which such restraints have been imposed by
the people itself on its immediate mandataries and agents.
Such are some of the most prominent functions of the constitutions of the several States. The Constitution of the
United States, designed to operate on State sovereignties,
as well as on the people directly, partakes of the character
of a league as well as of a constitution, as the latter term is
more strictly used.

Of these three great components, then, CONSTITU-
TIONAL LAW, STATUTE LAW, and CUSTOMARY or
COMMON LAW, the jurisprudence of our municipal sys-
tem is chiefly composed. . . .

Both constitutional and statute law have two great attributes common to each other, which render it indispensable to examine them together. They are both written; in
cases of doubt they are both submitted to the same judicial
arbiter. It is plain that differences will arise in the construction of written laws. The history of private discussions
and of public controversies, of contracts and of treaties,
and more than all the religious annals of our race, show
the feebleness and imperfection of language, and the sad
facility with which it lends itself to the various interpretations put upon it by ambition, fraud, or even honest difference of judgment. To settle these differences in regard to
the civil conduct of mankind, some tribunal is necessary. . . .

In the early ages of the English system, it appears that
the line between the Judiciary and the Legislature was not
distinctly marked, and that Parliament, consisting of one
great chamber in which sat both Lords and Commons, not
only made, but interpreted the law. But it has now long
been settled in England, that the interpretation of statute
law belongs to the judiciary alone, and in this country they
have claimed and obtained an equal control over the construction of constitutional provisions. This treatise is, then,
devoted mainly to a consideration of constitutional and
statute law, and of the control exercised by the judiciary
over it.

It is plain that the matter is of great moment. On the
one hand, the nature of the case, the frequency of doubt,
the impossibility of recurring to the legislature or to popular sovereignties for the removal of difficulties, and the
general analogies of our system, require the power of the
judiciary to be extended over the subject; while, on the
other hand, unless their authority be very carefully exer-

cised and confined within strict limits, the boundary between the legislature and the judiciary would be gradually
effaced and the most valuable parts of the law-making
power practically fall into the hands of that branch of the
government which is not intended to have any share whatever in the enactment of laws.

NOTES

[1] Without written warrant, there arises a law which use has
approved, for customs of long standing, tested by the consent
of those using them, are themselves a second law.

A LIST OF SUGGESTED READINGS

This list by no means pretends to be a full bibliography of a subject on which the secondary literature is immense. It is only a somewhat arbitrary selection of works most apt to interest the "general reader" or the practicing lawyer or jurist who has a limited time to spend looking backward over the history of his profession.

Cahn, Edmond Nathaniel, *The Moral Decision; Right and Wrong in the Light of American Law*, Bloomington, Indiana, 1955.
——, *Supreme Court and Supreme Law*, Bloomington, Indiana, 1954.
Chafee, Zechariah, *Free Speech in the United States*, Cambridge, 1941.
Chase, Frederic Hathaway, *Lemuel Shaw, Chief Justice of the Supreme Judicial Court of Massachusetts*, Boston, 1918.
Cohen, M. R., "Legal Philosophy in America," in *Law: A Century of Progress* (New York, 1937), II, 266.
Corwin, Edward Samuel, *National Supremacy; Treaty Power vs. State Power*, New York, 1913.
——, *The Doctrine of Judicial Review, Its Legal and Historical Basis*, New York, 1914.
——, *John Marshall and the Constitution*, New Haven, 1919.
——, *The Twilight of the Supreme Court*, New Haven, 1934.

Corwin, Edward Samuel, *Liberty against Government,* Baton Rouge, 1948.

———, *A Constitution of Powers in a Secular State,* Charlottesville, Virginia, 1951.

Frankfurter, Felix, *The Commerce Clause under Marshall, Taney and Waite,* Chapel Hill, 1937.

Handlin, Oscar and Mary, *Commonwealth: Massachusetts, 1774–1861,* New York, 1947.

Hartz, Louis, *Economic Policy and Democratic Thought: Pennsylvania, 1776–1860,* Cambridge, 1948.

Holdsworth, William Searle, *A History of English Law, Volume VI,* Boston, 1927.

Horton, John Theodore, *James Kent,* New York, 1939.

Howe, Mark DeWolfe, *Readings in American Legal History,* Cambridge, 1945.

Hurst, James Willard, *The Growth of American Law: The Law Makers,* Boston, 1950.

———, *Law and the Conditions of Freedom in the Nineteenth-Century United States,* Madison, Wisconsin, 1956.

Keitt, Lawrence, editor, *Annotated Bibliography of Bibliographies of Statutory Materials of the United States,* Cambridge, 1934.

Kent, William, *Memoirs and Letters of James Kent,* New York, 1898.

Levy, Leonard W., *The Law of the Commonwealth and Chief Justice Shaw,* Cambridge, 1957.

McCloskey, Robert Green, *Essays in Constitutional Law,* New York, 1957.

———, *The American Supreme Court,* Chicago, 1960.

Pound, Roscoe, *The Spirit of the Common Law,* Boston, 1921.

———, *An Introduction to the Philosophy of Law,* New Haven, 1922.

———, *The Formative Era of American Law,* New York, 1938.

———, *The Development of Constitutional Guarantees of Liberty,* New Haven, 1957.

Primm, James Neal, *Economic Policy in the Development of a Western State: Missouri, 1820–60,* Cambridge, 1954.

Story, William W., *Life and Letters of Joseph Story,* Boston, 1951.

Warren, Charles, *History of the Harvard Law School and of Early Legal Conditions in America,* New York, 1908.

——, *A History of the American Bar,* Boston, 1911.

——, *The Supreme Court in United States History,* Boston, 1922.

——, *Congress, the Constitution, and the Supreme Court,* Boston, 1925.

——, *Odd Byways in American History,* Cambridge, 1942.

Wright, Benjamin F., *American Interpretations of Natural Law,* Cambridge, 1931.

——, *The Contract Clause of the Constitution,* Cambridge, 1938.

INDEX

345
M 64